TAKE A LOOK

Observation and Portfolio Assessment in Early Childhood

SECOND EDITION

Sue Martin

Centennial College, Toronto

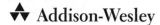 Addison-Wesley

An imprint of Addison Wesley Longman Ltd.

Don Mills, Ontario • Reading, Massachusetts • Harlow, England
Melbourne, Australia • Amsterdam, The Netherlands • Bonn, Germany

Publisher: Brian Henderson
Managing Editor: Linda Scott
Editor: Suzanne Schaan
Design, Cover Design, and Page Layout: Anthony Leung
Production Coordinator: Alex Odulak
Manufacturing Coordinator: Annette Darby

Photo credits:
Cover; background photos for Chapters 2, 3, 5, 6, 8, 9, 11; pp. 55, 106, 133, 149, 204, 235, 284: *Adobe Image Library: Children.* Copyright © 1998 Adobe Systems Incorporated. All rights reserved.
Background photos for Chapters 1, 4, 7, 10: Copyright © Corel Corporation.
pp. 1, 43, 83, 90, 97, 118, 124, 163, 175, 211, 219, 222, 236, 249, 261, 304, 317, 339, 346: Sue Martin.

The credits on page xii constitute an extension of this copyright page.

Canadian Cataloguing in Publication Data

Martin, Sue
  Take a look: observation and portfolio assessment in early childhood

2nd ed.
Includes bibliographical references and index.
ISBN 0-201-39602-5

1. Child development—Research.   2. Child psychology—Research.
3. Child development—Evaluation.   4. Child psychology—Evaluation.
5. Observation (Psychology).   I. Title.

BF722.M37 1999   155.4'072   C98-931638-6

ISBN 0-201-39602-5

Printed and bound in Canada.

A B C D E -WC- 02 01 00 99 98

Contents

Preface

Take a Look: Observation and Portfolio Assessment in Early Childhood is intended for early childhood educators, student teachers, practicing teachers, and parents who are interested in improving observation and assessment processes for children from infancy through the elementary school years. *Take a Look* covers the history, philosophy, and practice of observing, recording, and analyzing children's behavior. Focusing on the individual child, the book explains the need to gather information about each child and suggests a variety of techniques for recording the data. Unless caregivers and educators take a look at how the children are developing and responding to the environment, they will not be able to provide appropriate programs.

This book differs from others in its approach to the observer's own skill development. Perceptions are refined as the observer gains greater insight into why observation is the most effective means of evaluation. With practice, the observer acquires new techniques for recording information and learns to make valid and supported inferences about the child. The emphasis on evaluation is vital, as observations are too often filed away without adequate exploration, resulting in an undue reliance on standardized test results to give developmental information.

While adults responsible for young children may know that observation is the most effective way to understand the children, they often lack the tools to do the job properly. *Take a Look* will help students and practitioners build skills and become increasingly effective in their various professional roles. The observer's perspective always leaves room for improvement, but the more you look, the more likely you are to perceive objectively and evaluate accurately.

An outline of the book

Chapter 1 explores why, what, when, and how to observe, and provides an overview of the principles behind the use of observation and portfolio assessment as developmentally appropriate evaluation. Chapter 2 focuses on child development and how it can be observed, outlining the developmental domains and various theories of development.

Chapters 3–7 each explore a different style of recording, defining the methodology, indicating features of the particular method, and demonstrating how it can be used. Chapter 8 addresses portfolios and child studies, pulling together elements from each of the methods previously explained and showing how collections of various observational records and other information can provide the most detailed and effective technique for profiling the individual child.

Chapter 9 deals with measuring outcomes, discussing the philosophy and use of outcome-based education and the pros and cons of this approach. Chapter 10 gives an overview of the uses and limitations of standardized screening and assessment tools, which are often administered by professionals from outside the agency or school to help make accurate evaluations of developmental progress.

Chapter 11 shifts away from the child's behavior to focus on the child's environment. Indicators of appropriate children's environments cover notions of quality, inclusion, physical well-being, nurturance, and learning. These lists can form an effective evaluation tool if used as the basis of a checklist, rating scale, or questionnaire.

In addition to the specific learning outcomes in each chapter, the book as a whole helps students achieve the following four outcomes:

- Learners will discuss the historical events that have led to the practice of observation and portfolio assessment in early childhood, and they will articulate a philosophy of authentic assessment.
- Learners will compare and contrast a variety of observational methods to determine their usefulness.
- Learners will develop a comprehensive observation and record-keeping system suitable for the needs of an early childhood agency.
- Learners will analyze observational and contextual data to create holistic and sympathetic assessments of individual children.

Features of the second edition

The success of the first edition, the call for help in measuring learning outcomes, and the need for an improved focus on observable characteristics of children's development led to this new edition.

Its new features include the following:

- a clearer and simplified text
- a new chapter on observing development (Chapter 2)
- a new chapter on measuring learning outcomes (Chapter 9)
- observation samples that represent examples of good practice in observing, recording, summarizing and analyzing data
- a focus on what each method of recording can reveal about child development
- notes on observing and assessing children with special needs
- an expanded *Instructor's Manual* that includes exercises, observation charts, a test bank, and answers to the Focus Questions.

Focus Questions: Each chapter begins with a series of questions that enable readers to review their current understanding and skill level. The focus questions start the process of learning with reflection and provide an overview of the content. Answers are provided in the *Instructor's Manual* for review.

Learning Outcomes: Each chapter has its own learning outcome that summarizes the knowledge readers will gain.

History Notes: An historical perspective is offered at the beginning of each chapter to explain the evolutionary stages that have brought us to our current philosophy and practice. Views about how children develop have changed dramatically in a relatively short period; the history notes help us understand these changes in how children are perceived and in how records are kept to monitor their progress.

Definitions: Clear explanations of the methods of observation and information gathering are essential to understanding, choosing, and using each. The definitions help readers access basic information quickly and efficiently.

Features: The characteristics of each observational method are fully described. "Key Features" boxes provide quick summaries of important points that will help students choose an appropriate method for each situation.

Using the Methods: Advantages/Disadvantages: All data collection techniques have positive and negative aspects; concise lists clearly indicate the strengths and weaknesses of each observational method. These lists will help students select appropriate methods and avoid common pitfalls.

Child Development Focus: Each standard method of observing and recording data is reviewed with a clear indication of which developmental domains are addressed or likely to be highlighted.

Taking a Special Look: Students and practitioners alike may encounter children with a wide variety of special needs, whether developmental, linguistic, or cultural. Boxed notes give information on how to observe children with special needs and what to keep in mind when analyzing these observations.

Watch out!: "Watch out!" boxes draw attention to key facts or issues that must be remembered.

Key Terms/Glossary: Key terms are shown in boldface the first significant time they occur in each chapter and are defined in the glossary at the end of the book. The glossary can be used as a quick reference tool to aid understanding of the text. The lists of key terms at the end of each chapter can be used to review and test knowledge.

Observation Samples: Samples that demonstrate good practice for the core observational and recording methods are included at the end of each chapter (except for Chapter 10, "Screening and Assessment"). As every observation is individual to the child, situation, observer, and chosen methodology, an "ideal" is difficult to supply, but all the samples have identifiable strengths.

Bibliography: The bibliography includes all references cited in the text as well as other books and articles that offer particularly useful information on topics covered in *Take a Look*.

Instructor's Manual

The *Instructor's Manual* includes the following:

Assignment Options: The assignments are designed to build skills in the use of observation methods as well as to aid appreciation of the philosophy of observation as developmentally appropriate evaluation. Individual and group exercises will help students improve their perceptions, make more objective recordings, and analyze data more successfully; they also support the development of critical thinking skills.

The assignments include examples to critique, along with criteria for assessing them. This evaluation process is an essential learning tool. Instructors will find the evaluation criteria helpful in teaching and in assessing students' work.

Chapter 10, "Screening and Assessment," does not give assignments because most readers will not normally administer standardized tests. As such tests may form part of a portfolio, however, the educator must know their place, be prepared to consult with other professionals about their use, and be able to interpret the results, comparing them with other data from observational sources. Some commonly used screening and assessment tools are described briefly in the *Instructor's Manual.*

Test Bank: The test bank includes matching, true/false, multiple-choice, and short-answer questions for each chapter.

Observation Charts: Blank charts for the different observation methods are provided in full-page format. These can be reproduced for student practice or made into overhead transparencies for classroom use.

Answer Key: Suggested answers are given for the Focus Questions that begin each chapter. Complete answers for the test bank are also provided.

Acknowledgments

Jacob, my dog, was better behaved while I was working on the second edition; he didn't eat the photos or do unspeakable things to the chapters as they were spread over the floor. Thanks, Jacob.

Andrew, my best friend and husband, has learned to do all kinds of domestic things so I could research and write; thanks a lot for enabling me to do what I wanted! Both Simon and Cassie have developed their own lives now they are older, but there was some price paid in that I was not as available to them as I might have been. Hopefully their early years set them on the right track, because they have learned to be wonderful independent people, and they were persuaded to limit their Internet surfing and Great Big Sea chat room conversations to allow me to use the computer!

A host of friends have supported me directly and indirectly, some because they understood why I was temporarily out of sight; Esther, Michael, Irene, and Mara were particularly sensitive. Pat managed to offer both personal support and sound professional advice for which I am most grateful.

Students and graduates of the programs I have taught contributed most significantly by offering me samples of their work, discussing many ideas and providing moral support. Sonia, Marriana, Shane, Wendy-Ann, Tanya, Ken, Keira, Wendy, Sara, Fabi, Mary M., and Mary C. were all particularly helpful. Thank you so much. The staff of the Centennial College Child Care Centres, and Marie and Linda the supervisors, have not only supported *Take a Look* but also been responsible for ensuring that there was congruence between its theory and their practice; I am appreciative of their personal and professional support.

The following people reviewed the first edition and suggested some of the changes implemented in the second edition: Carol Anderson, Durham College; Barbara J. Duffy, Okanagan University College; Paul Fralick, Mohawk College; Karen Nolan, Seneca College; Carlota Schechter, St. Joseph's College; Cheryl Taylor, The Institute for Early Childhood Education and Developmental Services; Karla Baxter Vincent, New Brunswick Community College (St. John). Karen MacKay Burns reviewed the manuscript for the first edition.

Thanks also to the faculty of Centennial College, Seneca College, George Brown College, Ryerson Polytechnic University, the University of Toronto Faculty of Education, and the Canadian Mothercraft Society, who contributed ideas and responses to the first edition of *Take a Look*. Also, thanks for my teaching and learning experiences in England and also in Vermont and Delaware in the U.S.A.; they provided me with interesting challenges that helped me to shape the book.

And finally, thanks to Suzanne Schaan, my editor at Addison Wesley Longman, whose attention to detail was phenomenal. May our conversations about Canadian English, English English, and American English continue.

Credits

The publishers acknowledge the following sources of material reprinted in this book and would gladly receive information enabling them to rectify any errors in references or credits.

p. 65: Laura E. Berk, *Infants, Children, and Adolescents.* Copyright © 1994 by Allyn & Bacon. Reprinted/adapted by permission.

pp. 153–55: *Exceptional Children: Inclusion in Early Childhood Programs* by K. Eileen Allen et al. Reprinted with permission of ITP Nelson.

pp. 166–67: *Infants and Toddlers,* 3rd ed. By LaVisa Cam Wilson, Linda Douville-Watson, and Michael A. Watson. Delmar Publishers, Albany, New York. Copyright 1995. Reproduced by permission.

pp. 168–71: *Observing Development of the Young Child* 4/e by Beaty, Janice, © 1994. Adapted by permission of Prentice-Hall, Inc., Upper Saddle River, NJ.

p. 195 (top): *Protecting Children,* Department of Health (Great Britain). Crown copyright is reproduced with the permission of the Controller of Her Majesty's Stationery Office.

p. 196: From *Genograms in Family Assessment* by Monica McGoldrick and Randy Gerson. Copyright © 1985 by Monica McGoldrick and Randy Gerson. Reprinted by permission of W.W. Norton & Company, Inc.

p. 293: Ontario Ministry of Education and Training, *The Arts: The Ontario Curriculum, Grades 1–8.* © Queen's Printer for Ontario, 1998. Reproduced with permission.

pp. 329–30: R. Langford et al., *Checklist for Quality Inclusive Education: A Self-Assessment Tool and Manual for Early Childhood Settings.* Barrie, ON: Early Childhood Resource Teacher Network of Ontario, 1997. Reprinted by permission.

p. 331: Reprinted by permission of the publisher from Harms, T., and Clifford, R.M., *Family Day Care Rating Scale (FDCRS), Scoring Sheets* (New York: Teachers College Press. © 1989 by Thelma Harms and Richard Clifford. All rights reserved.)

p. 333–34: Sue Bredekamp, *Developmentally Appropriate Practice in Early Childhood Programs Serving Children from Birth Through Age 8.* Reprinted with permission from the National Association for the Education of Young Children.

p. 334: Carol H. Schlank and Barbara Metzger, *A Room Full of Children.* Churchville, NY: Rochester Association for the Education of Young Children, 1989.

p. 336: Centennial College Early Childhood Education Programs and Child Care Centres, *Philosophy Check-In.* Toronto, ON: Centennial College, 1998. Reprinted by permission.

Observation: An Introduction

You well know that the teacher in our method is more of an observer than a teacher; therefore this is what the teacher must know, how to observe.

Maria Montessori (1913)

Observation can lead to the collection of valid, reliable information without intruding on or transforming the daily classroom life and without constraining the children's behavior so as to limit their demonstration of competence.

Tynette W. Hills (1992)

Early childhood education students use an in-class opportunity for nonparticipant observation of infants. Skill in objective recording needs to be gained from practice.

Focus Questions

1. Why do educators think that observation is important?

2. What can be learned from watching children involved in spontaneous activity?

3. How can observational information be recorded?

4. In recording information about children, how can judgments and assumptions be avoided?

5. How can observers reduce or eliminate personal biases that might influence their observations?

6. Can observers be sure that valid interpretations are made from objectively recorded observations?

Learning Outcomes

Learners will recognize a variety of reasons to observe young children, and use critical thinking to analyze recorded observations.

Learners will develop strategies to record observations and gather data professionally, and demonstrate appropriate sensitivity to the subjects of such recordings.

History Notes

The principles of **observation** are rooted in both the pure and social sciences. The scientific method accepts that no truth can be *proven*, even if it is generally accepted and *likely* to be true. In the pure sciences, scientists observe and experiment to determine how one variable changes with another, and try to find equations that relate the variables and theories that explain the equations. Social sciences follow modified processes of discovery but, like the pure sciences, are relatively objective and systematic methods of recording and analyzing reliable information. Biologist and writer T.H. Huxley in fact suggested that we are all scientists and that all phenomena can be explained using scientific methods.

In 1895, French philosopher Émile Durkheim established some principles for sociology. Using the traditional sciences as a model, he suggested that people and social information should be treated in the same way as any other data. Sociological studies of the early twentieth century provided the basis for our understanding of the necessity to study children's contexts as well as their behavior. In the same period, the increase in global travel caused people to think about social conditions and cultural practices that differed from their own; new ways of studying social structures, the concept of ecological systems, and ideas drawn from anthropology all contributed to current perspectives on the significance of the context of development.

At the time of the Industrial Revolution, people believed that **objectivity** could reveal an absolute truth regarding states of being and facts. Scientists now think that differences of perception alter the concept of truth; although objectivity is still highly prized, it is a means rather than an end in itself.

Empirical evidence is information gained from careful observation or experimentation; the data is processed in such a way that speculations can be made from analyzing the information. For example, Galileo was an empiricist concerned with planetary information. The early empirical psychologists, led by Wilhelm Wundt at the end of the nineteenth century, observed animal behavior. Our studies of child behavior can be traced to some of the empirical approaches of more than a century ago.

The school of **behaviorism** contributed to the focus on observing behaviors rather than on their underlying causes or explanations; this approach may have reinforced the move to observe individuals in experimental situations. Behaviorism called for an objectivity and cold detachment not characteristic of today's observational skills. To get to our current practice, we have combined the most useful features of scientific behavioral studies with a more compassionate and understanding view of children within their own context.

The art of seeing differs from the scientific approach to observing in that it concerns itself less with ultimate truths and does not prize objectivity so highly. This concept values the intuitive perceptions of the individual who can glean the essence of an event or individual experience. **Phenomenology**, one approach to revealing the essence of another's experience, was founded by the German philosopher Edmund Husserl over a century ago; more recently, writers such as French philosopher Jean-Paul Sartre and Max Van Manen have used phenomenology to show the value of an individual's experiences. While phenomenological processes should be used with caution, they have offered us reasons to appreciate personal perspectives when we observe children and to avoid assumptions when we try to understand their life experiences.

Observational studies need to be carried out using ethical methods of data collection and confidential treatment of that information. These principles have not always existed; social sciences have in the past mirrored other sciences in forgetting that real people are the subjects of study. Fortunately, we have borrowed from the traditional professions to establish ethical practices. Like physicians, observers are expected to follow appropriate protocols for accessing and storing information. Research methods that respect human subjects are usually required of those gathering information, whether the data is used for the care of the child or for the purpose of study.

Clearly, the principles that guide the practice of observation and portfolio assessment come from a variety of disciplines. The pure sciences determine objectivity: empirical evidence is gathered according to scientific and psychological approaches. On the other hand, the social sciences encourage intuitive responses: the observation focuses on the individual as both the subject of the research and the creator of a personal construction of experience. Documentation, permission, and confidentiality practices are guided by the professional requirements of doctors of medicine. The analysis of observational data draws on developmental psychology, biological sciences, ecological studies, maturational sequences, theories of cognition, sociology, anthropology, language studies, health sciences, educational principles, and so on. Thus, the origins of **authentic assessment** processes are extremely broad and eclectic.

People Watching

A mother gazes at her newborn infant. The baby looks at her. At first the baby's sight is unfocused, yet she is attracted by the configuration of her mother's face. The infant is, perhaps, "programmed" to have this interest. It encourages social interaction and leads to emotional bonding. Drawn to faces and signs of movement, the infant learns through watching as well as through her other senses. All babies are born to be people watchers.

"Don't stare," says a mother to her young child, in the expectation that she can shape the child's instinctive **behavior**. Socially acceptable behavior requires that observation be subtle. Required behavior is learned more by example than by verbal reinforcement; watching others is integral to the process of social learning.

Watch out!

Make sure that you don't stare at strangers who might misunderstand your motives!

Have you ever watched the hellos and goodbyes being said at an airport? If you were not too caught up in your own emotions, you might have wondered about the demonstrations of feeling, the honesty of expression, or the social or cultural determination of particular behaviors. What are the stories behind all those faces? If you have done this kind of thing, then you, too, are an observer.

"I did not expect her to do that," "She must be frustrated to have that reaction," or "He is a very quiet person" are all examples of informal observations. We all observe, deduce, and respond in all our communications with other people. Most adults go through this process without really considering what is happening.

The same process occurs when we are more conscious of making observations. The significant difference is that, when we use observation as a method for collecting information, we must do it carefully, systematically, and accurately.

Why Observe?

We observe children because we are drawn to them; we want to protect, nurture, and teach them. Every adult involved with young children in any role or capacity will observe the children for somewhat different reasons. The adults may be parents or other relatives, babysitters, caregivers, teachers, early childhood educators, psychologists, doctors, social workers, play therapists, students, child life workers (who work with children in hospitals), recreation leaders, camp counselors, or any other interested party. All of these have some care duties, but the kind of responsibility varies. The following list gives, in no particular order, some of the reasons that adults may observe children:

- to ensure safety
- to see if the child is healthy
- to notice changes in behavior
- to see what the child consumes
- to learn about the child's interests
- to see how long the child's attention span is
- to determine the child's physical skills and needs
- to tune in to the child's rhythms
- to assess a program's effectiveness
- to make inferences about cognitive activity
- to notice social relationships
- to deduce how the child is feeling
- to help design a program plan for an individual or the group
- to evaluate use of space

- to make written records of the child's development
- to assess the child for particular sensory disabilities
- to help appreciate the child's learning style
- to learn about the ages and stages of child development
- to help build skill in objective observation
- to determine the progression through stages of development
- to assess behavior with reference to "norms"
- to report information to other professionals
- to let a parent know how the child is developing
- to enable parents to seek professional opinions about the child's progress or perceived concerns
- to gain written documentation for legal purposes
- to record any regression in behavior
- to confirm or contradict a formal assessment
- to help change routines to be more effective
- to determine appropriate guidance strategies
- to determine when and how to "scaffold" (to extend the child's learning)
- to establish the frequency of a particular behavior
- to acknowledge the complexity of the child's play
- to determine the quality of interaction with an adult
- to record activities undertaken
- to look at the child's response to a new situation
- to evaluate the effectiveness of play as therapy
- to help determine the interaction among various aspects of development
- to gain insight into the child's personality and individuality
- to evaluate the appropriateness of the learning environment
- to determine the effect of the environment on the child

Watch out!

Always remember why you are observing!

The observation may take many forms. Informal, unrecorded observation is frequently used as it can be done while participating with the children. Narrative accounts of behavior do not rely on highly developed observational skills, and they are open-ended. Observers looking for particular behaviors might use a prewritten chart, checklist, or scale. (All of these methods will be dealt with in later chapters.)

Focus on the individual

"Did they like the creative activity?" a teacher asked an ECE student who came into the office. As the student replied, the teacher realized that she hadn't asked a very useful question. Imagining that each child's response to a situation is identical can be a mistake. The focus must be on the behaviors of an individual child far more frequently than on the group.

Watch out!

Some students are so busy studying "their" subject that they forget about the other children's needs!

If you can see only the general flow of action, you will not have insight into the set of individuals in your care. Without singling out children to observe closely, you are very likely to miss the particular skills that have been acquired and fail to acknowledge the areas of development that can be addressed.

Individuals do function within groups. Group dynamics can be better understood when the individuals in the group are first observed separately. For this reason, adults must learn to work at observing individual children and avoid making assumptions or generalizations. In time your observations can center on the interactions within the group, but first you will need to refine your skills at observing one child at a time.

Observation as authentic assessment

The strengths of observation as a form of **authentic assessment** are numerous. Observation

- enables adults to take responsibility for the process of the child's development
- is the key to evaluating development
- is significant because adults can bring about changes in a child's behavior
- focuses on what a child can do
- forms the foundation of effective individual program planning and group planning
- allows for variation and individuality of children in their development and needs
- presupposes no curriculum theory but can support almost all types of program planning

- can be more objective and tends to be less biased than standardized tests
- allows for understanding of each interacting aspect of development
- enables evaluation to be carried out in familiar surroundings
- can be quicker and more effective then other methods of gaining information about development
- encourages parental involvement and professional team work

The Observer's Role

"Watching the kids" is a phrase sometimes used to mean looking after or caring for children. It is interesting that the nonprofessional term accentuates a responsibility for observation.

There are conflicts in our jobs as caregivers, teachers, and parents. Consider a parent who spends a lot of his time watching his children and pointing out to everyone how advanced they are. He does not take responsibility for interacting or even being with them, but observes and expresses his pride in their accomplishments. Other parents and caregivers may be so busy doing practical domestic jobs that they don't take time to "stand and stare"—to watch with any sense of wonder or intrigue. Some are so involved with the children's activities that they do not notice their changing behaviors and increasing skills.

All adults involved with children need to observe constantly. Only a small amount of the information observed can be recorded or analyzed. Active involvement with the children can make more formal observations difficult. Some methods enable us to be interactive as we observe, but these require refined skill.

Nonparticipant observation

Early attempts at the more formal types of observing and recording need to be done while the observer is detached from the children. Students and skill-building teachers need to take themselves away from the children for **nonparticipant observation**. In the practice of observation, student educators' perspectives will alter and they will gradually notice things that they missed, be more objective about what they do see, and be more analytical about the information recorded. This nonparticipant role is a necessary part of learning to observe effectively.

Practicing teachers should, from time to time, remove themselves from direct contact with the children. This helps teachers watch more carefully what is happening and usually leads them to be more responsive. Taking the time to be a nonparticipant in the program does not mean prolonged time away from the children, however, and should never be an excuse to ignore a child's needs. Suitable supervision must always be made when the responsibilities change.

Watch out!

We need to observe all the time, but that shouldn't make us unresponsive!

With young children, it is useful to be a noninteracting observer from time to time. As long as the children's needs are met, they may not be affected if you remove yourself just far enough to be out of their personal space but within sight and earshot; sit on a small chair in a position that does not interfere with their activity and is not in a significant traffic area. Here are some suggestions:

- Avoid making the eye contact and facial expressions that initiate communications with the children.
- Wear comfortable but fairly plain clothes, avoiding anything that may be a lure to a child.
- Try to avoid obvious staring at a child, which could make her or him feel uncomfortable.
- Distance yourself so that you can see and hear the children but are not within their play area or personal space.
- Ensure that sufficient appropriate supervision is provided so that all the children's needs are met.
- If a child draws you into conversation, respond in simple sentences to explain what you are doing. Remember to follow through with any promises you make for doing activities later.
- Make regular times for nonparticipant observation so that the children get used to you doing it. Older children may learn to observe by imitating you.
- *Never use nonparticipant observation as an excuse for not being involved with the children when you should be responsible.*

Participant observation

Teachers who have gained skill in observing may make only brief recordings from time to time; they will mostly practice **participant observation,** done while they are involved with the children. If teachers have developed their skills, they will be responsive to casually observed information.

For training purposes, there are further ways of building skills in observation. Visiting child-care agencies and schools may provide opportunities. Using a college's on-site lab school facilities can be particularly helpful. A laboratory school can help students' skill development in several ways:

- Children can be brought to class for a "set-up" observation opportunity. The students will all see the same behavior and can learn to record and analyze appropriately.
- Observations in the lab school can be recorded for replay in class. Going over the material as a class can be a good practice, as what is seen is the same for everyone.
- Students can go into the lab school and observe as nonparticipants. Situations can be set up so that students can focus on the same aspect of development.
- Observation booths can enable students, individually or in groups, to observe children. Ideally, a sound system would enable them to pick up language and other sound. This is a nonintrusive way of observing, which does not influence the recording. Students can observe while others take the interactive role, setting up activities for the children.
- If the center is large enough, students may be able to do a placement at the lab school. As they get to know the children better than they would as a visitor, students can try out observational styles in nonparticipant and participant approaches.

The purpose of focused observation for the students in a class situation may need to be explained to the parents and teachers of the children to be observed. Of course, permission should be gained.

Professionalism and Confidentiality

When you receive a psychological or medical report, it may arrive with a confidential sticker attached, making it clear that the report contains information to which there should be limited access. An observation is also confidential material and should be treated as such. The circle of stakeholders involved in an observation, or those who require a degree of access to the information it contains, may be wider than you might at first imagine. This situation can present some challenges.

Watch out!

Keep all personal information confidential—not only the facts you are told not to share!

Who has, or should have, access to the formal records or informal notes that teachers and caregivers need to keep? While legal requirements vary, you must ensure that you interpret and practice **professionalism** and, when appropriate, **confidentiality** in regard to all the information that is stored or shared. The basic principle is that information about a child is the concern only of that child, his or her custodial parent or guardian, and anyone with whom the parent consents to share it. In taking responsibility for the care or education of a child, you need to ensure that any legal requirements regarding access to information and privacy are met. The agency or school must have a policy that determines who has access to information and in what circumstances.

At enrollment, most agencies and schools make an agreement with parents and guardians that observations and information gathering will occur. Student educators, however, must always request and gain parental permission before carrying out observations, documentation, and record keeping relating to a child. As a professional courtesy, students should provide parents with a corrected copy of any such studies.

All written records need to be kept in a secure, preferably locked, file. They should be labeled and dated. Files need to be updated regularly; all entries should be signed by their contributor. Any significant content must be communicated to the parents in an appropriate manner with any necessary explanations. Access to the child's file should be open to parents at any reasonable time. If you think that there is any cause to withhold information from a parent, it is quite probable that the content is inappropriate and possibly **subjective**.

It is easier to accept the need for confidentiality with formal documents. The challenge for practicing teachers is to maintain the same level of confidential treatment with all pieces of information regarding a child. Parents' comfort level regarding privacy is very personal and may be culturally determined. Avoiding risks is essential and may require careful organization. While you may think that a posted chart recording the feeding, sleeping, and elimination pattern of the day is acceptable for infants, you need to work out with a parent group an appropriate practice for your setting.

Permission Form

Child Observations, Case Studies, and Portfolios

Student and Parent Agreement

Without written permission I will not observe and record information about your child. Please sign in the space provided if you agree that I may make observations and study your child. It would be helpful if you could initial each of the boxes if you are willing for me to undertake any or all of the techniques of information gathering.

I _____ *(student name)* will not refer to the child in any written manner by his or her real name. Information recorded will be written objectively, treated professionally, and kept confidential.

_____   _____
(student's signature)   *(date)*

I _____
  (parent's name)

agree to have _____
                      (child's name)

observed ☐   photographed ☐   audiotaped ☐   videotaped ☐

by _____
  (student's name above)

at _____
  (agency/home)

for the purpose of study in child development at _____

(school/college) for a period of _____ *(weeks/months)* on the consideration that copies are made available to me, the parent, if I so request.

_____   _____
(parent's signature)   *(date)*

In the days when children ran out of school clutching their readers of varying proficiency levels, it was quite clear to the parents (as well as to the children themselves) who was at the "top" or "bottom" of the reading class. You can avoid this kind of practice.

Briefing parents about their children's challenging behavior might be an excellent idea. While it is useful to share daily observations, you must be sensitive about timing. Not only might the end of the day be the wrong time to deliver seemingly bad news; offering the comments when others might overhear is also inconsiderate.

Students are in a difficult position with regard to confidential record keeping. Their observations should not easily reveal the identity of a child to anyone who might accidentally come across the record. As students are learners, the observations may not be as objective as they could be, and the inferences they contain might not be appropriate. Deductions made by students may be based on insufficient information or analyzed on the basis of an inaccurate explanation of the behavior.

Schools and agencies have varying attitudes to students' access to children's records. It may be understood in some cases that students are in a better position to appreciate a child's behavior if some contextual information is offered; however, to many in supervisory roles, this presents an unnecessary intrusion into the family's privacy. Centers working with students need to make some decisions about the way permissions are sought (see permission form on page 12) and the amount of information about the child that is offered. It is true that information may bias an observer's objectivity in recording. An agency might request that observations made by students be countersigned by a staff member to indicate that permission to make the observation was given and that the observation is consistent with his or her knowledge. Feedback can be very useful for students, without breaching confidentiality; they may find that they have contributed new insights to the professional's knowledge of the child.

Objective Observation

You may be relieved to hear that it is impossible to be completely objective when observing children. But it is a hard task to move to an acceptable level of **objectivity** in all observation and recording. This idea is captured by Cohen and Stern (1978):

> For teachers observing the children with whom they work and live, absolute objectivity is impossible, and objectivity itself becomes a relative thing. As a matter of fact, it is to be hoped that no teacher would ever try for so much objectivity that she would cease to be a responsible and responsive adult to her group.

Total objectivity may be impossible, but that's no excuse for accepting subjective observations!

No two people will see the same child in identical ways. Two open and honest teachers can be asked to observe the same child. What they see and the sense that they make of it will depend on what they decide to look for and their particular perspectives. To scientists, this might appear to be an unacceptable variation; however, observers of children need to decide what is an acceptable degree of objectivity. According to the two teachers, they both tell the "truth," or their own version of it. How can you ensure that you keep to the truth when others see the child's behavior in a different light? How you see depends on your skill in observing, what you are seeking, and your own perspective. If these are the variables, you can improve observer reliability by increasing your skill, determining what you are looking for, and reviewing your personal perspective.

The Objectivity Continuum

Objectivity ◄————————► Subjectivity

- There are no absolutes.
- All observations fall between the two opposites.
- Objectivity is usually desirable.
- Subjectivity is not always "wrong."
- Appreciation of the reasons for the degree of objectivity is always essential.

Bias

Whatever stage we are at in our professional or adult life, we have had experiences that shape our perceptions. The way we take in information is determined by our previous experience and knowledge. We bring to situations previously acquired attitudes and beliefs. Some of these are well founded; others are born of some **bias** that comes from incorrectly understood information, negative experiences, or inappropriate generalizations. Most biases are subtle, and may be unrecognizable to others. Some biases may be much more blatant and recognizable to others and even considered to be acceptable.

Observers can eliminate many of their biases by acknowledging and confronting them. Eventually, observers will realize that there is more to observation than seeing. What separates human observation from a mechanical means of recording is how we *perceive* what we observe. The selection of how, when, and what to observe is a skill we must work on.

We come to observe with some useful preconceived ideas as well as inappropriate biases. While we must build a background knowledge base, we have to avoid biases when we can and address them when they do exist.

> **Taking a Special Look: Observing exceptional children**
>
> How we see people may be shaped by our experience and our emotions. If we have little knowledge of **exceptional children**, we could be fearful or negative. It helps both you and the exceptional child to speak positively about who he is and be clear about his abilities, rather than focus on his disabilities. Getting to know the child and increasing your knowledge about his condition will usually reduce any fears and help you relate to him. Children with below-average skill levels in one or more domains may have abilities in other areas that you can see more easily if you observe with a positive outlook.

Teamwork

Many people have a role in caring for, nurturing, and educating each child. Where there is responsibility for a child, there is a need for observation and assessment of that child.

Parents are the most significant stakeholders in children's lives. They may be the adults who take the leading role in observing their children and responding appropriately to their needs. Quite naturally and spontaneously, a mother or father will watch a child; such observation may elicit a wide range of feelings and responses. This informal monitoring of the child's behavior, and of changes in health or development, may well be the most significant assessment that is ever done. The professional involved in the child's care must never forget that the child is a member of a family and that the family may be able to offer closer insights than the trained caregiver. No assessment could ever be complete without the inclusion of the parent's observations.

Watch out!

However skilled you become, you will never know a child as well as the parents do!

Front-line caregivers need to consider their observations in the light of what is known about the child. This is done most usefully in discussion with co-workers and parents. Interested parties may be able to exchange observations in a relatively informal way—frequently at the start or end of the day, or perhaps at nap-time for a younger child.

Supervisors and others involved in the delivery of care and education may add their own observations or help make objective inferences about the child. When observed behavior causes concern or is difficult to interpret, an "outside" professional, such as a psychologist, may be brought in. Legislation varies, but professional principles and good practice indicate that this should be done only after seeking parental permission, support, and involvement. Psychologists, occupational therapists, child-care consultants, and social workers will not be able to make a fair and appropriate assessment without input from the day-to-day caregiver and the parents.

The transdisciplinary play-based assessment (TPBA) model (Linder, 1990) offers the idea of holistic assessment, with the involved professionals working with the parents in a way that enables all parties to observe simultaneously and take the time to discuss deductions that have been made. Linder states, "Team discussion is critical, and having the same foundation improves team communication" (1990, p. 17).

Not all observations are, or could be, conducted when all those involved with the child are present. Communication systems should be in place to share information in convenient ways.

The team approach increases the reliability of inferences made from observation. This model also encourages each adult to take responsibility in the process. An indicator of good quality child care is the practice of teamwork in observation and program planning.

Choice of Observation Method

There is a wide range of methods of recording information. As you read this book, you might want to try some new ways or practice some of those familiar to you. When choosing a method, ask yourself the following questions:

1. Are you in a nonparticipatory role or do you have responsibility for the children as you observe?
2. Do you have the language skills to enable you to write detailed narrative descriptions?
3. Why are you observing? What are you looking for?
4. Is the purpose of observing to increase your skill or to benefit the child directly?
5. Do you appreciate what the various methods of information collecting will tell you—and can you choose appropriately?
6. Have you developed strategies to summarize and make sense of the observational information collected?

If in doubt about where to start, work through the methods presented in this book. They are offered in a sequence that is appropriate for observation students or skill-developing practitioners. Since informal observation is what everyone has done without training, continue to do this. Your skill will improve as you record, and your casual observations will gradually take on greater meaning as you continue the process. Narrative recordings require little interpretive skill and so may be a method of choice for the relatively unskilled. As you find new ways of charting behaviors, checking off behaviors on lists, and using styles that require inference in their recording, your understanding of child development will also expand. Your learning will accelerate if you study theories of child development at the same time as you improve your observations. Each will benefit the other.

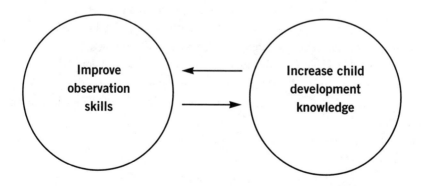

Observation as Part of an Assessment Procedure

Early childhood specialists focus more on the process of the child's learning than on its products. Observation of the process can tell us much about the child that would not be revealed by viewing only such products as the child's artwork and writing. It is important, however, not to disregard the significance of such products. If you can gather information about the child from various sources, and in a variety of ways, you will be in a better position to make evaluations.

Watch out!

Lack of observational skill can sometimes lead to poor assessment, but lack of child development knowledge will *always* mean poor assessment.

Formal **assessment** may require tests. (Tests are dealt with in Chapter 10.) The best of these have an observation component. Even in a structured play situation, children are in a better position to be evaluated more fairly than in a testing situation. A restrictive "testing environment" can create stress. Children can demonstrate their skills more readily in a situation that resembles what they are used to. Members of an assessment team are wise to get their data through a variety of methods to ensure that they include naturalistic observations.

The **portfolio** technique combines the best of the evaluation styles. A portfolio can contain observations, charts, products of the child's efforts, test results, parental contributions, medical notes, and any other pertinent information. It forms a record that can be added to at any time. The portfolio forms long-term documentation of the child's education, health, and experience to which those involved with the child may refer. As the child grows, she may choose items for inclusion in her own portfolio to form a personal record of achievement. Looking back at the child's life experience can stir the emotions and can supply significant information about her patterns of behavior. (A full explanation of the portfolio method is given in Chapter 8.)

Focus on emerging skills

Observation is not necessarily an exercise to identify "strengths" and "weaknesses" in children's behavior. Such value judgments are usually inappropriate in naturalistic observation. Observers should look at the skills that are present, rather than focus on what a child cannot do. Programs are more positive and more likely to be effective if they are planned to enable the child to build skills from "where he is" rather than from what he has failed to do. A more developmentally appropriate curriculum plan should result from focusing on **emerging skills**.

> ### Taking a Special Look: Emerging skills
>
> Whatever the developmental progress of a child, we need to support the skills that are emerging. Sometimes, when a child takes longer than average to acquire a new skill, the achievement seems even more amazing than for the child who had no particular challenge in that domain.
>
> Observing the ongoing progression of skill development should lead us to respond. When we see new behaviors, we need to find ways of supporting them. We are not trying to get the child to develop faster—development is not a race! Rather, we are trying to ensure that we maximize the child's potential in a nurturing way.

Summarizing information

Often confused with analysis, the observation **summary** is a categorization of the essential parts of the observation. In many open-ended observations, the summary may try to collect information to identify and list behaviors seen. It is not an interpretation but a review and organization of objectively recorded behaviors. Developmental domains might be used as categories in the summary.

In a more structured observation that looks for particular identified behaviors, the summary might contain information such as the number, frequency, duration, or triggers of those behaviors. The summary is intended to be a brief outline of significant observed behavior.

Analyzing the content of observations

Watch out!

Analyzing behaviors with reference to norms is easier than explaining behaviors according to theories—but the norms are only the beginning!

There are a few basic rules of **analysis**:

1. Focus on what was observed and recorded, not on other less accurate "bits of information."
2. Always separate the observation from its summary and analysis.

3. Do not make **inferences** unless you can support them; that is:
    a. identify the specific behavior(s) that lead(s) to such a deduction
    b. support your inference with reason(s), using inferential language carefully: "It appears that . . . on the basis of . . . I think that . . . demonstrates behaviors in excess of . . . norm for his age."
    c. **validate** each statement with the use of at least one (preferably all) of the following:
        i. observations made by others with similar inferences
        ii. use of theoretical explanations
        iii. comparison with recognized **norm**
    d. state the source of validation—professional input or book reference
4. Put on paper only what you consider to be professional and could defend against challenges. Avoid judgments, assumptions, and generalizations that cannot be substantiated regarding background, social, or contextual information. For example, do *not* say, "This occurs because he is an only child" or "He is much smarter than his brother" or "Her English is poor because her parents don't communicate with her."
5. Keep the analysis as well as the observation confidential. Some people may find the word "analysis" quite off-putting or coldly scientific.

Taking a Special Look: Attention deficit disorder

> Attention deficit, hyperactivity, and attention deficit disorder (ADD) are terms being used rather casually by some parents, teachers, and caregivers. These terms have very specific diagnoses and are not for the nonmedically trained to diagnose. Consequently, we should be careful about making inferences using these labels. It is better, without the benefit of a professional diagnosis, to describe behaviors objectively. Use your observation skills and describe exactly what you see!

"Analysis" is more easily understood as the "making sense of what I saw" section of the observation process. The easiest way to go about an analysis is to ask yourself, and then answer, a series of questions about what was observed. If the observation is set up to seek particular information, then that question needs to be addressed first. Unless you cite the source of "extra" information, it is best to stick to analyzing only what was in the observation just completed.

Structuring the analysis in a way that considers each of the developmental areas is helpful. Any section where there is no significant information can be left out. In practice, you might find the following suggested plan a good idea. Adapt it to fit your needs. Write it up according to the required style, either in an essay or in notes under the organized headings.

Watch out!

You will have to keep returning to this section on analysis as you learn about different observation methods.

Plan to Assist the Analysis of a Single Observation

BACKGROUND

- What was the reason for observing? (Was I seeking specific information?)
- Did the observation occur spontaneously? Was the child aware of being observed?
- What is my role as observer? (e.g., nonparticipant, etc.)
- Did I have any preconceived ideas about what I was going to see?
- What contextual information might be helpful?
- Who gave permission for or input into the process?

METHOD

- Why did I choose this method of observing?
- Were there any concerns regarding the procedure?
- Did the method reveal what I wanted? What was it?

CONTENT

Physical development

- What gross motor skills were demonstrated?
- What fine motor or manipulative skills were seen?
- What activity was the child observed doing?
- What responses did the child make to any sensory experience (sight, hearing, touch, smell, or taste)?

Social development

- What evidence was there of the child's sense of self?
- What kinds of connection was the child making with
  a. adults?
  b. other children?
- What adult interaction did I observe?

- Describe the quality of the interactions.
- What kind of self-help skills were seen?
- Were there any examples of independence or dependence?
- What did I see that indicated understanding of social roles and behavior?

Emotional development

- What demonstrations of feelings did I observe
  a. in language?
  b. in posture and body language?
  c. in gestures?
  d. in facial expressions?
- Was there indication of control of feelings?
- What attachments were evident?
- What moods did I see?

Play

- Did I see the child in onlooker, solitary, parallel associative, or cooperative activity?
- What type of play (if any) was observed? (e.g., one or more of imaginative, imitative, pretend, fantasy, sociodramatic, superhero, social constructional, functional, physical, or other)
- How long and involved were these sequences?
- Was the play self-initiated and self-supported?
- What props were used?

Language and communication

- What utterances were made? In what language?
- What indications of nonverbal communication did I observe?
- What kind of structure did the language have?
- How extensive was the child's vocabulary?
- How effective was the communication?
- What was the child's interpersonal style?

Moral and spiritual development

- Did any of the observed behaviors indicate an understanding of "rights" or "social justice"? If so, how?
- Were any of the behaviors pro-social in nature? (e.g., empathetic, altruistic, sharing, taking turns, helping others)

- Was there evidence of beliefs about any philosophical issues, such as creation of things, in the child's world?
- Did I see the child's curiosity and sense of wonder?
- Did the child demonstrate respect for the dignity of others?
- What indication was there of the child's categorizing himself or herself into a sub-culture? (e.g., racial, belief system, family make-up, dialect, etc.)
- What demonstration was there of an understanding of, compliance with, or rejection of any kind of rules or guidelines?

Personality

- Did I observe any behaviors that indicate temperamental type? (e.g., slow to warm, extrovert, orderly, etc.)
- What reactions to stimuli did I see?

Cognition

- What drew the child's attention? How long was the span of concentration?
- What behaviors indicated thought process?
- Did I notice any "mistakes" the child made?
- Did the demonstrated language or behavior show understanding of any of the basic concepts? If so, what? (e.g., color, shape, time, space, classification, relativity, seriation, conservation)
- Did the child "experiment" with materials?
- Was there evidence of conditioned responses?
- Did I see any trial and error strategies?
- What evidence might there be of an understanding of symbolism in language or behavior?
- Was there evidence of use of memory?
- Was any of the child's art representational?
- What behaviors indicated to me how the child perceives the world?
- Did the child use concrete objects to help perform tasks? Can the child use any forms of abstraction?
- What humor did the child initiate or respond to?

The whole child

- What outside influences affected what I observed?
- In what ways did I see aspects of the child's development interact?

Responses to the above questions should incorporate deductions that cite the section of the observation to which they are related and that are validated appropriately. For practice, you might like to use the following flow chart, which follows the process of critical thinking required in analyzing observations. The sample on page 35 shows the analysis of a single observation, while that on pages 36–37 shows the analysis of a number of behaviors in chart form.

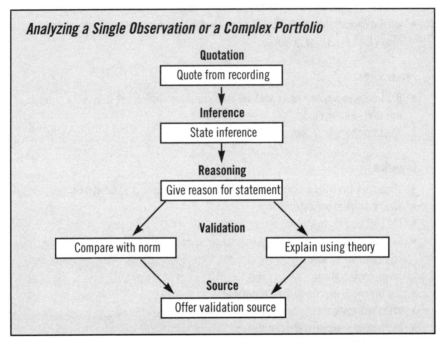

Analyzing a Single Observation or a Complex Portfolio

Quotation
Quote from recording

↓

Inference
State inference

↓

Reasoning
Give reason for statement

Validation
Compare with norm   Explain using theory

Source
Offer validation source

In each of the areas you will explore, ensure that all deductions and inferences can be supported. If such inferences are "checked" using this model, they can be evaluated for their objectivity and likelihood of being accurate. If your inferences cannot be validated, they should not be stated.

Using Observational Data to Plan

Those who teach teachers often say that students need to learn how to set goals and objectives for children. Such a philosophy makes people believe that achievement is only possible with goal setting. It disregards the idea that children will progress through the developmental stages, given appropriate support and open-ended experiences that enable them to operate at their own level. Learning and skill development are not dependent only on our overt intervention. There is a difference between making appropriate curriculum provision based on observation of the child's developmental needs and goal setting that is presumptuous in assuming that you know what the child's "next stage" is. However knowledgeable you are about patterns of development, it is rarely useful to set specific goals for children who are in the mainstream of our education and care agencies.

Watch out!

Much development happens without adult intervention—make sure that your plans really enhance the process!

Children with **special needs** that are identified and diagnosed may benefit from a more structured goal-setting approach because **objectives** can break down skills into component parts. These objectives can be addressed separately.

Interpretation of observational information is essential for all planning and curriculum design. Many inappropriate assessments have resulted in poor provision; the teacher's focus should be on supplying appropriate experiences and guidance to support children in their own efforts to struggle with new skills.

Whether or not you set goals may be inconsequential to how appropriate the program plan is. If you choose to set goals, you might be more focused on the child's specific needs; thoughtful programming must always have some deliberate intention.

Taking a Special Look: Early identification and intervention

Observing and recording development has a purpose beyond that of the school or child-care agency working directly with a child. Sometimes observation leads to the identification of potential concerns that need to be reviewed outside the agency. After repeating observations to see if the results are consistent, teachers and caregivers may suggest to the parent that further assessment from another professional might be helpful. Early identification of many conditions can be extremely beneficial for the child. In some cases, it may mean that an appropriate assistive device is supplied; in other cases, the teacher may follow the professional's directions to support the child more responsively. The long-term outcome is likely to be much better if action is taken early.

In some situations, a special plan of **early intervention** may be developed to support an infant, toddler, or preschooler. The plan can involve many different strategies to support the child's development and relationships. Psychologists or psychiatrists may try to assist before any potential problem rears its head. In other cases, where a developmental problem already exists, they will work with the child, parent, and caregivers or teachers to find appropriate ways of providing support.

Individual program plans

Individual program plans (IPPs) and individual education plans (IEPs) are commonly devised for children with identified special needs. But all children have individual needs that should be met. The IPP helps you in that task, by formalizing the process of converting observational and other assessment information into an action plan.

An IPP requires a team approach to piece together all available information about a child and come up with an appropriate response to the child's individual needs. At its best, it is a dynamic ongoing process that changes and is adapted in the light of new information.

Watch out!

Build an IPP from current performance levels rather than future goals!

Informal IPPs are devised regularly with parents and teachers working cooperatively to observe, evaluate, assess needs, and respond to them. In this case, it might not be a recorded plan. If there are specific concerns about the child's development, the IPP can be a much more thorough, written teamwork process with clearly defined intentions and practical suggestions or objectives.

A sample IPP can be found on page 38, and a sample IEP on pages 39–40.

Taking a Special Look: IPPs for children with special needs

The idea of the individual program plan is borrowed from the philosophy of those working with children who have special needs. We should find ways to support emerging skills; in this way, we assist development from the child's current skill level rather than jump ahead to the next stage. Designing activities to get a child to where he "should" be is not very helpful. For example, Juan, who is currently struggling to stand despite having malformed feet, is better assisted if we plan his individual program to include lots of activities to help him perfect this skill rather than set the goal of walking, which he may not reach for some time.

Individual Program Plan

Child's name: _____   Teacher:_____

Age/D.O.B.: _____   Date: _____

Persons participating: _____

Reason for program development: _____

Developmental domain	Observation summary (skills present)	Needs	Intentions	Practical supports	Person responsible

---

Individual Program Plan Review

Child's name: _____   Teacher:_____

Age/D.O.B.: _____   Date: _____

Persons participating: _____

Reason for program development: _____

Developmental domain	Previous intentions	Observed skills	Progress made	Newly devised supports	Person responsible

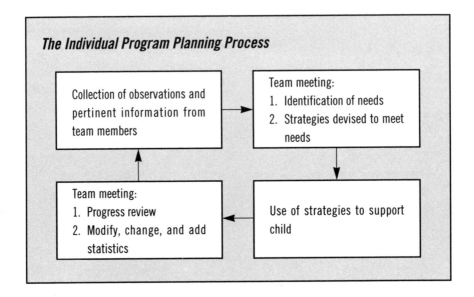

The Individual Program Planning Process

Collection of observations and pertinent information from team members	Team meeting: 1. Identification of needs 2. Strategies devised to meet needs
Team meeting: 1. Progress review 2. Modify, change, and add statistics	Use of strategies to support child

Observation as part of curriculum planning

A child's **curriculum** is his or her whole experience of life. What you may have thought of as "the program" or even "planned activities" is only a small element of that whole experience. When you take care to observe children in every aspect of their day, from waking through all kinds of family interactions and domestic scenarios as well as more carefully designed day-care or school experiences, you can appreciate the children's style, individuality, and social context, and how these affect their responsiveness and developing skills. As a trained observer, you may make useful inferences from observation in an agency or school setting. Those observations will be much more revealing if you have some previously acquired information about the child's family and background. Observing a child as widely as possible pays off in a picture of the "whole" rather than unconnected bits of information about some specific area of development.

The great challenge for teachers is to take time to observe the individual within the group while acknowledging the dynamics of that group and endeavoring to provide for the needs of each child. Teachers need acute observational skills, an understanding of the more **"normal" patterns** of development, and a philosophy of curriculum that recognizes that everything they provide, including themselves, is part of the curriculum provision. If children are enabled to operate at their own level, the variation of development within the group can be addressed; if changing environments are provided, children are able to build their own knowledge.

Translating what is observed into plans for meaningful activities and experiences is challenging for many reasons:

1. Observational information can only indicate the child's current competency level—this does not, of itself, dictate what skills need enhancing or what new ones could be acquired.

2. Observation and evaluation techniques require detailed analysis of the data if accurate inferences are to be made; analysis requires training and practice.

3. Naturalistic observation puts the emphasis for evaluation on the shoulders of the recorder.

4. The fact that a child is functioning at a particular level does not mean that the child will always develop in a particular sequence within a certain time frame or will always progress and not regress.

5. Programming for groups of children, each of whom is at a different developmental level, can be challenging if the variation is such that the needs differ.

6. Where teachers believe that programming should focus on developmental needs, they may find that working toward determined learning outcomes or the curriculum of a school board or other authority is not only limiting but impossible.

7. A process needs to be established to take the observational information into programming. This is a time-consuming activity that requires observational recording and analytical skills.

These skills are attainable, but teachers have to devote much time and hard work to achieve them. While teachers may struggle against making compromises, they should realize that some compromise is necessary in the most effective curriculum design.

As part of curriculum design, observation provides ongoing evaluation of each child's environment for development. By observing, teachers can know if their intentions for the children's learning are being fulfilled. How the children respond to experiences helps teachers see how the environment might be changed or modified to facilitate learning.

Teachers and caregivers may use observation as a means of assessing the achievement of previously set goals and objectives. While this may work for some teachers, it may not work for others, particularly if their educational philosophy is not one of goal setting.

Process of Curriculum Design

Observe ⟶ Record ⟶ Interpret ⟶ Plan ⟶ Implement

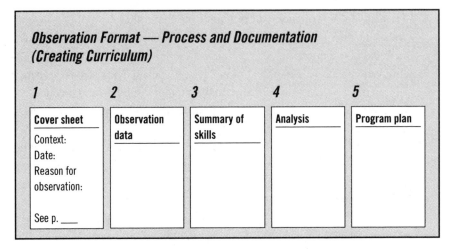

Observation Format — Process and Documentation (Creating Curriculum)

1	2	3	4	5
Cover sheet Context: Date: Reason for observation: See p. ___	**Observation data**	**Summary of skills**	**Analysis**	**Program plan**

Curriculum planning models

The most effective planning models are rooted in observation and an appropriate evaluation of the child. Such evaluation can be used to indicate current competence in each developmental domain, attempt to predict the sequence of skill acquisition, and provide open-ended experiences from which the child can consolidate or build skills.

Planning processes should ensure that the needs of the child and the goals of the program are met. Some teachers think that students learn to program effectively if they use a process of setting goals and objectives. This procedure may focus on curriculum areas rather than on developmental needs or interests. Some goals may be set within a developmental context, but the assumption will be that the goal should be set at the "next" stage of development. The educator may make incorrect assumptions or set a path to failure because refinement of a presently demonstrated competence might be more appropriate than a big jump to acquire a new skill.

Sequential models make assumptions about the stages in which component parts of a competence are acquired. These models work most effectively when planning to support physical skills. Even with a clear step-by-step explanation of the stages through which the child will develop, they show little sensitivity to the concepts of learning readiness or maturational levels. Children cannot always master skills even when the stages are specified and the necessary experiences are provided.

You may sometimes find that administrators' expectations regarding specified curriculum, competencies, or goals are not a "good fit" developmentally. If you program for the goal rather than the child, you may be unsuccessful. A compromise can be reached in an **input/outcome planning model,** which factors in both the child and the expectations. This model may be expedient for teachers under pressure to conform; they need not lose their integrity in their developmental focus. Ongoing, well-documented observation of the children may lead the administrator to change the expectations so that unrealistic or inappropriate outcomes are dropped (see Chapter 9 on outcome-based education).

Webbing models take into account the child's observed performance and curriculum goals. They try to relate all curriculum areas through a single topic or focus. These plans can generate many good ideas for constructing the learning environment; however, although they are intended to factor in observed information, their structure does not allow for it in any clear manner.

Topic planning may be based on notions of what is appropriate or desirable for the children to learn. This approach does not encourage optimal learning because it does not grow from the children's needs, interests, and abilities. Children may well get something from the topic, but it is likely to be limiting. Thematic approaches may have similar limitations but do, at least, acknowledge the need for interrelated learning experiences. Where the theme focus lends itself to open-ended activities, the children can operate at their own levels.

The gap between what the child can do independently and what the child can do with support should be understood when planning experiences. Vygotsky (1978) offers an excellent model for responsive curriculum in the theory of the **zone of proximal development** (see page 73). Sensitive observation of a child's behavior will indicate when and how to move in to assist learning.

Using planning models

Advantages

- Visual presentations enable teachers to conceptualize the plan easily.
- The plan can offer programming process rather than random "good ideas."
- Teamwork planning can be effective when a common planning model is used.
- A model can be selected to fit the program philosophy.
- The model may offer planning for developmentally appropriate experiences while meeting program outcomes.
- Most models are circular and ongoing.
- A model may easily build in a component for evaluation of its success.

Disadvantages

- Planning models depend on an understanding of curriculum design.
- The easiest options may be the least developmentally appropriate.
- The plan may be too abstract or not sufficiently flexible.
- If the plan is based on observation, perceptions may vary.
- Models may be used without a realization of their underlying premise.
- The model may not conform to the needs of administrators.

Planning models based on observation

The role of the teacher is as important to the curriculum as are the materials and set-up. These planning models based on observation may help you in your responsibility. More specific samples, showing a curriculum web and an integrative planning model, can be found on pages 41 and 42.

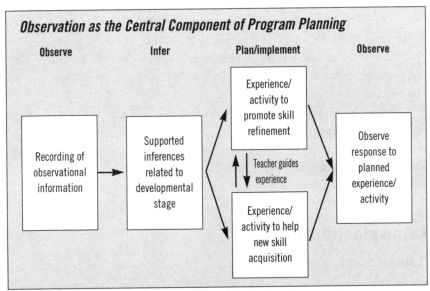

Observation as the Central Component of Program Planning

Observe — Infer — Plan/implement — Observe

Recording of observational information → Supported inferences related to developmental stage → Experience/ activity to promote skill refinement — Teacher guides experience — Experience/ activity to help new skill acquisition → Observe response to planned experience/ activity

This model is one desired by teachers practicing in a developmentally appropriate program, who use naturalistic observation as their primary tool for evaluation. The planning and implementation of learning experiences is supported by the teacher's guidance.

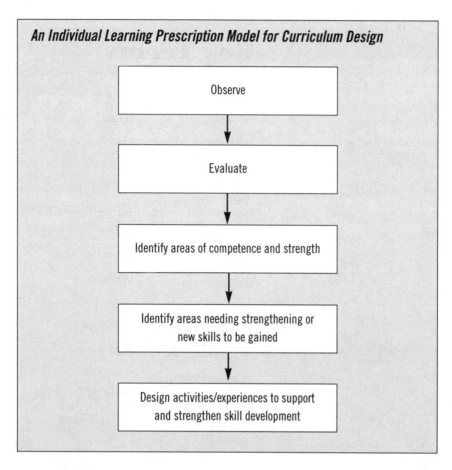

An Individual Learning Prescription Model for Curriculum Design

Observe

↓

Evaluate

↓

Identify areas of competence and strength

↓

Identify areas needing strengthening or new skills to be gained

↓

Design activities/experiences to support and strengthen skill development

This model shows a logical progression from observation to the design of an activity. It requires thorough analysis of observational data to identify "areas needing strengthening" or "new skills to be gained."

Key Terms

analysis

assessment

authentic assessment

behavior

behaviorism

bias

confidentiality

curriculum

early intervention

emerging skill

empirical evidence

exceptional child

individual education
plan (IEP)

individual program
plan (IPP)

inference

input/outcome plan-
ning model

nonpartipant obser-
vation

norm

normal patterns

objectives

objectivity

observation

participant observa-
tion

phenomenology

portfolio

professionalism

sequential model

special needs

subjective

summary

topic planning

validate

webbing model

zone of proximal
development

Observation Sample

This sample shows how a student uses a prepared form to assist her critical thinking. She makes an inference from her observation and supports it with a quotation from a theory.

Analysis Chart: Observations

Child's name: *Zoe*　　　　　　　　　　　　Date: *November 4, 1997*

Child's age: *2 years, 8 months*　　　　　　　Inference # *7*

Domain(s) of development *(If possible, state inferences in each developmental area.)*

The following inference concerns this/these area(s) of development:

Social-personal skills; imitative behavior

Having examined the evidence *(Make a statement that assesses the child's development—is it typical, atypical, or can you explain it using a theoretical model?)*

I infer that *Zoe shows some signs of preoperational thinking. She has internalized a behavior and imitated it.*

The source of my inference *(Which observation or bit of information led you to the inference?)*

Because I recorded *that she engaged in deferred imitation, where she imitated how her grandfather had placed a plastic cat-face mask on his face.*

My reasoning *(Give your own reasons for stating the inference.)*

I think this because *when I babysat a toddler, she held a baby doll in her arms and fed it with a toy bottle, just as her mother had done with her baby brother earlier that day when I had visited.*

Quote from norm (if applicable) *(Validate your inference with the use of either a norm, a theory, or both.)*

I found this quote from a normative development profile to support my inference:

N/A

Quote from theory (if applicable) *(Validate your inference with the explanation of a theory.)*

I found a theory that supports my inference. The theory is called *preoperational stage of cognitive development.*

This is a quote from the explanation of the theory: *"Many children between 24 and 30 months are entering Piaget's preoperational stage of cognitive development. The first sub-stage . . . is preconceptual, which occurs from about 2 to 4 years of age. . . . In deferred imitation the child imitates another person's behavior, even when that person is no longer present."*

The name of the theorist is *Piaget*

Author I found this in a book by *LaVisa Cam Wilson*

Title The book is called *Infants and Toddlers: Curriculum and Teaching (2nd ed.)*

Source The book/journal/article is published by *Delmar Publishers Inc.*

Date of publication: *1990*　　　　　　　　Page # of quote: *276–277*

Observer/assessor/recorder's name: *Wanda*

Observation Sample

This excerpt from an analysis chart is an example of using a structured approach to critical thinking. Observations are broken down by developmental domain. Explanations of behaviors use recognized theories and norms.

ANALYSIS OF DEVELOPMENT

Child's name: Carolina   Child's age: 18 months

SPEECH AND LANGUAGE DEVELOPMENT

Behavior observed	Inference	Reasoning
Followed caregiver when caregiver asked her to come	It's typical for children of this age to follow simple requests.	I believe this to be true because I have observed other children following simple requests.
Said hello on toy phone	It's typical for a child almost 12 months to start to use single words.	Children at this age learn through imitation, and the child hears "hello" many times a day.
Would sing before falling asleep	It seemed that the child was soothing herself before falling asleep.	Developmental Profiles states the child will do this as a way of releasing tension.
Would engage in rhythmic singing	It seemed that the repetitive sounds were the beginnings of speech.	David Elkind has noted that babbling and rhythmic sound speed up the acquisition of speech.

PERSONAL-SOCIAL DEVELOPMENT

Behavior observed	Inference	Reasoning
Watched the delivery man come in and followed him	Child seemed not to have a fear of strangers.	Child felt safe in her environment and does not have the concept of danger yet.
Imitated the adult's action by clapping hands	It's typical behavior for children of this age to imitate adults.	Child observed what adult was doing and then repeated the action.
Followed caregiver when caregiver asked her to come	It's typical for children of this age to follow simple requests.	I believe this to be true because I have observed other children following simple requests.
Clapped hands and danced to a familiar song	It's typical for children of this age to enjoy rhymed activities.	I have observed other children, and they all seem to like dancing and singing.

BIBLIOGRAPHY
Allen, K.E., & Marotz, L.R. (1994). Developmental profiles: Pre-birth through eight (2nd ed.). Albany, NY: Delmar.

Observer's name: Ken   Date: November 6, 1998

Validation by theory	Validation by norm	Source	Bibliographic reference
	Carries out simple directions and requests	K. Eileen Allen & Lynn Marotz	Developmental Profiles, p. 73
	Names everyday objects; imitates sounds	K. Eileen Allen & Lynn Marotz	Developmental Profiles, p. 63
	May sing as a way of winding down	K. Eileen Allen & Lynn Marotz	Developmental Profiles, p. 75
ne inability to babble uring the early months f life delays language cquisition.		David Elkind	Sympathetic Understanding, p. 21

Validation by theory	Validation by norm	Source	Bibliographic reference
ildren will show fear only fter they have the concept at they are an object that an be destroyed.		David Elkind	Sympathetic Understanding, p. 12
	Often imitates adult action in play	K. Eileen Allen & Lynn Marotz	Developmental Profiles, p. 74
	Carries out simple directions and requests	K. Eileen Allen & Lynn Marotz	Developmental Profiles, p. 73
	Children enjoy simple songs, dance, and music.	K. Eileen Allen & Lynn Marotz	Developmental Profiles, p. 64

lkind, D. (1994). A sympathetic understanding of the child: Birth to sixteen
3rd ed.). Boston: Allyn & Bacon.

Observation Sample

This simple IPP is based on behaviors recorded in observations. The child's needs have been determined. Activities are suggested to support skill development.

Individual Program Plan (IPP)

Child's name: Arjumand

Caregiver: Casz

Age/D.O.B.: April 9, 1996/1 year old

Date: April 15, 1997

Area of Development	Needs	Activities
Explores environment using fine motor skills (pincer grasp)	Small objects	Activity pillow with buckle, zipper, shoelace, and velcro Wind-up toys Putting small blocks in a bucket
Transfer objects from hand to hand	Small objects Chance to explore	Offer toys to Ashley when already has one Passing games (adapted version of "hot potato")
Feed self using a spoon	Opportunity Encouragement Exposure to spoons in a variety of situations	Kitchen play Sensory activities using spoons (e.g., oatmeal play)
Walk alone (began at the end of March)	Open space Encouragement	Gross Motor Room Walks of the center Nature walks outside Pull toys (e.g., wagons)
Climb on, over, and through objects	Climbing equipment Carpeted/padded areas Sturdy furniture	Slides Cushion ramps, stairs, and blocks Pillows Tunnels
Imitate actions and sounds	Music People Mirrors Toys with sounds	Songs with actions (e.g., "Row Your Boat") Copycat games; if he does something, you repeat it Walks outside so nature sounds can be imitated
Nod for "yes" and shake head for "no"	Opportunity to decide for himself Encouragement Reinforcement	Ask questions and let him tell you when he is done Repeat nods accompanied by you saying "yes"
Follow simple directions	Opportunity Praise Encouragement	Simple "Simon Says" games Head and shoulders, knees and toes Clean-up activities (e.g., put the toy on the shelf) Ask him to do things (e.g., "Please sit down" or "Come here, please")
Openly show affection toward others and his toys (likes to cuddle)	Trust Consistency Soft toys Praise Love	Songs about loving (e.g., Barney song, "I Love You") Pillows Teddy bears (washable) Cuddle Ashley throughout the day

Observation Sample

This thorough IEP was created for Jamilla, who has been identified as being in need of special support. Jamilla's resource teacher recorded the chart with Jamilla's regular teacher.

Child's name: Jamilla

Caregivers/Teachers: Ms. Trainor, Ms. Jessop

Age/D.O.B.: 5 years, 7 months

Date: May 7/98

Recorder: Ms. Jessop

Date of last IEP: April 9/98

Comment on success of previous IEP: Jamilla achieved the skills that were needed to perform the activities. There remains some concern about Jamilla's lack of social skills.

Developmental domain	Observation	Support	Response
Physical development: • gross motor	Jamilla watches other children in the playground. Walks around with adult supervisor.	Jamilla needs opportunities to become engaged with other children's activities.	Try parachute games and other noncompetitive games.
• fine motor	Jamilla has started to copy letters and joins in with drawing and "writing." She does some scribble shapes like letters in her name. She notices that other children can write their names.	Opportunities to develop fine motor control (and build self-esteem) are needed.	As Jamilla likes dramatic play, we could introduce a "post office" and writing center with writing pads, "stamps," envelopes, etc.
Cognition • number	Counting in sequence is no problem 1-20, but Jamilla can only count to 4 or 5 when actually counting objects.	Jamilla needs the chance to have fun with counting experiences.	Sociodramatic play could also have a table (for 6?) to set. Jamilla would enjoy "preparing" a meal for "guests."
• seriation	Jamilla gets confused when putting objects in any kind of sequence. She makes up her own reasons for pictures or objects to be the way she wishes.	Opportunity to seriate in play might add meaning to this.	Provide picture cards of growing seeds, buds opening, etc. (link with spring theme).
• patterning, matching, and sorting	When given assorted items, she can sort them according to color and kind but not according to two characteristics together. Jamilla likes to play with buttons, shells, and pine cones, making patterns with them. She plays with the materials by herself and rejects involvement with others.	The materials are already available, but these could be extended with other items.	Jamilla can be asked about her patterns--these involve sorting and patterning. She can be encouraged to articulate her reasoning for the patterns.

Developmental domain	Observation	Support	Response
Language • literacy	Jamilla appears to enjoy stories; she wants the same ones re-read. She follows the stories page by page. When sitting alone, she "reads" the story. At other times, Jamilla recognizes word shapes.	Provide other stories and opportunity to talk about the ones she likes. Pick up and reinforce her understanding of words in context.	Offer picture books for Jamilla to create stories. Provide books she likes and reinforce key words. Link words with everyday objects.
• language	Jamilla listens at circle time but only talks confidently one-to-one with an adult. She tends to play alone with a lot of self-talk.	She needs to build confidence.	Avoid forcing Jamilla, but provide opportunity for closeness with an adult.
Social development • play behavior	Jamilla tends to play alone. Sometimes she will play alongside others if she is interested in the activity (e.g., cooking).	Jamilla needs confidence to communicate, but her thinking tends to be egocentric. She needs time and play experience.	Encourage parallel play and provide opportunity for some association. Sharing tools may help.
• relationships with adults	Quiet moments alone with the teacher are the most happy times for Jamilla. She jumps up and down with enthusiasm when she starts talking. Soon she is immersed in conversation and she becomes composed again.	She needs one-to-one contact to build trust so that she can become more autonomous.	The new assistant could try to spend extra time so that Jamilla can build trust and begin to "branch out."
Emotions	Jamilla expresses her feelings in quiet communication but does not project her wishes to other children. At times, she is left out of the "girl play" because she can't negotiate.	Jamilla would be happier if she could find her way into the play with her peers.	Role-play situations may help. Strategies to overcome communication problems can come in children's stories.

Observation Sample

This web outlines an individual curriculum plan for a child in Grade 1. Moving out from observing the child's interests and abilities, the teacher plans activities to lead to desired achievements or learning.

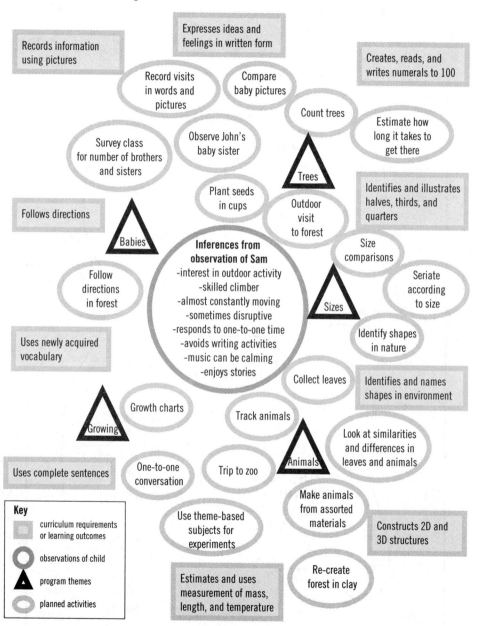

Records information using pictures

Expresses ideas and feelings in written form

Creates, reads, and writes numerals to 100

Record visits in words and pictures

Compare baby pictures

Count trees

Estimate how long it takes to get there

Survey class for number of brothers and sisters

Observe John's baby sister

Trees

Follows directions

Plant seeds in cups

Outdoor visit to forest

Identifies and illustrates halves, thirds, and quarters

Babies

Inferences from observation of Sam
-interest in outdoor activity
-skilled climber
-almost constantly moving
-sometimes disruptive
-responds to one-to-one time
-avoids writing activities
-music can be calming
-enjoys stories

Size comparisons

Seriate according to size

Follow directions in forest

Sizes

Uses newly acquired vocabulary

Identify shapes in nature

Collect leaves

Identifies and names shapes in environment

Growth charts

Track animals

Look at similarities and differences in leaves and animals

Growing

Animals

Uses complete sentences

One-to-one conversation

Trip to zoo

Make animals from assorted materials

Constructs 2D and 3D structures

Use theme-based subjects for experiments

Re-create forest in clay

Estimates and uses measurement of mass, length, and temperature

Key

☐ curriculum requirements or learning outcomes

◯ observations of child

▲ program themes

◯ planned activities

Observation Sample

This integrative planning model focuses on the whole experience of the child related to a theme rather than on particular curriculum areas. The model leads to planning experiences and environments but does not determine expected outcomes; the open-ended activities allow each child to learn what he or she is developmentally ready to do. Teachers and caregivers can use their observations of the children to help plan motivating experiences and to intervene appropriately to support each child's learning. Observation of the children's responses also leads to modified or new activities.

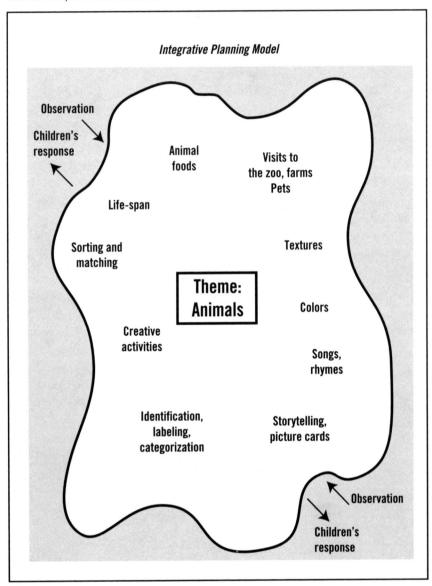

Integrative Planning Model

Observation
Children's response

Animal foods

Visits to the zoo, farms
Pets

Life-span

Sorting and matching

Textures

Theme: Animals

Colors

Creative activities

Songs, rhymes

Identification, labeling, categorization

Storytelling, picture cards

Observation
Children's response

Observing Development

2

And so we see that if we can develop a more delicate faculty of observation, we can really gain an insight into the true essence of human existence.

Rudolf Steiner (1924)

At its best naturalistic observation combines a keen eye with an informed and skeptical mind.

Lauren Adamson (1996)

Success is achieved if one is faithful to life, observing and examining it in its individual and general reference.

Friedrich Froebel (1826)

Any activity can demonstrate a child's development in various domains. A careful observer of these children playing together could comment not only on their physical skills but also on their social, emotional, and communication skills.

Focus Questions

1. What are the principles of child development that influence how we approach observation and data collection?

2. What do we need to look for when we observe the development of young children?

3. How does having developmental knowledge influence our perceptions of children?

4. How can the observational guidelines for each developmental domain be used?

5. Why should observers of children's development consider the interaction of developmental domains?

6. How might educators justify observation as part of their role?

Learning Outcome

The learner will identify characteristics of child development and use them to create observational strategies and interpret recorded data.

History Notes

Although the term **child development** seems common to us, the concept is relatively new. Child development is part of the larger disciplines of human development and **developmental psychology**, which have evolved in the twentieth century. For a long time before that, it was believed the primary difference between the infant and the adult was one of size! We now know that people commonly pass through some stages of growth in size but, more importantly, also undergo transformations in their psychological development.

The concept of developmental change is based on the principle that individuals undergo dynamic processes of maturing: bodily aging; physical skill acquisition;

changes in emotional perspectives, cognitive activity, self and social awareness, moral and attitudinal stances, language and communication abilities, spiritual and aesthetic sensibilities, and inner drives and motivations. Our understanding of each area has evolved separately.

The study of human biology dates back to medieval Europe and the dissection of cadavers. Within the last century, understanding of the bodily systems has grown remarkably, as has society's ability to promote health and optimal physical development through measures such as immunization, improved nutrition, wider availability of health services, and health education. Recently, we have seen advancements in our knowledge of brain development, genetics, and human biological functions. Growth, reflexes, brain activity, and other processes of change are more easily measured than they could be a generation ago. All these factors aid our understanding of developmental change.

Nonscientific approaches to understanding human life are found in cultures around the world. For thousands of years, both India and China have followed systems that promote health and support development. Native Americans also have spiritual and practical processes for ensuring balance and health. In many cultures and religions, the treatment of the human body is combined with spiritual rituals. Although the word *development* may not be used by many religions, allusions to the passage of time and changes of personal perspectives are common. According to some religions, the attainment of perfect balance, peace, or ultimate knowledge marks the end of one stage of life or the beginning of the next.

In Western thought, the idea of dynamic changes in the individual is rooted in the work of Jean-Jacques Rousseau, an eighteenth-century French philosopher, who initiated a conceptual leap in stating that he appreciated the individuality of even small children. Following Rousseau's example, the Swiss educational reformer Johann Heinrich Pestalozzi constructed his own theories about children's needs and stages of development, based on his experience working with children and observing their capabilities. Pestalozzi emphasized the need to encourage problem solving so that children could progress to higher stages of thinking. Friedrich Froebel, a German educator, worked with Pestalozzi for two years early in the nineteenth century and was influenced by his thinking. Froebel, who created the concept of kindergarten (or "children's garden"), formulated an approach to education that addressed children's developmental needs, paying more attention to mental development than to physical growth.

The science of psychology developed at the end of the nineteenth century in Germany, where Wilhelm Wundt created the first laboratory for studying conscious experience. In the United States, one of Wundt's students, Edward Bradford Titchener, tried to develop a "mental chemistry" by analyzing experience as basic elements. William James, an American psychologist and philosopher who was influenced by Charles Darwin's theories, considered the science of animal behavior and such topics as religious experience and abnormal behavior. Darwin's principle of natural selection also provided significant insight into the science that would be called genetics. Educational psychology evolved from these early studies and those of behaviorism.

Behaviorism was introduced by John B. Watson early in the twentieth century. He focused on behavior as the only way to measure the relationship between stimulus and response. He soon accepted the notion of conditioned responses put forth by the Russian physiologist Ivan Pavlov—a theory best known to us through "Pavlov's dog," who salivated on hearing a bell because he was usually fed at the sound of the bell. B.F. Skinner also studied animal behavior, in controlled environments, and concluded that behavior is strongly influenced by the environment. Another type of behaviorism, called cognitive behaviorism, developed from the stance that thought processes lie behind observable behaviors.

In opposition to the study of specific behaviors as separate elements, Max Wertheimer advanced the Gestalt theory. He believed that experiences should be studied as a "whole," not broken down into constituent parts. This school of thought shaped studies in personality and perception.

In the late nineteenth century, **phenomenology** provided a new approach to understanding human experience by studying personal experiences or "essences" from the point of view of the subject rather than that of the "objective" world. Early phenomenologists were the German philosophers Edmund Husserl and Martin Heidegger. An informal method of phenomenology is used today when educators study the essence of the child's experience as well as objectively recorded observational information.

Another influential psychological perspective is Sigmund Freud's psychoanalytic approach, developed in the late nineteenth and early twentieth century. He considered the mind to be like an iceberg, mostly hidden from view. He thought that much of human behavior is driven by unconscious thoughts, and proposed a theory of developmental stages that focused on body parts and functions. Although his work has been much criticized, it is still held in high esteem and has prompted studies that rework the initial theoretical base—for example, work by Alfred Adler, Karen Horney, and Carl Jung. Erik Erikson, an American psychoanalyst, used some of the Freudian concepts of life stages, but he considered these as psychosocial dilemmas or crises. He thought resolution of these crises was necessary for satisfactory personal development.

The study of emotions is a relatively recent phenomenon, since early psychologists felt emotion was too subjective for their scientific approach. Katharine Bridges found emotions to be relatively universal in expression. However, more recent studies on the social context of emotional expression assert that social learning is involved in most aspects of body language. In the 1960s, Desmond Morris carried out studies that linked human behaviors to those of our predecessors, the apes, and also explained many behaviors in group social contexts.

Jean Piaget, a Swiss psychologist, can be considered the father of the developmental perspectives we accept as fact today. A biologist by training, Piaget knew the importance of careful observation in his work on cognition. He surmised a series of increasingly complex structures of thought that are observable through analysis of a child's behavior. Piaget created a model for understanding cognitive changes as a process of adaptation involving assimilation, accommodation, and equilibration, and he theorized that individuals construct their own knowledge. Although Piaget has been criticized for ignoring the requirements of memory for some cognitive functions and for underrepresenting the abilities of young children, his work drives much of our understanding of children's thinking and learning.

Language studies have biological, physiological, social, cognitive, and cultural aspects, so discerning their origins is difficult. At one time, it was speculated that language was just absorbed, gained because of the social standing of the parents or learned purely by imitation. Jerome Bruner (1966) and Lev Vygotsky (1978) have given us the most meaningful understanding of how language is acquired and how language learning can be "scaffolded" or supported by parents and teachers.

The contemporary view of human development is complex and has changed since the theories of Rousseau and Pestalozzi. Today's version of the developmental principle emphasizes the **context** of development as well as the stages through which individuals proceed. Development is seen not as a linear progression but as a dynamic interactive process. Current perspectives on development identify the interacting forces of nature and nurture as codeterminants. John Dewey (1963) suggested that "heredity is a limit of education" and that "recognition of this fact prevents the waste of energy and the irritation that ensue from the too prevalent habit of trying to make through instruction something out of an individual which he is not naturally fitted to become." On the other side of the nature/nurture balance, theorists such as Piaget have shown that **environment** is an important factor in development.

Observing the Development of Young Children

What we see when observing young children depends on what we know about how human beings grow and develop. The philosophy of observation and authentic assessment, and therefore of this book, is based on the following fundamental principles:

Human beings

- are unique and individual and yet have characteristics that are common to all
- need to form attachments and develop within a social network
- tend to share patterns of maturational changes
- inherit many attributes and potentials, but their experiences of life influence how they develop
- are diverse in their appearance, patterns of development, beliefs, lifestyles, occupations, and needs
- demonstrate individual temperamental styles that tend to remain fairly constant throughout life
- develop within, shape, and are shaped by social contexts that are part of wider ecological systems
- adapt to changing environments and circumstances, thereby creating an individually constructed knowledge of the world
- develop in patterns of continuous and discontinuous change, some elements of development increasing gradually and constantly and others changing in surges and plateaus
- are especially sensitive to particular kinds of stimuli at certain times in their development
- undergo many changes during their lifetime, some observable and others internal
- are influenced by **social, biological,** and **psychological clocks**
- demonstrate similar basic emotional expressions whatever their culture or location, but social emotions are learned within a context
- continue to develop throughout their life span, each stage of which is equally significant
- can be raised in an environment that supports and optimizes development, but they cannot progress faster than their own timetable for development
- may deviate from expected patterns of growth and development or have **special needs,** and they may sometimes require special health, nurturance, or educational interventions

The developmental process

Definition: Child development

Child development is the dynamic process of change and progression that enables each individual to become increasingly independent, knowledgeable, skilled, and self-sufficient.

Child development depends on maturational processes and environmental conditions that can optimize each individual's genetic potential. Theories of child development, like those of life-span development, consider each human being as highly individual in appearance, style, and needs, but recognize the existence of reasonably predictable patterns of adaptation, changes in thinking structures, and skill acquisition among most of a population. Child development models can help us understand the role we can play in observing young children and supporting their development.

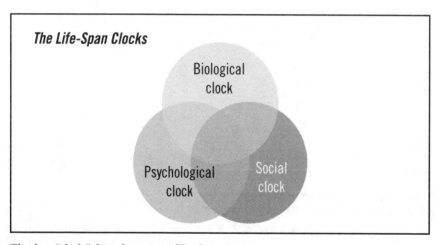

The Life-Span Clocks

Biological clock

Psychological clock

Social clock

The three "clocks" drive the process of development.

Taking a Special Look: Developmental delay

For a variety of reasons, some children may have slower than average development. The developmental delay may be general or specific to one or two domains. The caregiver or teacher may identify a cause for concern and approach the child's parents, or a parent may bring a concern to the caregiver or teacher. It is then the professional's responsibility, along with the parent, to observe the child closely, focusing on the particular area in question and the child's development in general.

Developmental Domains

One way to look at a child's development is to consider the developmental domains and how they interact. Although we divide the domains for ease of study, they also need to be seen as a dynamic whole. Within each person, this development happens differently, with external factors influencing developmental outcomes.

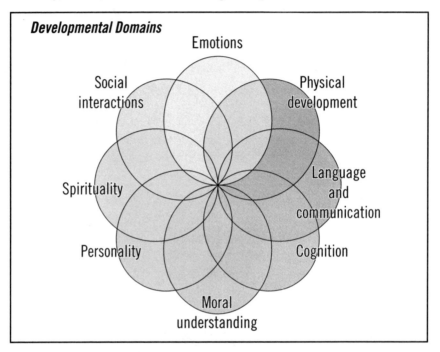

Developmental Domains

Emotions

Social interactions

Physical development

Spirituality

Language and communication

Personality

Cognition

Moral understanding

Taking a Special Look: The use of norms

Looking at the typical behaviors of children at particular ages and stages gives us an idea of what is average, but this **norm** does not imply that children "should" be at a certain level of achievement. The norm is just one way of viewing children's skill development, and it can give us an idea of how they are progressing. When we use the yardstick of the norm over a period of time, we can identify the children's rate of development in each domain. The fact that a child takes nine months to achieve skills that the average child accomplishes in about six months can tell us about the child's pattern of development.

If we can see that a child's skills are lagging behind those of other children, we may need to pay closer attention. Whatever the skills demonstrated, we need to support that development, document further observations, and, if necessary, refer the child to a specialist.

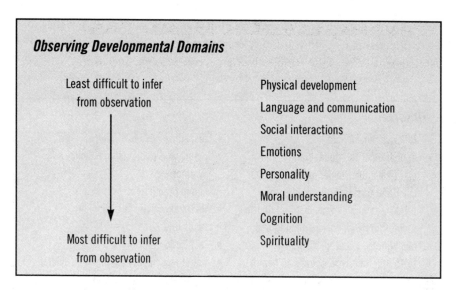

Observing Developmental Domains

Least difficult to infer
from observation

Physical development

Language and communication

Social interactions

Emotions

Personality

Moral understanding

Cognition

Most difficult to infer
from observation

Spirituality

This sequence is offered to highlight the challenge to the observer in making sense of observational information. It is based on the idea that behaviors that are clearly observable are easier to interpret. The sequence focuses on the evaluation of the child's progression through developmental stages. (It is not intended to be a hierarchy of difficulty in attributing theoretical explanations as to why the behavior is demonstrated.)

Physical development

Physical development has two basic aspects: **gross motor skills** refer to the development of the large muscles of the body; **fine motor skills** concern the control of the small muscles. The **cephalo-caudal principle** explains that the typical sequence of bodily control starts with the head and proceeds from there downward; the **proximo-distal principle** explains that control usually begins at the center of the body and proceeds to the extremities. **Sensory acuity** changes rapidly in the early months of the infant's life, with all five senses operating at an optimal level by the age of about 2 years. Bodily proportions change throughout development, with the head being larger in proportion to the rest of the body in infancy and the body gaining in proportional size through later stages.

Growth is an integral part of development but concerns only increase in size. Even with good nutrition, there may be individual patterns of weight gain and height increase. The basic needs of food, shelter, clothing, and protection must be satisfied for healthy physical development to occur. Children can fail to thrive if their physical or emotional needs are not fulfilled.

Sequences of skill development are common to most children, but they may occur at differing rates. Physical development is the most easily observed group of developmental changes. A sample observation can be found on page 78.

Observe:

- reflexive movements
- appearance: skin tone, quality, and clarity; posture; facial expression; hair color and texture; nail quality; eye brightness and clearness, pupil dilation; facial symmetry; ear positioning and cleanliness; sweat, personal odor
- teeth: number, type, color, and health
- skin marks: freckles, spots, birthmarks; cuts, bruises; acne, milia; urticaria, heat rash, cradle cap, diaper rash, etc.
- neck: angle and symmetry
- body temperature
- level of consciousness: uptime, downtime, trance, and sleep
- sleep: types, times, rhythms, and length
- appetite
- responses to foods: allergies, sensitivities, indigestion, colic, etc.
- abdomen: shape, protrusions, etc.
- increases in height
- body symmetry
- weight
- distribution of body fat
- muscular tone and definition
- alterations in body proportions
- sexual characteristics
- use and acuity of senses: sight, hearing, touch, taste, smell, and multimodal sensory acuity
- responsiveness to stimuli
- mouth and palate: shape, color, and symmetry
- sound production
- levels of activity and passivity
- heart rate
- respiration
- bowel movements: continence, color, consistency, frequency, and amount
- urination: continence, color, frequency, and amount
- bodily fluids: drooling, discharges, etc.
- fontanels (in children under 2 years old)
- mobility
- leg positioning and straightness
- large-body skills: walking, running, jumping, kicking, etc.
- foot position: inward pointing, outward pointing
- right- or left-footedness
- endurance
- hand coordination
- fine motor/manipulative skills: holding, throwing, catching, squeezing, drawing, piano playing, etc.
- right- or left-handedness
- self-help skills: dressing, undressing, toileting, feeding, etc.
- repetitive behaviors: habits and patterns of physical behavior

Observing Physical Development

Child's name:_____   Observer: _____

Age/D.O.B.: _____   Date: _____

Context/setting: _____

What gross motor skills do you observe? _____

_____

_____

_____

_____

What fine motor skills do you observe?_____

_____

_____

_____

_____

Describe the child's physical appearance and health indicators.

skin color/tone:_____

hair color/texture/length and condition: _____

eyes: _____

senses: _____

nails: _____

teeth: _____

foot position (inward/outward pointing): _____

head size in proportion to trunk/legs:_____

body shape: _____

body fat distribution:_____

posture/alignment/body symmetry: _____

legs (straight/bowed): _____

injuries (scars/bruises/etc.): _____

bowel control:_____

bladder control: _____

self-help skills: _____

observable habits: _____

identifying features: _____

height: _____

weight: _____

respiration: _____

health signs (and symptoms): _____

left/right hand preference: _____

Language and communication

Language development leads to two-way interpersonal communication. It involves both hearing and the physical ability to produce sound, but it also concerns the other sensory abilities. Language requires experimentation with sound, repetition of human sounds, attachment to adults, and various forms of reinforcement. There appear to be **sensitive periods** early in life for language development; it is thought that human beings have a "pre-wiring" that enables them to acquire language as long as certain conditions allow it to flourish. Stages of first-language learning are clearly observable, but the underlying explanations of how language is acquired are more complex. Language learning is the forerunner of literacy. Children who are exposed to more than one language may be at an intellectual advantage in later development.

Observe:

- crying: types and length
- eye gazing
- eye contact
- two-way communication
- cooing
- vowel-type sound production
- babbling
- seeking adult company
- responding to "mother-ese" or "parent-ese"
- attaching to adults
- game playing
- modulated babbling
- listening
- repeating consonants
- pointing
- gesturing
- making requests
- protesting
- drawing attention to self
- experimenting with sounds
- imitating sounds
- understanding language
- using holophrases
- taking turns
- making pronunciation errors
- producing whole words
- language with gesturing
- uttering two-word phrases
- using phrases of three or more words
- asking questions
- answering questions
- using grammar/rules of language
- listening to stories
- labeling objects
- naming people
- rhythmic sound production
- repeating rhymes
- creating stories
- creating rhymes
- singing
- pretend playing
- role playing
- storytelling
- cooperating with other children
- communicating in associative play and activity
- social conversation

- responding to social overtures
- initiating social relationships
- expressing feelings
- collaborating on projects
- making grammatical errors
- clarifying misunderstandings
- mixing two languages
- recognizing written letters
- recognizing own name
- writing own name
- understanding the experiences and feelings of others
- reporting and planning
- lying/variations of telling the "truth"
- comparing and interpreting

- inferring
- decoding
- encoding
- imagining
- reasoning
- predicting sequences
- inquiring about people, places, objects, and ideas
- socially acceptable communication
- drawing conclusions
- copying word shapes
- early writing
- story/letter writing: simple or complex
- symbolizing
- representing ideas

Taking a Special Look: Responding to cues

Young children can send out different **cues** or messages to us through their body language, gestures, and expressions. We must recognize that they have individual ways of communicating. Children with some special needs may need to be supported with communication strategies, and sometimes assistive devices, so that they can be better understood. For example, a visually impaired infant may not maintain eye contact, smile, or imitate an adult in the same way as a sighted infant. The caregivers need to observe any visual responses she does have and provide communication modes that she can perceive, such as through her other senses. If caregivers observe such a sensory deficit, they should share their observations with the parents, who may have similar observations, and seek further professional assessment; in this example, the child will probably need glasses.

Although infants cannot express themselves through language, they communicate in other ways. Their development in this domain can be observed through such signs as facial expressions, gestures, eye contact, and crying.

Social interactions

Social development involves both the concept of self and the relationships the individual has with others. Early **attachments** to primary caregivers are necessary for children to start building a sense of themselves. There may be particularly sensitive periods for the formation of these personal relationships and long-term consequences if such relationships are not established. Children need other people so that they can learn what is socially acceptable; much of this knowledge is gained through imitation. Social learning involves internalizing role models, so **social play** involving pretend games is very important. **Social interactions** can be readily observed when children are at play, in domestic situations, or in their natural environment with other adults or children. A sample observation can be found on page 79.

Observe:

- eye gazing
- reciprocal communication
- bonding to adult
- cues for attention
- egocentricity
- relationships with primary caregivers
- relationships with family members
- multiple attachments
- relationships with strangers
- stranger anxiety
- separation of "self" from others
- self-concept
- onlooker activity
- solitary play
- trial-and-error learning
- personal achievement
- individual problem solving
- identification of own needs
- articulation of personal needs
- strategies for meeting personal needs
- parallel play
- genderless play

- recognition of existence of others
- perspective shifting
- associative playing
- sharing skills
- imitative learning
- acknowledgment of sameness and differences
- same-sex friendships
- acceptance as member of a group
- identification with group activities or beliefs
- opposite-sex friendships
- categorical self
- pretend playing
- role playing
- team activity and problem solving
- cooperative playing
- developing strategies for collective success
- caring for others
- unconditional love

Observing Social Interactions

Observer: _____ Date(s): _____

Context(s)/setting(s): _____

	Child's appearance	Activity/materials	Involvement with self/others	Category of social play or activity
Infant				
Toddler				
Preschooler				
School-age child				

Observing Cooperative Activity

Children's names: _____ Ages/D.O.B.: _____

_____ _____

_____ _____

_____ _____

Observer: _____ Date: _____

Context/setting: _____

Type of activity: _____

Materials: _____

_____

How the play/activity started: _____

_____

How the activity progressed: _____

_____

_____

Adult involvement (if any): _____

_____

Evidence of leadership: _____

_____

Evidence of following instructions: _____

_____

How "rules" were set or followed: _____

_____

What agreement or disagreement was demonstrated: _____

_____

How difficulties were resolved: _____

_____

Evidence of sharing/empathy: _____

_____

Emotional development

Emotional development involves the expression and control of feelings. All infants express basic **emotions** in similar ways. However, feelings become more complex as children understand more about themselves, others, and the world. Early emotions are influenced by the bonding relationship with a parent. Typical stages of emotional conflict are experienced throughout childhood. At first, infants strive for a trusting relationship; they then focus on becoming independent and showing initiative, and struggle for a clear sense of self-worth. **Social emotions** express feelings shaped by social experiences. Emotions can be observed by interpreting behaviors, expressions, posture, and gestures, but inner conflicts and the subtleties of complex emotions may be harder to analyze.

Observe:

- facial expressions
- eyes: openness, direction, pupil dilation, symmetry
- eyebrows: shape and position
- creases on forehead
- mouth: open or closed, tilted
- head tilt: direction and angle
- nose: flared or relaxed
- cheeks: puffy, pinched, etc.
- skin: patchiness, color, sweat, etc.
- breathing: rate and depth
- posture
- positioning of arms
- state of consciousness
- attachments
- separations
- patterns of sleep
- eating patterns and appetite
- speed of movement
- gestures
- cues
- regression/progression in play, language, or other developmental domain
- response to stimuli
- egocentricity

- perspective changing
- pretend playing
- intentional communications
- role playing
- control of anger
- building confidence
- expressions of love
- use of comfort objects
- habitual behaviors
- labeling of emotions
- congruence between stated feelings and behavior
- fantasy playing
- making friends
- recognizing own emotional needs
- meeting personal needs
- sustaining friendships
- reactions to sensory experiences
- self-regulation
- creativity/destructiveness
- response to guidance strategies
- returning to plateau states of emotion
- coping with crises
- using personal style to advantage
- acknowledging the feelings of others

Observing Attachments and Separations

Child's name:_____   Observer: _____

Age/D.O.B.: _____   Date: _____

Context/setting: _____   Caregiver(s)/parent(s):_____

Child's routine contact with adults (e.g., 6 p.m.–8 a.m.: Mom; 8 a.m.–6 p.m.: 2 ECE teachers):

_____

_____

_____

Indicators of attachment (e.g., eye contact, physical closeness, etc.) to:

Adult #1: _____   Role: _____

_____

Adult #2: _____   Role: _____

_____

Adult #3: _____   Role: _____

_____

Adult #4: _____   Role: _____

_____

Behaviors at the time of separation from:

Adult #1: _____

Adult #2: _____

Adult #3: _____

Adult #4: _____

Behaviors one hour after separation from:

Adult #1: _____

Adult #2: _____

Adult #3: _____

Adult #4: _____

Personality

Personality involves the individual's **temperament**, awareness of self, and ability to manage life's challenges. Temperamental styles tend to be observable soon after birth and are thought to remain fairly constant throughout life. However, life experiences can alter how people deal with their temperament, and adults can be influential in shaping how children see themselves and cope with events. Temperamental styles have observable characteristics, but personality types can be difficult to label, because personal characteristics and patterns of behavior need to be observed over a prolonged period. Chess and Thomas (1996) offer a model for identifying temperamental types that is useful for teachers and caregivers trying to respond to different temperamental styles (see page 192). A wide range of personality assessments are available, but there is merit in observing a child naturalistically rather than performing tests that disregard situational variables.

Observe:

- activity level
- rhythms and daily patterns
- pace of activity
- timing of responses
- adaptability and openness to new experiences
- extroversion or introversion
- response to success or failure
- response to being touched
- emotional stability or instability
- intensity of reactions
- agreeableness
- consistency of reaction patterns
- personal space (physical)
- need to be with others or be alone
- pattern of self-control
- responses to stressors
- pro-social or antisocial style
- reality or fantasy
- positive or negative perceptions
- self-concept
- identification with adults
- leading or following others
- sex-role performances
- creativity
- optimism/pessimism
- confidence or diffidence
- habits
- honesty or dishonesty
- seeking of emotional or practical support
- conscientiousness
- role playing
- degree of autonomy
- mood quality and changes
- distractibility
- attention span
- persistence
- sleep and wakefulness
- body type: ectomorph, endomorph, or mesomorph
- responses to auditory stimuli
- reponses to visual stimuli
- intensity
- stability
- sensitivity

Moral understanding

Moral understanding involves the intellectual and social skills of understanding the difference between right and wrong and being able to behave according to those principles. **Morality** develops from understanding social roles and responsibilities and may be shaped by religious beliefs and culturally determined roles. Because cognitive skills are required to be able to think from the perspective of others and to manipulate ideas about what is ethical or morally right, this developmental domain is difficult to observe. **Pro-social skills** are easier to observe, but the ability to behave appropriately or desirably is not necessarily indicative of moral understanding. It is thought that stages of moral understanding can be observed through children's responses to moral dilemmas.

Observe:

- concept of self
- egocentricity
- perspective taking
- attachments
- guilt
- view of punishment
- response to consequences
- response to lack of consequences
- appreciating the concept of winning and losing
- pleasure seeking or pain seeking
- pleasure avoidance or pain avoidance
- cause-and-effect understanding
- risk taking
- thrill seeking
- labeling of "good" and "bad"
- understanding the role of authority
- remembering parameters of behavior
- control over own emotions and behavior
- metacognitive processes concerning morality
- choosing to demonstrate "good" behavior or "bad" behavior
- linking events to causes

- identification with adult figures
- role playing
- super-hero playing
- fantasy playing
- understanding specific rules
- following rules
- identifying emotions and feelings
- apologizing
- accepting apologies
- making up rules
- lying
- cheating
- behaving unsociably
- matching "punishments" and "crimes"
- inflicting "punishments" on others
- justifying behaviors and actions
- internalizing religious beliefs
- internalizing philosophical perspectives
- making moral judgments on the basis of abstract ideas
- stating personal beliefs
- advocating for what is "right"
- advocating for social "causes"

Cognition

Cognition involves the process of knowing, thinking, and understanding. Early learning is shaped by experimentation, play, imitation, stimulus–response, and reinforcement. Stages of cognitive development differ in their complexity as well as in the amount of information that is learned. Infants' understanding is acquired through their sensory exploration of the world and is highly egocentric. Later, thinking patterns change as children are able to deal with concrete ideas and some symbolism. Through intellectual stimulation and brain maturation, children gradually learn to deal with abstract ideas and multifaceted tasks. Information is processed according to these changing mental structures; an internal construction of the world is created. We can understand what children are thinking from what they say, what they do, and the mistakes they make.

Cognitive development is an extremely difficult process to observe and to make appropriate inferences from. Brain activity can be observed through various types of electronic scans and can be studied as neurological activity, but this doesn't help us understand thinking in everyday situations! Theories of cognition can help us to untangle the complexities of children's thought processes. A sample profile using the theory of multiple intelligences (see page 73) can be found on page 82.

Observe:

- reflexive behaviors
- exploration
- experimentation
- curiosity
- sensory acuity
- sensory discovery
- attachment behaviors
- responses to stimuli
- imitation
- constructing meaning
- object/people permanence
- trial-and-error behavior
- use of symbolism
- pretend playing
- role playing
- attention span
- emergence of language
- use of language to express ideas
- response to ideas
- concrete thinking

- classifying
- sorting
- matching
- seriating
- counting
- one-to-one correspondence
- cardinality
- magical thinking
- sequencing
- spatial relationships
- decoding
- encoding
- conserving ideas
- concentrating or focusing on single ideas
- identifying people, objects, and places
- asking questions
- discriminating
- patterning
- discovering properties of materials

- using logic
- predicting outcomes
- following sequences
- estimating size, time, quantity, etc.
- convergent problem solving
- creative problem solving
- aesthetic understanding
- following instructions
- understanding time sequences
- remembering people, objects, and places
- considering viewpoints of others
- construction
- searching for challenges
- expressing a problem
- goal setting
- reading and understanding
- investigating a problem
- producing ideas
- using rational arguments
- combining ideas
- designing objects
- making models
- using metacognitive strategies
- using metalinguistic strategies
- arranging the learning environment
- developing strategies for problem solving
- carrying out plans
- cooperating in activities

- investigating nature
- recalling facts
- learning by rote
- overextending rules
- creating rules
- pressing individual interests
- using research methods
- scribbling
- attempting to spell
- making errors
- identifying and solving problems
- making free associations
- scientific discovery
- recording events
- brainstorming
- debating
- paraphrasing
- comprehending
- making inferences
- refining solutions
- summarizing information
- making objective comments
- making value judgments
- deferring gratification
- stating hypotheses
- analyzing research
- assessing situations
- synthesizing ideas

 Taking a Special Look: Patterns of development

Skills are almost always gained in the same sequence, even though they may be demonstrated at varying rates. For a child with special needs whose development is somewhat uneven, you may observe that some domains of development are further advanced than the rest. Frequently, one aspect of development will affect another, so we sometimes need to respond in different ways. For example, you may need to arouse the interest of a child who has a hearing deficit by providing visual rather than auditory stimulation. Watch closely to see the reactions to your stimuli and respond accordingly.

Observing Mathematical Thinking

Child's name:_____   Observer: _____

Age/D.O.B.: _____   Date: _____

Context:_____

Observation task	Original presentation	Transformation	Observed response
Number	Are there the same number of pennies in each row?	Now are there the same number of pennies in each row, or does one row have more?	
Length	Is each of these sticks just as long as the other?	Now are the two sticks each equally as long, or is one longer?	
Liquid	Is there the same amount of water in each glass?	Now is there the same amount of water in each glass, or does one have more?	
Mass	Is there the same amount of clay in each ball?	Now does each piece have the same amount of clay, or does one have more?	
Area	Does each of these cows have the same amount of grass to eat?	Now does each cow have the same amount of grass to eat, or does one cow have more?	
Weight	Does each of these two balls of clay weigh the same amount?	Now (without placing them back on the scale to confirm what is correct for the child) do the two pieces of clay weigh the same, or does one weigh more?	
Volume	Does the water level rise equally in each glass when the two balls of clay are dropped in the water?	Now (after one piece of clay is removed from the water and reshaped) will the water levels rise equally, or will one rise more?	

Source: Laura E. Berk, *Infants, Children, and Adolescents*. Copyright © 1994 by Allyn & Bacon. Reprinted by permission.

This observation chart provides the opportunity to see how a child "conserves" ideas. Some preschool children understand constancy, while others will not grasp this concept until they are older. Remember that responses may reflect language limitations rather than conceptual errors.

Spirituality

Spirituality is concerned with personal reflections, a connection or relationship with a power or person outside the self, and an appreciation of the significance of people and things. Not all child-care professionals consider this developmental domain significant, and those who do may have difficulty defining it. For some, spirituality involves appreciating beauty, developing aesthetic values, and demonstrating care for the world and its people. For others, it is strongly associated with a religion or philosophy of belief about our creation, the nature of existence, and our role in the world. Spiritual development can involve an increased awareness, understanding, or practice in any of these areas.

Spiritual development is possibly the most challenging area of human development for observers. Philosophical thought obviously involves cognition, but there is more to spirituality than logic and mental gymnastics, and even that part of spiritual thought is not easily observed. Our observation of children's actions and words may only hint at a surface explanation for something that is much deeper.

Observe:

- curiosity
- appreciation of beauty
- meditation and prayer
- listening to music
- appreciating art forms
- acknowledgment of nature
- wonder
- joy
- connection with predecessors
- futuristic thought
- symbolism
- recognition of signs
- premonitions
- intuition
- identification with culture/ethnicity
- rituals
- ceremony
- social responsibility
- rites of passage

- imagination
- discussion of the purpose of life
- philosophical thought
- religious understanding
- appreciating the efforts of others
- pro-social behavior
- fantasy
- magic/imagination
- interest in literature
- creative activity
- expressing love
- experiencing the intensity of emotions
- forgiving
- accepting forgiveness
- appreciating movement and dance
- experiencing success or failure
- poetry
- magical thinking
- connectedness with family, friends, etc.

- romance
- striving for justice
- fun experiences
- transcending the "here and now"
- advocating for peace
- stillness
- membership in a group
- enjoying myths and legends
- appreciating the "essence" of an experience
- birth experiences
- belief in the sanctity of human life
- dreaming
- being solitary
- giving thanks
- celebrating
- fasting
- reciting mantras, creeds, scriptures
- metaphysical thought
- comparing and contrasting world religions
- analyzing why events happen
- making a pilgrimage
- attributing "bad" things to the devil or Satan
- knowledge of nirvana, heaven, hell, the underworld, etc.
- singing and chanting
- acknowledging icons, symbols, altars, and other holy objects
- belief in an afterlife
- worshiping
- belief in the soul or other immortal element of human beings
- listening to an inner voice
- social advocacy
- mysticism
- punishment and retribution
- belief in sacraments and other practical signs of spiritual occurrences
- knowledge or wisdom
- belief in being saved
- belief in reincarnation
- healing
- mindfulness
- communication with the "creator"
- interpreting dreams
- belief in God, the Divine, Krishna, etc.
- near-death experiences
- expressing or experiencing wholeness
- atoning
- acknowledging auras, karmas, atmospheres
- expressing ethical perspectives and behaving according to ethical principles
- identifying a moral in a story
- interest in the supernatural or occult
- communion
- love for people or for God
- giving to the poor or needy
- belief in immortality
- animism
- identification of archetypes
- initiations
- belief in extraterrestrial forces
- arguing from a specific religious or moral standpoint
- visiting historic/holy places
- superstitious beliefs and practices
- perspective taking
- expressing feelings
- being in a state of depression, sadness, bereavement, loss, etc.
- living in the moment
- interpreting scriptures, holy books, and moral stories

The interaction of the domains

When we observe any child, we see a flow of behavior that is not labeled as belonging to any one developmental domain. In fact, we should make sure that we do not think of any behavior as being physical, cognitive, or so on; every behavior involves interacting domains. Since no area of development should be considered without seeing how it might relate to the others, we need to observe carefully and consider the **whole child**. If, for example, we observe language skills, we must remember that they are dependent on social skill development, cognitive processes, emotional ties, and the physical skill of sound production. The sample observation on page 80 shows how various domains can be observed in play.

Watch out!

Try to review all domains of development, even though some areas are easier to interpret than others!

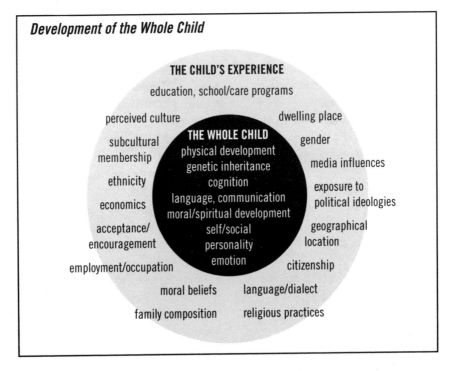

Development of the Whole Child

THE CHILD'S EXPERIENCE

education, school/care programs

perceived culture   dwelling place

subcultural membership

THE WHOLE CHILD
physical development
genetic inheritance
cognition
language, communication
moral/spiritual development
self/social
personality
emotion

gender

media influences

ethnicity

exposure to political ideologies

economics

acceptance/ encouragement

geographical location

employment/occupation   citizenship

moral beliefs   language/dialect

family composition   religious practices

The child is at the center. Each interacting aspect of the child's development is affected by all of the environmental factors that contribute to her or his experience of the world. You observe the behaviors that help you to make inferences about the whole child's development.

Observing a Preschooler's Development

Child's name: _____   Observer: _____

Age/D.O.B.: _____   Date: _____

Context/setting: _____

Appearance: _____

_____

Sensory exploration/discovery: _____

_____

Physical skills:

    a. gross motor: _____

_____

    b. fine motor: _____

_____

Language/communications: _____

_____

Evidence of pre-operational thinking: _____

_____

Demonstration of conceptual understanding: _____

_____

Self-help skills: _____

_____

Social/pre-social skills: _____

_____

Demonstration of emotions: _____

_____

Personal style/temperament: _____

_____

Play behaviors: _____

_____

Personal interests: _____

_____

Observing an Adult's Assistance in a Child's Learning

Child's name:_____   Observer: _____

Age/D.O.B.: _____   Date: _____

Context/setting: _____

Observe a child in a play sequence or semi-structured learning activity. _____

_____

What can the child do without adult assistance? _____

_____

_____

Describe how the adult "moves" in the situation. _____

_____

_____

What strategy is the adult using to support the child's understanding or skills? _____

_____

_____

How does the child respond? _____

_____

_____

What can the child do now with the adult's support?_____

_____

_____

How can the child become able to do this independently?_____

_____

_____

Observing Play

Child's name: _____   Observer: _____

Age/D.O.B.: _____   Context/setting: _____

What interests the child? _____

_____

_____

Describe the kinds of play the child engages in. *(isolate, onlooker, parallel, interactive, explorative, physical, functional, pretend, cooperative, sociodramatic, etc.)* _____

_____

_____

Describe the complexity of play. *(use of symbols, use of tools and objects, complexity of rules in interactive play, etc.)* _____

_____

What are the emotional characteristics of this play? *(smiles a lot, talks during play, aware of others; follows, leads; etc.)* _____

_____

What knowledge does the child have to possess to play this way? *(how things work, units of measurement, social roles, etc.)* _____

_____

Describe the use of materials. *(appropriate, inappropriate; destructive, creative; repetitious; imitates others, shows others; etc.)* _____

_____

What skills does the child have to possess to play this way? *(drawing, constructing, creating, measuring, etc.)*

_____

What is the use of language during play? *(quiet, talkative; positive, negative; talks to self, talks to others, responds verbally to others; asks questions, explains, describes, labels items; uses words/phrases/sentences; etc.)* _____

_____

Describe the social characteristics of the child's play. *(relationship and involvement with others)* _____

_____

_____

Principles of Development

Understanding developmental theories

We should be aware of not only the developmental domains but also some other important ideas that can shape how we observe, what we see, and how we interpret that information.

The child as the constructor of knowledge

Piaget's (1954) theory of developmental psychology offers a profound view of children's **construction of knowledge**. He observed and described play sequences that indicate that young children learn through direct experience. Their understanding needs to come from first-hand experiences; caregivers may orchestrate the events, but the children must play themselves. Piaget's theory reinforces the need to observe children's activities and to be present in those activities to ensure that the children can construct meaningful learning. Where necessary, caregivers have to intervene, reconstruct the physical environment, and then continue to observe.

The adult's role as facilitator of learning

Froebel (1826) described the adult as a gardener in the child's garden. Teachers and caregivers need to watch what is happening and supply the necessary nurturance, tools, or practical help required. They must be keen observers and learn when and how to assist the children's development.

A pro-social ethos

Moral understanding depends on children's maturational stage as well as their environment. The strongest influence on children's value systems is usually their parents, but they also receive many strong messages from the media and the other adults around them. Social learning theorists such as Bandura (1977) explain this process as imitation and deferred imitation, but the way children construct their own values is more involved than imitation alone. A complex interplay between children and their environment enables them to search for meaning. Their cognitive level shapes how this happens; children can only internalize "right" and "wrong" according to their own personal reality.

Positive guidance strategies and strong role models can influence how children learn to behave, but children acquire much moral and pro-social learning through conversation with adults. When we listen to what they tell us and respond with thought, children know that we take their thinking seriously and care about them. In addition, we can observe their play behaviors and intervene to label a behavior, clarify a moral issue, or nurse hurt feelings.

The zone of proximal development

Vygotsky (1978) discusses a **zone of proximal development** that explains how children can be supported to new learning. Through an observation process, caregivers identify what each child knows or can currently accomplish. They use a variety of strategies to help the children perform at a new level of skill or acquire new knowledge. Bridging the gap between what each child can do with and then without assistance allows caregivers to help learning and allows the children to be successful. This principle underlines the need for careful observation and appropriate intervention in the children's activity.

The principle of scaffolding

Bruner (1966) developed a theory of **scaffolding** by studying how adults help children gain new language skills. He noticed that many mothers aided their children's language by extending the learning that had already been gained. Mothers observed their infants closely and provided a "scaffold" for new language by using various support strategies. This model applies to many different situations where caregivers observe children and can help the children's learning. A sample observation of scaffolding can be found on page 81.

Multiple aspects of intelligence

In the last few years, interest had increased in Gardner's (1993) work on **multiple intelligences,** in which he hypothesizes that there are seven or more different forms of intelligence: spatial, logical/mathematical, linguistic, bodily/kinesthetic, musical, interpersonal, and intrapersonal. He suggests that, if we observe the style of different children, we can see that they think and operate in different ways. Without valuing any intellectual type over another, teachers and caregivers should offer differing learning experiences to accommodate all types of learning; both the approach to learning and the content of what is to be learned will vary. The work of Goleman (1997), on what he calls **emotional intelligence,** reinforces the need to observe and value ways to control, manage, motivate, and recognize emotions in others and to handle relationships. Both theories clearly indicate that caregivers must observe personal styles in order to meet the children's needs. A sample multiple intelligence profile can be found on page 82.

Attachments

Bowlby (1965), Ainsworth (1972), and others have done significant research on the necessity of early attachments. Caregivers should observe the processes of attachment and separation that children experience. Without the emotional ties of attachment, all other aspects of development may seem irrelevant. With infants, the attachment relationships with primary caregivers should be strong and well supported. With all ages, caregivers must observe how the children make transitions from one adult to another and find ways of supporting them through separations. Strong emotional ties will lead to trusting relationships.

Cultural diversity

Many of the children we care for and educate come from very different backgrounds from our own. This **cultural diversity** can be positive for us all, because we not only benefit from the breadth of experience of our community, but can also find that the multicultural climate stops us from making assumptions about those who seem to be like ourselves. We can observe the behavior of people from different cultural groups, but we must avoid making **stereotypes** and generalizations from one family's behavioral patterns. Those behaviors may be particular to a family or even an individual. Asking questions can offer really helpful information; genuine inquiries are rarely rejected, but the parent should be approached in an appropriate manner. Inviting parents to participate, in whatever way they can, might also allow you to get to know each other better and provide a stronger bridge between home and child care or school.

Taking a Special Look: Assessing children from diverse cultures

Children from other cultures can face social and linguistic challenges within the North American community. If such children also have special physical or developmental needs, caregivers and teachers must approach the assessment process with extra care. Methods of authentic assessment will allow a child to demonstrate her abilities and needs clearly. If at all possible, the child should be assessed in her native language to avoid misunderstandings and to ensure that a limited command of English is not interpreted as a limited ability to communicate or understand. Similarly, a person from, or at least familiar with, the family's culture should be present at meetings with the family, both to help the family understand the child's needs and to ensure that the family's beliefs and values are understood and respected by the caregivers and other professionals involved with the child.

Ecological systems

Because human development occurs within a social system, caregivers must know about children's social networks and as much as possible about their broader ecological systems. Bronfenbrenner's (1979) **ecological systems model** of concentric circles (see page 195) explains how a child's development is influenced by a wide variety of social, political, economic, and religious aspects of the environment. Caregivers should do their best to appreciate these interrelated factors that shape the development of the children they care for. Possible strategies include conducting sociological studies, observing local environments, keeping up to date with economic and employment issues, finding out about social challenges in the community, and establishing good communication with parent groups. Contextual questionnaires can supplement this data (see pages 254–57).

Early intervention

Until recently, it was thought to be inappropriate to interfere with a child's development in its very early stages. Any remediation or accommodation was thought to be unnecessary unless the child had an extreme physical disability. The Greenspans' (1985) work demonstrates great success in **early intervention** with infants and toddlers who are experiencing emotional and social challenges in their relationship building. Caregivers need to observe many aspects of early development, especially those involving how babies relate to adults. Early observation and identification of social difficulties may have life-long effects.

Sensitive periods of development

The entire life span provides a time for a flow of change, but certain sensitive periods are particularly important for learning specific skills and acquiring cognitive processes. Observations of the imprinting behaviors of young birds led Lorenz (1937) to develop this theory, but it can also be applied to other aspects of development. Language learning, in particular, is much easier for a young person acquiring a first or subsequent language. Bowlby (1965) believed that maternal bonding to a newborn needs to happen immediately after birth, or else subsequent attachments will be spoiled.

Although some people debate whether the stage or skill will actually be missed if it does not develop during the sensitive period, it may not be possible to make up for some early deprivations. In the case of a neglected child who was not exposed to language or social learning, her ability to gain a full language was severely reduced; she was able to say only a handful of words when she received concentrated teaching. Some mechanisms do exist to overcome certain short-term deprivations or limitations; in principle, however, some key experiences need to be provided at the right moments.

Developmental diversity

One result of having more children with diagnosed special needs integrated into mainstream settings is an increased need to accommodate a wider range of development within any group of children. The positive aspect of **developmental diversity** is the greater likelihood that teachers and caregivers will treat the children as individuals; however, the integration also presents a curriculum and assessment challenge. Observation skills need to be finely honed, and a wide range of assessment tools is necessary. Being able to conduct some standardized assessments may be helpful, depending on the caregiver's role and responsibilities (see Chapter 10). It will always be necessary to read reports from educational psychologists and be able to interpret the summary or results. Any individual program plan (IPP) that has been developed will have to be carried out. It is preferable that such a plan be a team activity; however, teachers can find themselves carrying out the plans of psychologists or other interventionists, so they must be able to understand what is required and to observe and record the child's responses.

Health issues

In order to notice that a child is looking or behaving in ways that are different from usual, caregivers need to know about typical appearance and usual patterns of behavior. Baseline observations are usually made on a daily basis but are not recorded unless there is a need to document the information. They can give us clear information about a child's state at the start of the day, which then acts as a useful reference point for later physical or behavioral changes. Pimento and Kernested (1996) suggest that caregivers take time to observe and assess growth, personal hygiene, emotional health, developmental skills, and a range of physical and behavioral signs and symptoms.

Assessing development through observation

Advantages

- The observer knows what to look for.
- Analysis of data is more straightforward.
- Data collection can meet the needs of educators.
- The data collected are focused and pertinent.

Disadvantages

- The observer may be biased by a particular developmental theory.
- Developmental knowledge takes time to acquire.
- Analysis may disregard pertinent information that was thought to be irrelevant.
- Prescribing learning requirements from open-ended observations can be too subjective.
- The data are collected using formats that are not tested to be valid or reliable.

Key Terms

attachment

behaviorism

biological clock

cephalo-caudal principle

child development

cognition

construction of knowledge

context

cue

cultural diversity

developmental diversity

developmental psychology

early intervention

ecological systems model

emotion

emotional intelligence

environment

fine motor skills

gross motor skills

language

morality

multiple intelligences

norm

personality

phenomenology

physical development

pro-social skills

proximo-distal principle

psychological clock

scaffolding

sensitive period

sensory acuity

social clock

social emotions

social interaction

social play

special needs

spirituality

stereotype

temperament

whole child

zone of proximal development

Observation Sample

This recording documents the child's physical attributes and skills that were observed during recess time. The recording is written fairly objectively with useful details.

Observing Physical Development

Child's name: _James_ Observer: _Danielle_

Age/D.O.B.: _6 years, 2 months_ Date: _March 3, 1998_

Context/setting: _recess for Grade 1 class_

What gross motor skills do you observe? _Walking, standing, running forwards, to the right, and swerving; jumping down from the climber, sitting, jumping over skipping ropes on the ground, kicking a large ball (right foot)_

What fine motor skills do you observe? _Grasping with left and right hands, pointing to an item, pincer grasp (right hand), throwing ball through hoop, catching small ball, threading grasses through fencing with fine motor control, holding hands, pressing hands down on ground, shoveling sand_

Describe the child's physical appearance and health indicators.

skin color/tone: _fair skin, pink flush on cheeks (cold day), downy face_

hair color/texture/length and condition: _light brown, straight, somewhat lank, "bowl cut" style_

eyes: _gray-brown, long eyelashes, eyes set wide apart_

senses: _response to sound, visual stimuli, smell (fish tank), taste? touch?_

nails: _short and bitten on left hand; left thumb is sore_

teeth: _white, full set of first teeth, need cleaning, no cavities/fillings?_

foot position (inward/outward pointing): _slightly inward pointing, right more pronounced_

head size in proportion to trunk/legs: _1.6_

body shape: _slim build_

body fat distribution: _chubby cheeks but fairly flat abdomen and little fat on legs_

posture/alignment/body symmetry: _appears symmetrical with upright posture_

legs (straight/bowed): _straight legs_

injuries (scars/bruises/etc.): _knees have small grazes_

bowel control: _yes_ bladder control: _yes_

self-help skills: _can dress himself, use bathroom, wash, brush teeth; difficulty with shoelaces_

observable habits: _nail biting_

identifying features: _bushy eyebrows, small mole on upper lip_

height: _4 ft. 8 in._ weight: _44 lb._

respiration: _22 (30 after running)_

health signs (and symptoms): _normal temperature, active_

left/right hand preference: _right-handed, right-footed_

Observation Sample

This chart allows the teacher to review an entire play sequence to highlight its important characteristics. The recording contains some inferences as well as objective recording.

Observing Cooperative Activity

Children's names: _Damian_   Ages/D.O.B.: _5 yr., 6 mo._

      Cara   _4 yr., 11 mo_

      Jessie   _5 yr._

      Malachi   _5 yr., 3 mo._

Observer: _Shakila_   Date: _May 28, 1998_

Context/setting: _Preschool room, 3:30 p.m._

Type of activity: _Dramatic play_

Materials: _Dress-up clothes including hats, capes, and old shoes_

How the play/activity started: _Jessie was pretending to bake muffins when Cara asked if she could join._

How the activity progressed: _Jessie said Cara should do the dishes. Cara said she wanted to bake. Damian walked by and said boys are chefs, not girls. Damian continued conversing and entered the pretend kitchen area._

Adult involvement (if any): _The ECE asked Damian what made him think only boys were chefs. He shrugged and continued to take items out of the oven._

Evidence of leadership: _Jessie tends to initiate play activity; others follow, but she does not sustain interest._

Evidence of following instructions: _Cara followed Jessie's suggestion to wash dishes, but she soon found "baking" more interesting. She said she would "make eggs and ketchup" so Damian set the table and Malachi sat waiting to be served._

How "rules" were set or followed: _All group members agreed to the social rules of domestic play._

What agreement or disagreement was demonstrated: _Jessie did not pursue her direction to Cara; they were caught up in the play._

How difficulties were resolved: _Because each child took a "role," there was little to resolve._

Evidence of sharing/empathy: _The playthings were shared as was taking turns in conversation and the division of domestic "tasks."_

Observation Sample

This play observation was recorded during and after the sequence observed. This structure allows the teacher to look at the most important aspects of development that can be seen in play.

Observing Play

Child's name: _Rachel_   Observer: _Jerry_

Age/D.O.B.: _2 years, 8 months_   Context/setting: _Child's home, April 10/98_
Rachel is home in the afternoon after nursery school. Rachel is diagnosed as being "gifted." Observed for 48 minutes.

What interests the child? _Rachel focuses on two puzzles--one 8½ x 11 of Pooh Bear and the other a large floor puzzle of Piglet._

Describe the kinds of play the child engages in. *(isolate, onlooker, parallel, interactive, explorative, physical, functional, pretend, cooperative, sociodramatic, etc.)* _Rachel plays by herself in solitary activity except when she engages her mother._

Describe the complexity of play. *(use of symbols, use of tools and objects, complexity of rules in interactive play, etc.)* _Rachel follows a left-to-right sequence using trial and error, guessing, and matching pieces._

What are the emotional characteristics of this play? *(smiles a lot, talks during play, aware of others; follows, leads; etc.)* _Rachel appears to have little expressed emotion except when she tries to get her mother's attention. She is then excitable and whines._

What knowledge does the child have to possess to play this way? *(how things work, units of measurement, social roles, etc.)* _She needs to understand what the puzzle demands of her. She needs a knowledge of space and shape, and the ability to match colors and fit shapes together using a variety of cognitive strategies._

Describe the use of materials. *(appropriate, inappropriate; destructive, creative; repetitious; imitates others, shows others; etc.)* _Rachel handles the material (puzzle pieces) with care, manipulating them in her hands._

What skills does the child have to possess to play this way? *(drawing, constructing, creating, measuring, etc.)* _As well as the cognitive skills, she needs to be able to sit for a prolonged period and use fine motor skills._

What is the use of language during play? *(quiet, talkative; positive, negative; talks to self, talks to others, responds verbally to others; asks questions, explains, describes, labels items; uses words/phrases/sentences; etc.)* _She talks as she plays. At times she focuses on the real world and what she is doing. At other times she talks to Pooh and Piglet as though she is "in" the pictures. She uses complex sentences with correct grammar, tense, etc. "Piglet wants to go on a picnic; he liked it when Pooh shared his honey last time."_

Describe the social characteristics of the child's play. *(relationship and involvement with others)* _Content playing by herself, Rachel appears to want her mother's company more than her practical assistance. She wants Mom to do it "her way."_

Observation Sample

In this sample, both the child and the adult have been observed. The recording focuses on the specific responses that the adult makes to assist learning. This is an example of scaffolding.

Observing an Adult's Assistance in a Child's Learning

Child's name: _Pegah_   Observer: _Cory_

Age/D.O.B.: _1 year, 11 months_   Date: _June 8, 1998_

Context/setting: _Home child-care setting--in living room with two older children. Caregiver is present._

Observe a child in a play sequence or semi-structured learning activity. _Pegah is looking at a small bound book._

What can the child do without adult assistance? _She can point to pictures in the book (of baby animals) and say "dog, dog."_

Describe how the adult "moves" in the situation. _The caregiver sits by Pegah and says "lamb" and "calf" for the appropriate pictures._

What strategy is the adult using to support the child's understanding of skills? _The caregiver repeats "lamb" and makes the sound "baa, baa."_

How does the child respond? _Pegah looks at the book, points to the lamb, and says "log." The caregiver repeats "lamb" until Pegah says "lab."_

What can the child do now with the adult's support? _Pegah says "lab" for "lamb."_

How can the child become able to do this independently? _If she is supported in hearing "lamb" and seeing the picture, singing songs about lambs, seeing a stuffed toy lamb, and seeing lambs on television, this may reinforce "lamb."_

Observation Sample

This multiple intelligence profile demonstrates the child's intellectual type. This information will help teachers and caregivers provide appropriate learning experiences.

Multiple Intelligence Profile

Child's name: Tam   Observer: Ryan

Age: 6 years, 11 months   Date: May 17, 1998

Sources of data: Running records, conservation test, checklist observation, and interview

Contect: School-age child care and Grade 2 class

Musical

Logical/
mathematical

Bodily/
kinesthetic

Linguistic

Spatial

Interpersonal

Intrapersonal

Summary: The observational data pointed to Tam being strongly mathematical; he has intense and prolonged interest in all types of construction and the drawing of architectural diagrams. Although competent in language, Tam prefers the media of music and movement to express himself. He appears interested in making social relationships as long as they focus on his interests. If not, he soon loses the base for the relationship. He seems independent yet is not particularly reflective on his own abilities. When asked about what he liked doing, he mentioned the construction games, but he wasn't sure if his skill was strong in this area.

Tam responds to physical challenges and, although he did build intricate structures, his fine motor skills are not particularly well developed. It appears that his activity derives from his thought processes and problem solving rather than his physicality. Tam has interest in playing the piano, but he is frustrated that he cannot get results quickly.

Recently Tam has become involved with camping with his family. Tam enjoys building campfires, putting up tents, and pretending to be in the wilderness. Although he likes outside pursuits, he can often watch others rather than be involved in action; when he cannot lead, he opts out rather than follow directions.

Narratives

3

What is important in collecting anecdotes is that one develops a keen sense of the point of cogency that the anecdote carries within itself.

Max Van Manen (1990)

Observing young children at play, one is struck by the length of time that a child can spend blowing bubbles and learning about their characteristics, dressing up in adult or super hero clothes and trying on various roles, exercising creative talent while making a collage of found materials, figuring out how to build a snow creature or listening attentively to a story.

Ada Schermann (1990)

Narrative observations help us notice what the child is doing in a more objective, detailed way. A narrative of this girl's play will help evaluate her fine motor, language, and cognitive skills.

Focus Questions

1. How can you record a child's behavior to capture every detail of action, reaction, posture, gesture, and communication without using a video camera?

2. What can you discover by describing in detail a randomly selected sequence of a child's play activity?

3. How can you avoid interpreting your observations according to your own biases?

4. For people whose writing skills are not very strong, what are some creative ways to record detailed descriptions of behavior?

5. Anybody can write down what he or she sees—what difference does it make to observe children with a trained eye?

6. Writing down particular incidents in which a child is involved may be amusing, but how can you choose really significant episodes to record?

Learning Outcome

Learners will record observations objectively using a variety of narrative methods that suit the purpose of observing.

History Notes

Accounts of children's development were not always derived from observation. Early theorists, such as the seventeenth-century English philosopher John Locke, arrived at their notions about children from philosophical speculation rather than observational material.

Jean-Jacques Rousseau, a French philosopher, took much more interest in real children. He was intrigued with the observations of children made by explorer Captain James Cook in Tahiti in the eighteenth century. Using these recordings, he compared the Tahitian children's behaviors with those of their European counterparts. Possibly the earliest forms of human observations, called "Baby

Biographies," were made by Johann Pestalozzi in the late eighteenth century. These were day-to-day recordings of the development of young children and infants. Pestalozzi studied the behavior of his $2\frac{1}{2}$-year-old son for a short period and made significant **inferences** about the importance of the mother's role in the child's life.

Early educators, philosophers, and psychologists frequently studied their own offspring. Charles Darwin wrote anecdotal accounts of his son's behavior in an attempt to explore his development. Sigmund Freud used narrative accounts of early childhood experiences to formulate his theories of infantile sexuality.

Specimen descriptions of behavior were first used by Fletcher Dresslar in 1901 in *A Morning's Observation of a Baby*. These descriptions recorded behavior "intensively and continuously." A succession of observers helped to validate narrative recordings as an acceptable method of study.

The school of **behaviorism** was founded by John B. Watson in the early twentieth century. The behaviorists focused on the objective measurement of behavioral reactions. Their research centered on experiments with animals, which were carefully set up and meticulously recorded. While the experiments gave an opportunity for narrative recording, it was not the naturalistic type of observation with which narratives are usually associated.

The behaviorists looked at the total response of an organism and relied on objectively observed behaviors to make inferences. The developmental psychologists had different views, which involved making inferences about the causes of behavior and the patterns of development by writing detailed narrative accounts of children in naturalistic settings. The most significant developmental psychologist was Jean Piaget. His background as a biologist and observer of natural science led him to observe and record the behaviors of his own children. These observations form the most important series of anecdotal records yet written. From them, he drew far-reaching conclusions about the sequences of a child's development.

Narrative Observations

 Definition: Narrative observations

Narrative observations are those in which a written sequential account of what is perceived is recorded.

Describing behavior

The recording of a child's **behavior** in a narrative description is a direct noninterpretive method, in most cases. If the observer is skilled, an accurate record of the behavior can be made; for the less practiced, the method can lend itself to accidental **inferences** and **assumptions**. The greatest challenge of all narrative recording is to include as much detail as necessary to describe what happens, and the way in which it happens, so that readers of the record can get an accurate "visual" impression. The goal will be to record very much like a video camera. (The use of an actual video camera is covered in Chapter 7.)

Narrative recording goes further, though, because by looking for the minute details of behavior, you will perceive it more closely than if you were to record it on tape. The process of narrative recording enables you to be a better observer and furthers your own learning.

Child Development Focus

Narratives can be helpful in observing and recording
- gross motor skills
- fine motor skills
- social interactions
- spontaneous language
- play patterns
- interests

"But I can't write down everything," many students say—and they are correct! It is impossible to ensure that you have a description of every muscle movement, blink of the eye, and breath the child takes. Describe as much as you can of what is going on—so there is a degree of selection, even if it is inadvertent or due to the limitation of language. By recording, you learn to see more clearly.

Watch out!

Detail is the essence of a narrative, but don't focus on one aspect of behavior and forget the others!

Even when you intend to record all nuances of behavior, the practicalities mean that you must use whatever skill you have to write as quickly as possible everything that seems significant. Your early observations will most likely contain a lot of information involving **gross motor skills** and **language**. Later, you may add some detail of **fine motor skills**. As you practice the method, you will probably be able to add descriptions of posture and eye contact, and more detail regarding the subtleties of communication. As you build your skill in writing narrative recordings, you will also develop your ability to "see" with new eyes.

Watch out!

Improve your written English skills and your narratives will also improve!

Finding the right words can be difficult when describing behavior and indicating the quality of actions. A review of some of the components of narrative may help you:

1. **Adjectives:** These are the describing words, used to qualify or define. Use them to signify *how* something is being done—for example, a *loud* noise made the *sleeping* infant startle.
2. **Verbs:** These are the action words; they tell *what* is being done. These are the most significant words in a narrative as they indicate the type of behavior observed—for example, she *skipped*, he *ran*, she *jumped*, he *sorted* the counters.
3. **Adverbs:** These words describe the *quality* of an action or *modify* a verb—for example, he rose *quietly* from the chair, not saying anything, straightening his knees *slowly* as he twisted his ankles *sharply* to pass the book to the teacher.
4. **Sequencing:** The sequencing of events can also be a hurdle to those people who are not good at telling stories in the *order* in which they happen. Some cultural groups find this a particular challenge, as their language or tradition may emphasize different elements of a story line. Writing down what happens, as it happens, can help with sequencing difficulties.
5. **Tense:** Purists would have us write what is happening in the present tense—for example, he *squats* down and *picks* up the book. Others are mainly concerned that the tense be consistent—for example, he *squatted* down and *picked* up the book. Unless otherwise directed, use the one that you find the most comfortable.
6. **Observer bias:** The direct recording of behavior in narrative styles has less scope for **bias** than the interpretive methodologies like sampling. There is a risk, however, that the observer sees from a biased perspective. Descriptive

words may themselves seem biased—for example, to describe a child as *smiling* may suggest happiness whereas the word *grin* may have broader connotations. The observer may have a subjective feeling toward the observed child and consequently record, as fact, something that might be a negative interpretation—for example, the description of a child *whining* might be a subjective observation. The selection of one anecdote rather than another may in itself contain further bias—for example, the anecdote you select shows a preschooler being uncooperative when more often than not she is observed to cooperate and share.

Biased data presented for analysis result in inadequate, invalidated, subjective inference with little usefulness. (See Chapter 1 for a more detailed explanation of observer bias.)

Types of narrative observations

Narrative observations can take the following forms:

1. **Running record** (pages 89–94): A **running record** involves a written description of the child's behavior. The observer should be separate from the child to be observed and without immediate responsibility for the child or for other children in the area (**nonparticipant observation**). The method involves recording exactly what the child says and does in sequence as it happens. The observer can attempt this method with little previous observation skill, but increased practice enables the observer to record more detail, to describe more accurately, to avoid assumptions, to be aware of personal biases, and also to make better use of the **data** that are collected.

2. **Anecdotal record** (pages 95–99): An **anecdotal record** requires the observer, usually a practicing teacher or student teacher, to write a brief account of a selected incident or behavior soon after it occurs. Anecdotal records are frequently used because they can be written up at the end of the working day and are an appropriate method of recording developmental stages. They require some expertise on the part of the recorder to choose significant sequences of behavior.

3. **Diary record** (pages 99–101): A **diary record**, or a day-by-day written account of the child's behavior that is dated and timed, may incorporate features of the running record or anecdotal record as the observer thinks appropriate. This record can offer some of the **contextual information** that could help explain the behaviors. It may be used as a vehicle for an ongoing dialogue between caregiver and parents. Particularly useful for caregivers working with infants or children with **special needs**, this method enables rigorous record keeping.

4. **Specimen record** (pages 101–102): A **specimen record** gives the precise detail of the play or other behavior of one child with such description and clarity that reading the account evokes a mental image. This method may be carried out for a particular reason and therefore be undertaken at a predesignated time—for example, to determine the child's attempts to communicate or to use a particular limb. Alternatively, the observation may have no specific focus but offer an opportunity for thorough observation of the child in **spontaneous play** to investigate interests, choices, or **play patterns**. Most often, this intensive recording method is used by a psychologist or teacher not working directly with the child.

Running Records

▶▶ Key Features: Running record

- objective observation of one child
- open-ended
- written account recorded at time of observation
- detailed
- records most actions
- records all speech
- records whatever occurs
- naturalistic
- nonparticipatory

Writing descriptive sequences of children's activity is particularly useful for teachers or caregivers whose philosophy incorporates a **child-centered** approach to planning the curriculum. Open recordings enable observers to record whatever behaviors are demonstrated rather than look for specific behavior categories. Children's play is unstructured and directed by themselves. If we can observe children in action in their natural setting, what we see is the children being themselves.

Observers face the challenge of recording whatever they happen to see, since the focus is not on specific behaviors. They also require good descriptive skills and the ability to record a number of behaviors in quick succession. A running record, however, is often the method of choice for students starting an observation course, because it does not depend on strong knowledge of child development.

When looking for a particular behavior, you may well see it because you are expecting to. If you are looking for nothing in particular, you may run the risk of not interpreting correctly what you do see—but you are more likely to be more objective.

Depending on when you undertake your running record, you are likely to see a variety of behaviors. As you write down what you see, you must not include any inferences. Leave them for your **analysis**, where you will have to validate your comments. Sample running records can be found on pages 107–11 and 112–14.

In the effort to write what you see, you might find yourself writing "He played" or possibly "She went." Such phrases do not describe with sufficient accuracy what actually happened. Write down specifically how the child moves and what he does rather than using vague interpretive terms.

Running records are useful when planning parent interviews. Having some substantial information to share with parents helps caregivers and parents work together. At this time, teachers may request the informal observations of a parent and add them to the collection of information about a child.

Regular **assessments** may involve the running record along with other assessment or observational tools. These records may be presented at a case conference

Running records frequently contain unexpected happenings because they include anything that occurs. This girl reacted with a mixture of alarm and delight when a dog slipped into the yard as a visitor arrived.

with the parents, at which a multidisciplinary or co-worker team may plan the required curriculum.

The running record is the most frequently used method for learning about children in every aspect of their development. Teachers, students, and parents gain; the process benefits everyone.

Taking a Special Look: Naturalistic observation of children with special needs

Narrative methods of observation and recording are sufficiently open-ended to make them suitable for children who have special needs. For example, Rianna—who was diagnosed with cystic fibrosis as a toddler and is now 3 years, 5 months old—has a fluctuating activity level. On some days, she is very mobile and plays alongside other children of her age; on other days, she is quiet, more reflective, and less active. Rianna's teacher is keen to record her development in each domain. A running record allows for detailed recordings without any intrusion into Rianna's activity.

Using running records

Advantages

- This method can be used by untrained observers.
- Observation is less likely to be affected by bias when written at the time the behavior occurs.
- A description of a child's behavior can be used for a variety of purposes—for example, developmental assessment, parent meetings, program planning, or learning about child development.
- Observational data can be used by other professionals for objective analysis.
- This method provides the opportunity to record all behavior, including the unexpected.
- The record may indicate the need for further observation/assessment using other methods.

Disadvantages

- Successful recording requires fluent use of language.
- Observer bias may not be obvious where assumptions are made.
- The observer needs to be away from responsiblities with the children.
- Writing the record can be a long and laborious task.
- Inferences may be difficult to draw from a bulk of data.
- Observation can only be undertaken with one child at a time.

Method charts for running records

Split-page format

Running Record

Child's name: _____ Observer: _____

Age/D.O.B.: _____ Date: _____

Reason for observation: _____

_____

Context: _____

_____

_____

_____

Time	Observation	Comment/explanation

This chart enables the observer to log the time of events described. The "Observation" column is used for a detailed description of the behavior, recorded as it occurs. The right-hand column allows for comments that clarify or explain what is happening (this section is not to make inferences).

Full-page format

Running Record

Child's name: _____ Observer: _____

Age/D.O.B.: _____ Date: _____

Reason for observation: _____

_____

Context: _____

_____

_____

_____

Time	Observation

Although a running record can be written on any paper, an organized chart can be helpful. The left-hand margin keeps track of the time.

Categorizing format

Running Record

Child's name: _____   Observer: _____

Age/D.O.B.: _____   Date: _____

Reason for observation: _____

_____

Context: _____

_____

Category of behaviors: _____

_____

Time	Observation	Classification

This chart offers the possibility of writing a running record in note form or in detailed narrative. Time is recorded as behaviors occur. After the recording, the observer categorizes each play or behavior sequence according to the required classification (for example, for social play, the categories would be Onlooker, Solitary, Parallel, Associative, or Cooperative).

Anecdotal Records

▶▶ **Key Features: Anecdotal record**

- may focus on one or more children
- observer chooses what is significant to record
- written account recorded after observation
- details highlights of action
- frequently recorded as a series of occurrences
- naturalistic
- participatory or nonparticipatory

Although open to subjectivity because the observers choose to record particular behaviors, the anecdotal record is often used by psychologists, teachers, caregivers, parents, and students.

The most basic forms are those recorded by parents in a **baby book** or log book of development. As the child gets older, caregivers and parents can use this method for formal record keeping for meetings with parents or, most effectively, for a log of developmental or behavioral changes. Students may learn from recording anecdotes while working with children or during observational opportunities when not engaged with the children.

Piaget recorded anecdotal observations of his own children in the 1920s. Later, his observations were more systematic and focused on asking children questions, but his early observations enabled him to formulate his cognitive theory. Recording what seemed noteworthy enabled Piaget to study the child's behavior, by noticing the child's mistakes or misunderstandings.

The choice of event to record can be challenging for the untrained or inexperienced. Parents may be able to identify a significant behavior worthy of recording because of the change it indicates from previous behavioral patterns. A new strategy may be demonstrated or an **emerging skill** may be seen. These would be opportune moments to record.

Watch out!

The anecdotal record is useful only when the observer chooses significant behavior to record!

The degree of description required is dictated only by the necessity to detail the essential elements of the anecdote. The appropriate level of detail can be tested by having other people read the anecdote, to see if they can appreciate its significance. In a similar way, there is no set length of narrative for an anecdotal record. Usually a paragraph or two is adequate, as the context and behavior can be captured in that length. A sample anecdotal record can be found on pages 115–17.

Anecdotal records can be kept by researchers or psychologists and classified under behavioral types, social play categories, temperamental styles, cognitive activities, child's age, and so on. In this way, they can be resourced or cross-referenced so that key elements can be drawn together as required.

Practicing teachers may have a card index system, record information on tapes for each child, or keep a daily log book that can be completed by parent or child. Caregivers responsible for infants may find this a particularly easy and effective way to pass information back and forth from home to agency.

Caregiving in a private home environment is particularly challenging because there is little time to write up observations. The anecdotal record enables the caregiver to make a few written notes while remaining a participant.

Time constraints are difficult for all those who work with young children. Toddlers' teachers may find the anecdotal record convenient and efficient. Fragmented bits and pieces of activity typical of the toddler can be written up as anecdotal records. They could be recorded at naptime, if the caregiver is lucky.

Accidents, potential child abuse, or serious incident reports may be written in an anecdotal form. Dated anecdotal records of a child's behavioral changes and health observations may be required as evidence in a court situation and considered to be important documentation.

 Taking a Special Look: Observing indicators of abuse or neglect

Observations may lead teachers and caregivers to think that a child has suffered some kind of abuse or neglect. It is not for them to investigate the situation; that is the task of the child-care protection agency, which must be notified not only if there is proof or evidence of abuse, but also if there is reasonable cause for such a concern.

Particularly useful observations in these cases include dated anecdotal records or diary accounts that detail the observation of physical marks, unusual or disturbing behaviors, anything significant that the child tells you, or artwork that the child has produced. Be very careful not to enter into questioning the child, which can be counterproductive in the long term even though you might think that it could have a therapeutic function. Questioning can plant suggestions in the child's mind and could also undermine possible legal action.

Using anecdotal records

Advantages

- A brief account of what happened is easy to record.
- Short anecdotes are easy to write.
- The observer can record behavior soon after it occurs.
- This method is a useful means of recording behavior for record keeping and communication with parents.
- Data can form a useful selection of significant behaviors.
- The anecdotal method can be used by almost anybody.
- The observer can concentrate on more than one child.
- The observer can remain as a participant in the program.
- The record may form the basis of documentation used for legal purposes.
- This method can be used as a learning tool for students.

Disadvantages

- The observer needs to decide what behavior is pertinent to record.
- Time delay can involve observer bias.
- This method relies on the observer's memory.
- Selective recording can be biased.
- The record may offer insufficient contextual information.
- The observer requires skill to record most significant behaviors.

Parents and caregivers may wish to write down what they judge to be significant. An anecdotal record can capture the essence of the moment.

Method charts for anecdotal records

Basic recording system

Anecdotal Record

Child's name: _____   Observer: _____

Age/D.O.B.: _____   Date: _____

Reason for observation: _____

_____

_____

Time/date: _____

Context: _____

_____

Observation anecdote: _____

_____

_____

Time/date: _____

Context: _____

_____

Observation anecdote: _____

_____

_____

Time/date: _____

Context: _____

_____

Observation anecdote: _____

_____

_____

These anecdotal forms can be used in a card index system or in a log form for each child.

Accident/serious occurrence

Anecdotal Record						
Date	Time	Name of child	Incident	Teachers present	Action	Parent informed (sign)

This chart is useful when spread over the open pages of an accident book. The incident should be described as fully as possible—a drawing might be included.

Diary Records

▶▶ **Key Features: Diary record**

- objective observation of one or more children
- selects highlights of activity
- written account recorded regularly after observation
- may contain reflections or analysis within text
- naturalistic
- nonparticipatory or participatory

Diaries may be the oldest of all narrative recording methods. They involve little technology or expertise, and the diarist chooses what is significant to record. Diaries usually involve a series of anecdotal recordings; the level of detail can vary. A diary may be an open communication or a private record of events.

The same diary technique can be used for keeping an up-to-date account of the development of an individual child or a group of children. The significant area of development is selected and written up on a frequent, usually daily, basis. The style is often anecdotal, but other forms of recording can be included.

A parent may initiate this activity, as the daily process of recording results in a valuable document. Teachers and others may also want to keep an open diary as a dialogue between themselves and parents; it may encourage parental involvement where little had previously been demonstrated.

Using diary records

Advantages

- Observations are easy to record.
- This method keeps a daily record of behavior.
- The diary is a valuable tool for communicating between parents and caregivers.
- The diary provides a valuable record or "keepsake" for parents and/or agency.
- This method may be used alongside other methods of observation.
- The diary can be used as a learning tool for students as part of a child study.
- The record is useful in determining behavioral changes and revealing behavioral patterns.
- Observations may be written about one or more children at a time.
- Diaries are frequently helpful to teachers in reviewing previous months'/years' programs or children's progress.

Disadvantages

- The choice of content might be subjective.
- The observer requires persistence to keep the record going daily.
- The need to interpret data is easily overlooked.
- Situations usually require further observation. A diary alone may be insufficient.
- Inferences may be subjective.
- The selection of information may be influenced by observer bias.

Method charts for diary records

Daily log

Diary Record

Date: _____

Caregiver observation: _____

_____

Caregiver signature: _____

Parent signature/comment: _____

Date: _____

Caregiver observation: _____

_____

Caregiver signature: _____

Parent signature/comment: _____

Date: _____

Caregiver observation: _____

_____

Caregiver signature: _____

Parent signature/comment: _____

This system allows for a daily anecodote to be recorded and shared with the parent. Another style could include equal space for parent observations. The caregiver can also be given an update of what occurred at home.

Infant observation log

Infant Observation Log

Child's name: _____ Date: _____

Age/D.O.B.: _____ Caregiver's name(s): _____

Feeding: _____

Diapering: _____

Sleeping: _____

Played with: _____

New interests/achievements: _____

Caregiver signature: _____

Read by parent (signature): _____

These sheets can be copied and left on a clipboard for each infant each day. After a week, they can be kept in a binder, for each child, which the parent may want to keep. The "new interests/achievements" category may be completed as an anecdotal record.

Specimen Records

The most detailed narrative recording, the specimen record, is described by Goodwin and Driscoll (1980) as "a comprehensive, descriptive, objective and permanent record of behavior as it occurs." It is the most challenging of the narrative methodologies because of its comprehensive and open-ended nature.

Watch out!

Don't attempt a specimen record until you are skilled at the other narratives!

This type of recording cannot be undertaken while the observer has responsibilities for the child or other children. It requires skill on the part of the observer to record all the behaviors of the child. All possible detail should be recorded, including all gross and fine motor movement, actions and reactions, description of posture, gesture, facial expression, and all utterance including the exact language used.

Specimen records can use a variety of coding systems that help the observer capture detail. Coding systems can be harder to read but form a more detailed picture of the behavior. They may be written by re-running a video-recorded sequence—particularly in a detailed movement study. Rarely, if ever, do practicing teachers have the time or reason to do this kind of observation. Sometimes, however, they will read specimen records prepared by psychologists; such records offer greater depth than normal classroom observation usually allows.

Using specimen records

Advantages

- The specimen record gives a rich, detailed narrative description of all behavior.
- The data collected can be analyzed by one or more professionals.
- These records are useful for case conferences and may be used in research work. They are less likely to be affected by observer bias than other narratives.
- The record may focus on one behavior category or be entirely open-ended.
- This method provides an opportunity to observe unstructured play activity.
- The record may establish causes of behavior.
- The observation may indicate development in one or more domains and show the necessity to observe using other methods.

Disadvantages

- The observer requires refined skill to record.
- The observer needs to be a nonparticipant in the children's program.
- This method is heavily dependent on the written language skill of the observer.
- The observer can observe only one child at a time.
- The record may incorporate complex coding to enable the recorder to include sufficient detail.
- Specimen records are frequently used by professionals without full contextual information and may not involve appreciation of the whole child.

Recording Narrative Observations

How to record, summarize, and analyze a narrative observation

1. Decide on your reason for using the narrative method.
2. Choose one of the narrative styles that fits your reason for recording.
3. Check that you have parental permission.
4. Prepare a method chart to meet your needs.
5. Write the observation as it happens, or as you select behaviors to record after they occurred, in a rich, descriptive narrative.

6. Write up your "neat version" of the observation as soon as possible, making only additions that you are certain help your description but do not change the content.

7. Review your data and summarize the information according to developmental domains. (List, but do not explain, behaviors you have observed in each domain.)

8. Explain the observed behaviors with reference to norms and theories.

9. Make inferences about the behaviors following the process of analysis in Chapter 1 (pages 19–21).

10. Develop an action plan or learning prescription on the basis of your findings.

Ways to make narrative recording easier

- **If your writing is a problem:** Try using a tape recorder. Speak your observation into it, using rich, descriptive language. Write up the observation as soon as possible before any of the detail is lost.

- **If English is your second language:** You could try writing your observation in your own first language using the method as described. Translation may be necessary if your work is for an assignment or for record keeping. Be aware of how translation can affect objectivity.

  Or, tape record your observation in your first language to capture the detail and then translate as you put it down on paper.

- **If you cannot write fast enough:** Try using a map indicating movement to accompany the observation.

  Or, videotape the observation and take your time writing your version on paper, using the pause and replay buttons frequently until you have the descriptive narrative written down.

  Or, observe the child with another observer recording simultaneously. Afterward, sit down together and discuss your perceptions. If possible, write a narrative together.

  Or, use a form of shorthand. If you do not know standard abbreviations, you can study them. Try using R. instead of Richard, chdn. instead of children, and so on.

- **If your language lacks sufficient descriptive powers:** Write your observation in point form and add the adjectives, adverbs, or whatever is missing afterward with the help of a teacher or colleague who observed at the same time or from whom you can get language support.

  Or, prepare lists of adjectives, adverbs, and even verbs to help you write up your observation.

Each of the above strategies may help students or teachers who have particular difficulties in writing. These skill-building ideas can help but must always be mentioned in the observation, as they may affect the accuracy of a recording.

Taking a Special Look: Terminology for exceptionality and differences

Positive language can help shape our attitudes to children with special needs. A child is a person first and foremost; his or her individual identity should come before any descriptor of ability or of any professionally diagnosed condition. It is more sensitive and appropriate to speak of "a child who is partially sighted" than to say "a blind child." Observe children and describe their behaviors from a positive perspective.

Inappropriate language can be demeaning, teasing, impersonal, or judgmental; it often ignores the child's potential and focuses on disability rather than ability. Appropriate language considers the child first and then describes the child's condition, family, ability, or behavior as objectively as possible.

More appropriate terms	Inappropriate terms
Dana has epilepsy.	an epileptic
Percy has a hearing deficit.	the deaf kid
Bert's social skills are sometimes inappropriate.	a "behavior" child; a misfit
Kinga needs special help with . . .	a slow learner; retarded
Dora has learned to tie her shoelaces.	educable retarded; trainable
Rivka has a developmental delay.	a below-average child
Cory (child's name alone)	spotty Scotty (or other rhymes)
Ho is new to the country.	a "Chink" (or other demeaning references to country of origin)
Sharina's skin is a rich brown color.	ethnic children; "fuzzy tops"
a child who has exceptionalities	a special-ed kid
a child with a disability	a handicapped child
a child with a disorder	an abnormal child

A narrative observation could capture in detail these girls' involvement in their activity and their interaction with each other.

Key Terms

analysis

anecdotal record

assessment

assumption

baby book

behavior

behaviorism

bias

child-centered

contextual information

data

diary record

emerging skill

fine motor skills

gross motor skills

inference

language

narrative observation

nonparticipant observation

play pattern

running record

special needs

specimen record

spontaneous play

Observation Sample

This sample running record offers an extremely objective and descriptive recording of the child's behavior. A diagram assists the process of recording. The student then summarizes the data and provides a self-evaluation.

All observations need to include sufficient background information, such as that given here on the front page, to make the recording meaningful. Permission to record must always be sought from the parents, as shown on page 2 of this assignment. Note that the permission form shows the child's real name, while the observation uses a pseudonym to preserve confidentiality.

---

1 of 5

Observation Assignment

Front Page

Student name: _Sue Fung_   Student number: _000-888-000_

Section number: _062_

Assignment method: _Running Record_

Date due: _February 12, 1998_   Date handed in: _February 12, 1998_

Child's name (pseudonym): _Patrick_

Child's age (years/months): _2 years, 8 months_

Date of observation: _February 2, 1998_   Time of observation: _2:10-2:25 p.m._

Setting: _Day-care setting. Children are in free play time. There is a wide choice of activity_

Parent's name: _Mr. P. Yuen_   Phone # if released: _N/A_

* _The observation recording is translated from Chinese._

Each assignment has specific criteria. Please check with the assignment description and direction given in class.

Declaration by student

I have followed the assignment description and instructions given in class about confidentiality and privacy. I confirm that appropriate processes for making this observation have been undertaken and that permission has been gained from the parents. A copy of this observation will be given to the parents if they desire.

Sue Fung

Signature of Student

Permission Form

Child Observations, Case Studies, and Portfolios

Student and Parent Agreement

Without written permission I will not observe and record information about your child. Please sign in the space provided if you agree that I may make observations and study your child. It would be helpful if you could initial each of the boxes if you are willing for me to undertake any or all of the techniques of information gathering.

I ___Sue Fung___ *(student name)* will not refer to the child in any written manner by his or her real name. Information recorded will be written objectively, treated professionally, and kept confidential.

___S. Fung___   ___Feb. 2, 1998___
(student's signature)   *(date)*

I ___Peter Yuen___
(parent's name)

agree to have ___Johnny Yuen___
          (child's name)

observed ☑   photographed ☒   audiotaped ☒   videotaped ☒

by ___Sue Fung___
(student's name above)

at ___University Settlement Recreation Center-ESL child-minding division___
(agency/home)

for the purpose of study in child development at ___Centennial College___

(school/college) for a period of ___1 week___ *(weeks/months)* on the consideration that copies are made available to me, the parent, if I so request.

___Peter Yuen___   ___Feb. 2, 1998___
(parent's signature)   *(date)*

Patrick is sitting with his legs beneath his buttocks; then he stretches both legs and sits on the floor. He holds a plastic strawberry in his left hand and a knife in his right hand, and he uses the knife to cut the strawberry in half. He grasps the two pieces of strawberry in his left hand and puts them on a plate. Then, he puts the knife down on the floor; he picks up a cup with both hands, moves the cup toward himself and puts the straw, which sticks in the cup, in his mouth. It appears that he is sucking something from the cup.

He puts the cup down on his left side, and he bends his body forward and stretches his left hand to get a plastic tomato and holds it in his palm. He moves his upper body backward and turns it to his left side. He puts the tomato on the floor and uses his left thumb and forefinger to support the tomato. Then, he holds the knife in his right hand and cuts the tomato. He releases one half of the plastic tomato from his left hand and uses his thumb and forefinger to get a plastic lemon. He puts it on the floor, supports it with two fingers and cuts it with the knife he is holding. He puts the knife down, grasps a half of plastic tomato and sticks it with the half of lemon. He holds the knife in his right hand and cuts the tomato-lemon, which is put on a plate and supported by his left thumb and forefinger.

He puts the knife down again, leans his upper body and stretches his left hand toward John, who is sitting opposite him. He frowns and grasps the plastic fruit that John is holding and pulls it toward himself. After getting the fruit from John, Patrick holds it in his left hand. He raises his left hand and uses it to hit John's head. After an instructor tells him not to hit others, he throws the fruit away.

He stands up, bends to the floor and picks up a cup using both hands. He straightens his body and walks to the instructor; he lifts the cup and has the straw touch her lips. The instructor asks him, "What's this?" He replies, "Orange juice, for you." After the instructor asks him to get an apple juice for her, he smiles and bounds to the place where all the plastic fruits and plates are located. He holds the cup in his left hand; he puts his right palm on top of the cover, seizes the edge by the fore-finger, middle finger, ring finger and baby finger of his right hand, and pulls the cover away. He moves the cup toward his nose; it seems like he is smelling something in the cup. Then, he uses his right hand to press the cover on top of the cup. He holds the cup with two hands, walks to the instructor and stretches both hands toward her, smiles and says, "Apple juice." After the instructor has finished the juice, he throws the cup away, as he smiles and hums a tune.

He runs and then jumps into the play tent. He sits with his legs beneath his buttocks among balls and holds a ball in each hand. He raises both hands, looks up and says, "Cinderella" in a loud voice. He throws the balls away, leans his body forward and puts his hands on the floor. He stretches both legs; I think that he is trying to stand up. However, his right foot steps on a ball, and his body leans to the left. Then, he puts his hands on the floor again, stands up and jumps out of the tent.

He laughs and runs after John and says, "Goooo . . ." in a high-pitched loud voice. He runs around the room, stops next to the slide and jumps up and down with both hands raised. At this moment, John is throwing balls from the tent. As the instructor asks John to stop throwing and pick up the balls, Patrick helps them to pick up the balls near him and throws them overhand into the tent. Then, he laughs and runs after John, follows John, creeps under the slide and lies with his chest down. He puts both elbows on the floor and both palms under his chin.

When snack is ready to be served, he creeps forward and puts both hands on the floor to help himself stand up. Then, he runs to the right side of the room, grasps the back of a chair with two hands and walks with his body leaning backward. He puts the chair next to the table and sits down. He stretches his right hand and grasps a cup by using thumb, forefinger and middle finger. He pulls the cup toward himself; after the instructor asks him to wait for others, he pushes the cup forward next to the plates, moves his hands back and puts them on his thighs. While waiting for the instructor to allot the food, he puts his right hand on the edge of the table and says, "I want to eat." Then, he pulls the plate toward himself with thumb and forefinger. He grasps a cookie by using his thumb, forefinger and middle finger and puts the cookie in his mouth. He holds his cup with his hands and moves it toward his lips.

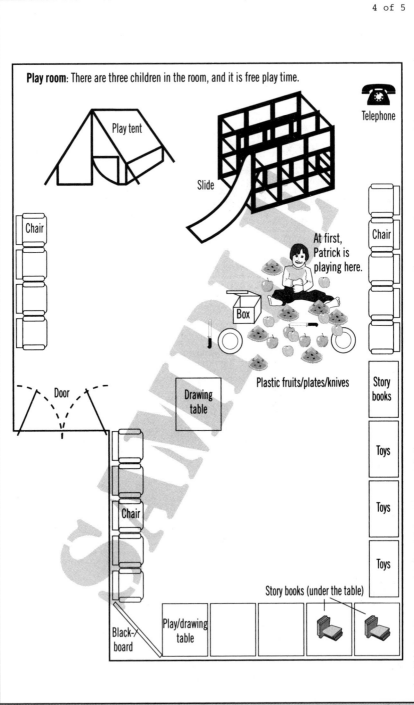

Play room: There are three children in the room, and it is free play time.

Telephone

Play tent

Slide

Chair

Chair

At first, Patrick is playing here.

Box

Plastic fruits/plates/knives

Story books

Door

Drawing table

Toys

Toys

Chair

Toys

Story books (under the table)

Black-board

Play/drawing table

SUMMARY

Physical Skills

Gross Motor:
- sits with his legs beneath his buttocks (squats)
- moves his body forward and backward when he sits
- pulls a plastic fruit toward himself from another child
- bends his body to pick up an object when he is standing
- walks steadily
- jumps out from the play tent and jumps up and down
- throws balls overhand into the play tent
- runs without falling
- creeps under the slide

Fine Motor:
- holds a plastic fruit in his left hand and a plastic knife in his right hand
- holds a cup with both hands and puts straw in mouth
- uses thumb and forefinger to support a plastic fruit
- holds an object in each hand and sticks the two objects together
- pulls a cover off a cup by using four fingers to seize the edge and putting his palm on the top
- picks up an object by using thumb, forefinger and middle finger (tripod grasp)
- uses thumb and forefinger to pick up food and feeds himself without assistance

Social Skills:
- grabs a plastic fruit from another child and hits the child with the fruit
- offers a cup of "juice" to another person
- friendly, eager to please, for example, gives the instructor an "apple juice"
- helps other children pick up balls
- plays parallel to another child (runs after the child and follows him to creep under the slide)

Emotional Skills:
- frowns when he grabs a plastic fruit from another child
- smiles and hums after the instructor drinks the "juice"
- laughs and says, "Goooo" loudly when he runs after another child

Cognitive Skills:
- sticks two pieces of plastic fruit together
- cuts a whole plastic fruit in half by using a plastic knife
- identifies the name of the object in the cup
- knows a cover should go with a cup
- picks up his own chair before having snack

Language and Communication:
- pushes the cup toward another person and lets the straw touch her lips
- tells her, "Orange juice, for you"
- laughs and says, "Goooo" in high-pitched, loud voice
- says, "Cinderella" loudly when playing alone in the play tent
- tells the instructor, "I want to eat," and puts his right hand on the edge of the table

Observation Sample

This running record offers an objective, flowing description of activity. Alongside, the recorder offers explanations of what is happening and some inferences about the child's behaviors.

Running Record

Child's name: _Mandy_ Observer: _Daisy C._

Age/D.O.B.: _2 years, 6 days/October 30, 1996_ Date: _November 5, 1998_

Reason for observation: _To observe all of Mandy's behaviors as they spontaneously occur during observation period, to help assess her development in all domains (emotional, social, physical, cognitive)._

Context: _Observation took place outside in the playground after afternoon snack. There were thirteen toddlers in the playground at the time of the observation. The weather was sunny and cool, so the children were dressed in coats, hats, and mittens. Five other children were also in the same play space with climbers and tricycles._

Time	Observation	Comments
3:50 to 4:10	Mandy is sitting on a tricycle with her feet placed flat on the ground, facing forward. She is grasping the handles, wrapping her hands around the handlebars. She climbs off the tricycle, swinging her right leg over the seat, both hands remaining in same position as above, while looking in the direction of another tricycle.	She has physical skill of sitting astride tricycle. Puts her feet on the ground rather than on the pedals. Good coordination allows her to climb off tricycle with ease, while appearing to focus visual attention on another object (tricycle).
	Mandy runs toward the other tricycle, climbing on by swinging her right leg over the seat, hands placed on the right side of the handlebars. Putting each foot on a pedal, she attempts to propel the tricycle forward. Her right foot slips off the pedal. She takes her left foot off the left pedal and moves the tricycle forward, using her legs and feet, both feet forward, pushing backward at the same time.	Effective coordination also displayed in her ability to run toward the other tricycle. Appears to understand that tricycle can be propelled by using pedals; however, has difficulty keeping her feet on pedals and quickly resorts to using her feet on the ground to move forward.
	Stops tricycle and looks over left shoulder in the direction of another child's father. She	Appears very aware of what is happening around her, implying her ability to scan her

Time	Observation	Comments

says, "John, your daddy is here!" Continues to sit on tricycle, watching John's daddy. After a moment, Mandy climbs off the tricycle and runs toward the riding car John had been sitting in. She climbs in and pulls the car door shut with her left hand and grips the steering wheel, one hand on each side, and propels forward using her feet, one in front of the other, to push the car forward.

surroundings to assess what is going on.

The above is further supported when Mandy immediately runs to the riding car as soon as John vacates it. When she looked for John after seeing his dad, she also noticed the toy he was using.

She places her left hand on the back of the car, puts her left foot on the ground, pushing the door open with her right foot, and climbs out. A caregiver comes over to Mandy and takes her hand, saying, "Come, Mandy, we'll wipe your nose." Mandy takes her hand and walks to the Kleenex box. She stands and lets caregiver wipe her nose. Mandy stands beside caregiver for a moment, then walks toward another caregiver.

Good large muscle coordination once again displayed. Margaret easily climbs into the car, using a series of twisting, supporting, and maneuvering motions to get herself in and out.

Mandy understands simple instructions—both the instruction to go with the caregiver and what was going to happen (wipe nose).

Caregiver says, "Hi, Mandy. Your shoe is untied; let me tie it for you." Mandy says, "No, I want Daisy to do it." Caregiver says, "Okay, Daisy will do it!" Once her shoe is tied, Mandy climbs the stairs on the climber, holding onto the railing with her left hand, alternating feet up the stairs. She sits down at the top of the slide and pushes herself down, each hand on one side of the slide. At the bottom, some other toddlers begin screaming, and Mandy stands up and screams as well. She runs back to the stairs and climbs to the top again, sliding down the slide. Lands on her bottom, flips over on hands and knees, looking up the slide. Gripping sides of slide, Mandy climbs up on hands and knees, sliding her hands up as she goes. At the top, lets her feet slip into a straight position, lying prostrate on the slide. Lets go with hands and slides down on her belly. Repeats this activity two more times.

Mandy is able to assert her independence by making her wishes known, verbally.

Good large motor control displayed here. Mandy climbs stairs with ease, alternating her feet. She easily maneuvers her body down the slide.

Joining the other children by imitating their screaming indicates, once again, that Mandy is aware of what is happening around her and is prepared to join in when she feels she would like to. May indicate her enjoyment of other toddlers' company.

Mandy enjoys using her motor skills in creative ways, exploring new ways of doing things.

Time	Observation	Comments
	At the bottom of slide, Mandy stands up from a crouch position, runs to climber stairs and climbs, using alternating feet and left hand on rail. Another child is sitting at the top of the slide. Mandy begins to scream in a frustrated voice. Caregiver says, "Mandy, Paul will slide down, then it is your turn." Mandy watches Paul slide down, then she slides down, on her bottom. Stands up from crouch position and walks toward a caregiver. She says, "I want to go on bike" (looking at a "big wheel" trike).	Evidence of Mandy's egocentricity. She has difficulty "sharing" the slide with another child, but understands that she will get her turn when Paul slides down. She accepts this and waits her turn. Evidence that Mandy can express herself verbally.
	Caregiver holds bike steady while Mandy climbs on. Mandy tries to propel trike forward with her feet, but the front wheel is turned sideways. The caregiver says, "The handles are backward, Mandy. Let's turn them around." Mandy climbs off trike, helping caregiver turn handles around. She climbs back on the trike and moves it forward using alternating feet. Goes a short distance, then climbs off.	Climbing onto yet another style of trike/riding toy, Mandy displays typical 2-year-old curiosity and exploration skills.
	She stands and looks around the playground. Walks toward another child on a tricycle and says, "Ride bike?" Other child pedals away. Mandy walks toward a mom picking up her child. She walks to caregiver and says, "I get up," while her arms stretch out in caregiver's direction. Caregiver picks her up. Mandy smiles and laughs. Stays in caregiver's arms for a couple of minutes, until caregiver says, "I have to put you down, Mandy, to see what is wrong with Michael, Okay?" Mandy gets down and follows caregiver in the direction of Michael. Stops and looks toward two other children, who are standing facing each other. Mandy walks toward them, stops, and observes. Walks away and wanders around the playground. Walks toward two children playing with a wagon. She follows the wagon as another child pulls wagon around the playground.	Behavioral indication of Mandy's comfort level with her environment and the people in it. She approaches another toddler with confidence, then a caregiver for some personal attention. Indication of her emotional well-being--she is able to approach a caregiver for a cuddle when she feels she needs one. Understands why caregiver needs to put her down; but, stays close until she finds something of interest to her. Evidence that Mandy enjoys the company of other children, but still tends to play solitary. Evidence of onlooker-type social play. She doesn't join in, but remains close to the action.

Observation Sample

This student has used anecdotal records to record significant behaviors in different developmental domains. The summary comments make tentative inferences about the child's performance.

Anecdotal Records

Observer's name: Sherry Lacroix

Child's name (pseudonym): Jenna

Age: 6 years, 4 months

Date: Thursday, January 29, to Friday, February 20, 1998

Setting: Child Care Center, Preschool room

     17 children and 2-3 adults

Purpose of observation: To observe the portfolio child in a natural setting to record behaviors unique to her. To select from the anecdotes the specific behaviors, and to use these for the purpose of the final analysis of her portfolio.

Date of observation: Thursday, January 29, 1998

Time: 10:40 a.m.

Context: Preschool room during circle time with all the children.

Jenna is sitting down cross-legged in a circle with all of the other children; she is listening to the caregiver read them a story. After the story is finished, several of the children, including Jenna, put up their hands and offer questions and comments. Jenna puts up her hand; the caregiver asks Jenna what she would like to say. Jenna says, "I think Jeremy is having a very good day. I think he deserves a round of applause." The caregiver says that it is a good idea, and all the children clap their hands for Jeremy.

Summary: Jenna appears to be showing signs of some pro-social behavior; she seems to be able to see things from another child's perspective and feel empathy for him. Jenna appears to have the ability to think about other people's feelings and show a sensitivity toward them. This can be seen in the above anecdote; Jenna seems to recognize the type of day a particular child is having and acknowledges it in her own way. Jenna appears to be becoming less egocentric; she now is able to put others in a primary role, showing increased pro-social behavior.

Date of observation: Friday, January 30, 1998

Time: 11:15 a.m.

Context: The children are going to the gymnasium for gross motor activities.

The children walk to the gymnasium and sit down on the floor. Jenna puts up her hand; the caregiver acknowledges Jenna and asks her what she would like to say. Jenna asks, "Can we do exercises?" The caregiver says yes and asks her what kind of exercises they should do. Jenna pauses; she stands up with her legs straight and her feet slightly apart. Jenna bends at the waist and reaches her hands to touch her toes. The caregiver says,

"All right, let's touch our toes ten times." The children touch their toes. Jenna then says, "How about leg lifts?" Jenna lies down on the floor and demonstrates to the caregiver what she has said. The children follow Jenna and do five leg lifts.

Summary: Jenna appears to have improved gross motor skills and coordination. She seems to be able to demonstrate specific exercises with relative ease and confidence. Jenna seems to use her cognitive abilities to think of different exercises, and to use her gross motor skills to carry them out in front of the class.

Date of observation: Friday, February 6, 1998

Time: 4:05 p.m.

Context: Preschool room at a table. Earlier in the day, Jenna and a caregiver had put together a puzzle; it was time for clean-up and the caregiver told Jenna they could do another puzzle later.

Jenna comes over to the caregiver she was playing with earlier in the day and asks, "Remember when you said we could finish the puzzle--well, could we finish it now?" The caregiver says yes. Jenna and the caregiver walk over to a table with two other children. Jenna picks out a Mickey Mouse puzzle containing 100 pieces. Jenna tries to fit several pieces together until she finds the one that will fit. The puzzle is completed and the caregiver asks, "How many pieces of the puzzle are we missing?" Jenna points to the empty spaces with her fingers; she replies, "One, two. Two pieces are missing." Jenna then says, "Let's keep this one together on the table. Let's do another one." Jenna stands up and walks over to the shelf and picks up another puzzle.

Summary: In the developmental area of social competence, Jenna appears to be able to interact positively with both adults and peers. She seems to be able to work cooperatively in a group all striving for one goal. Jenna appears to have a good sense of memory when she asks the caregiver about the puzzle they could not complete earlier in the day. Jenna seems to have an expanded concentration span to finish a large puzzle and wants to do another; she seems to be able to solve math questions the caregiver asks her. Jenna appears to have well-developed fine motor skills to fit together the small pieces in the puzzle. Jenna appears to enjoy cognitive games such as puzzles; this is seen when she remarks, "Let's do another one."

Date of observation: Friday, February 20, 1998

Time: 11:55 a.m.

Context: Just before lunch is about to begin, the caregiver asks the children to go to the washroom and wash their hands.

Jenna is sitting on the floor; she stands up and begins to walk to the door. Jenna stops and turns her head, looking behind her, then turns around and walks to a younger child who is standing still. She takes his hand and says, "Come on, Benjamin." Jenna takes Benjamin's left hand and walks with him out the door. The two children turn left and walk down the hallway and turn right into the bathroom. Jenna puts her hands under the fountain sink and washes her hands. She walks over to the paper-towel dispenser and pulls out one paper towel, dries her hands, and throws the paper towel into the garbage. Jenna turns around and walks toward the water fountain where Benjamin is standing. She bends down slightly, puts her arms around Benjamin's waist, and carries him over to the paper-towel dispenser. Benjamin grabs a paper towel; she puts him on the floor; he disposes of the paper towel. Jenna walks back to class beside Benjamin.

Summary: Jenna appears to have acquired many pro-social skills. She has developed a positive relationship with her peers; she shows sensitivity toward a younger, smaller child who has trouble reaching the paper-towel dispenser. She seems to be becoming less egocentric and has the ability to see things in a new perspective and help out when she can. Jenna appears to show her cognitive abilities when she responds to certain situations. She realizes the need for this child to get a paper towel; he cannot reach it, so she implements her own plan to fix the problem. Jenna shows her emotional development in a sensitivity toward others and in her general interaction with her peers; she seems to try to help others whenever the need arises.

Samplings

4

Just as the word "time" is central to time sampling, so the word "event" is central to event sampling. Although both methods use the word "sampling," their procedures and results can be quite different.

Warren R. Bentzen (1993)

This method (event sampling) proves to be very efficient in reducing observation time and has the added bonus of providing data that could be summarized easily and subjected to statistical analysis.

D. Michelle Irwin and M. Margaret Bushnell (1980)

Cooperative play can be encouraged if time, space, opportunity, and materials are available. Sampling this type of activity can help in understanding the children's social skills and assist in programming.

Learning Outcome

Learners will select and use sampling techniques to identify patterns of behavior.

History Notes

To get around the problem of the amount of time required to carry out narrative recordings, new ways of collecting information were devised in the 1920s. **Samplings** enabled preselected **behaviors** or snapshots of behavior to be charted and quantified more efficiently. Thus, researchers could observe a larger number of children and make more significant inferences.

Irwin and Bushnell (1980) cite Willard C. Olson at the Institute of Child Development at the University of Minnesota as the first to use **time sampling** as a technique, in 1926–27. This study focused on the nervous habits of children. At about the same time, Mary Cover Jones used a form of **event sampling** when recording observations of preschool children's emotions. This was a more scientific testing situation than the forms of event sampling that are used today. Studies of children in the 1930s and 1940s used these techniques in a variety of forms. Some used samplings to analyze the content of narrative recordings, others to measure behavior in a more scientific manner. Further work concentrated on recording behaviors in a naturalistic way, focusing on spontaneous activity. Possibly the best-known work of this period was Mildred B. Parten's (1932–33) study of children's play, which valued the spontaneous play of young children. She categorized social behavior using the terms that are commonly understood today—unoccupied, onlooker, solitary, parallel, associative, and cooperative. Parten's work shows the use of clear behavior categories, a practice that observers should continue to follow through well-stated definitions of the behaviors they are seeking to record.

The use of both time sampling and event sampling in research work has increased over the last fifty years. The data that have been collected and analyzed form the basis of our current knowledge of the sequences and patterns of child development.

Sampling Observations

 Definition: Sampling observations

Sampling observations are those in which examples of behavior are recorded as they occur or behaviors are recorded as they are demonstrated at previously decided intervals.

Sampling behaviors or events is an indirect or interpretive style of observing children. Practicing teachers may choose to record them frequently because of their very specific nature and the speed at which results can be produced. Recording information while involved in activity with the children can be challenging; some samplings can be done without disengaging from the children for any significant length of time.

 Child Development Focus

Samplings can be helpful in observing and recording
- patterns of behavior
- what triggers or causes a behavior

Samplings may assist in
- avoiding negative behavior sequences
- behavior reshaping

Event Sampling

Event sampling is a method of observation that records occurrences of behaviors called **events**, which are examples of a previously selected category of behavior. Event sampling is most frequently focused on one child at a time but may be constructed to record behaviors of a number of children simultaneously. Varying formats enable the following aspects of the behavior to be highlighted:

- **frequency:** how often the behavior occurs
- **duration:** how long the behavior continues
- **causality:** what triggered the behavior
- **severity:** the degree to which the behavior can be considered serious or a cause for concern

Event sampling is frequently used to analyze behaviors that present a challenge, but it can also be used for other observational purposes.

▶▶ Key Features: Event sampling

- focuses on behavior of one child
- defines behavior to be sampled
- records occurrences on a chart
- aims to establish behavioral causes and patterns
- naturalistic
- participatory or nonparticipatory
- interpretive method of recording

Watch out!

The behavior you record must be seen fairly frequently or you'll have nothing to put on your event sampling chart!

ABC format

The ABC format is possibly the most useful of the event sampling methods. The "ABC" indicates

A: the **antecedent event**—the "happening" just prior to the behavior example cited

B: the **behavior**—the example of the behavior category you are looking for

C: the **consequent event**—the effect, consequence, or event that occurs after the example given

Event samplings can give clear indications of the causality of the behaviors recorded. With the ABC format, the trigger or cause for the behavior may become apparent. Viewing the antecedent enables us to see if there is an identifiable pattern involved in which responses are elicited by particular stimuli. The stimulus–response pattern may be initiated by the child but could also come from the teacher's behavior, a routine occurrence, or an environmental factor. This method enables the observer to see possible effects as well as causes of the behavior. Examples of event samplings using the ABC format can be found on pages 136–40 and 141–42.

Behavior categories

Sampling techniques involve categorizing sets of behaviors. An **operational defini-tion** of the behavior to be observed is essential for the success of the observational recordings; without, it the observation will be built on quicksand. The definition needs to be more than a list of behaviors that fall within a broad category; it must offer a clear explanation of what will be recorded.

Choosing, then defining, the behavior category can be troublesome. As behavior is a continuous flow of activity, it is hard to segment, so observers must be clear about what they are seeking. Categories can be broad or specific according to needs, but they must be precise. A useful way of clarifying your thinking is to ask yourself, "What range of behaviors am I expecting to see?" The commonality of the set of behaviors should become apparent.

For example, if you expect to see examples of hitting, biting, and shouting, you will see that the commonality is anger or aggression. Consider the following definitions of "anger" and "aggression":

> Anger: This is a behavior in which the individual demonstrates rage and passionate resentment.
> Aggression: This is a behavior in which the individual demonstrates acts of violence or verbal anger.

Creating your own definition of aggression might be more useful because you could include all action and communication. Your definition could be more open-ended and therefore likely to cover other examples of the behaviors you might see.

Narrower categories can be useful if you are looking for a specific behavior. In that case, you might choose a precise category. Instead of choosing a category like social behaviors, you might need to be more exact if you are seeking examples such as altruism or empathy.

For example, when explaining to a new assistant teacher the particular behaviors of individuals in your class, you realize you want to highlight those children with an obvious habit, because you want the assistant to help you analyze the causes. Observing all repeated behaviors does not give you information that you want about nervous tics, nail biting, and so on. The term "habitual behavior" is more useful to you.

Defining the behavior to be observed limits the parameters of the observation while supporting its objectivity. The examples of behavior that fall into a category may be more than you anticipated—the operational definition will allow for that.

Taking a Special Look: Behavioral challenges

Sometimes a behavior causes us to wonder what is going on for the child to make her or him act this way. We can be so frustrated that we feel the behavior is happening more often than it actually is. This situation is an excellent opportunity to conduct an event sampling, which will enable us to examine the possible cause or triggers of the behavior, try to determine how significant the behavior is, and see how frequently it is really happening.

For example, Karl, aged 5 years and 7 months, has been diagnosed as visually impaired, so various strategies have been used to help him become independent. Recently, Karl seemed to withdraw from the other boys with whom he usually played. Sitting alone, he would rock himself back and forth, bang his head repeatedly, and sometimes rub his eyes and shake his hands in front of them. After carrying out an event sampling over several days, documenting each occurrence of these solitary and self-destructive behaviors, the teacher could see a pattern and a possible cause: the behaviors were consistent with a decrease in his visual acuity. Karl could not sustain the relationship he previously had with the other boys because he could not see well enough. The teacher's observation led to a referral to an ophthalmologist. With a much stronger prescription for his glasses, Karl regained some of his sociability and entered into activities with the other children.

Using event sampling

Advantages

- This method of recording is quick and efficient.
- Behavior can be charted in convenient units.
- Information can be recorded more quickly than with narrative observations.
- Sampling may be blended with other methods—for example, with a detailed narrative account, rating scale, and so on.

- This method may reveal behavioral patterns, frequency of behavior, and cause and effect of behavior/event.
- It is possible to observe and record more than one child at a time.
- The results are easily interpreted into appropriate program planning/behavior modification strategies.
- An observation can be recorded at the time or soon after its occurrence.
- Teachers involved with children can record as they interact in the program.
- Sampling may offer information about duration of behavior.
- Sampling may indicate the severity of recorded behavior.
- Some basic formats can be selected by consulted professionals and, with only a little instruction, can be carried out by parents and caregivers.

Disadvantages

- Sampling lacks the detail of narrative recordings.
- A high degree of selectivity and inference is required in categorizing observed behavior.
- Sampling breaks up the natural continuity of behavior into separate units.
- This method may encourage judgmental inferences.
- Sampling relies on repetition of behavior—not useful for infrequently observed behaviors.
- Any observation not recorded immediately is more likely to be affected by observer **bias**.
- Sampling relies on the skill of the observer to choose an appropriate methodology, define the behavior category, and evaluate the child's behavioral patterns.

Seemingly happy as he eats his lunch, this boy, who has Down's Syndrome, suddenly burst into tears a moment after the photograph was taken. An event sampling of these occurrences revealed a significant behavior pattern.

Method charts for event sampling

ABC *format*

Event Sampling

Child's name: _____   Observer: _____

Age/D.O.B.: _____   Date(s): _____

Behavior: _____

Operational definition: _____

_____

Examples of behavior: _____

_____

Reason for observation: _____

_____

Time	Antecedent event	Behavior	Consequent event

*This chart enables the observer to record the chosen behavior as it occurs, giving information about what was observed immediately prior to the sample behavior and also what happened afterward. Detailing the surrounding events gives the observer clues to the possible causes or triggers for the behavior, gives a **tally** of occurrences, and can provide a more detailed set of information that may be helpful in understanding the child's behavior.*

Frequency count

<table>
<tr><td colspan="3" align="center">**Event Sampling**</td></tr>
<tr><td>Child's name: _____</td><td colspan="2">Observer: _____</td></tr>
<tr><td>Age/D.O.B.: _____</td><td colspan="2">Date(s): _____</td></tr>
<tr><td colspan="3">Behavior: _____</td></tr>
<tr><td colspan="3">Operational definition: _____</td></tr>
<tr><td colspan="3">Examples of behavior: _____</td></tr>
<tr><td colspan="3">Reason for observation: _____</td></tr>
<tr><td>**Time**</td><td>**Tally count**</td><td>**Total**</td></tr>
<tr><td></td><td></td><td></td></tr>
</table>

Here the observer records the occurrences of the selected behavior as they happen. This method can be useful for a practicing teacher because it can be done efficiently without a break from the responsibilities with the children. No detail about the behaviors can be recorded.

Duration chart

<table>
<tr><td colspan="3" align="center">**Event Sampling**</td></tr>
<tr><td>Child's name: _____</td><td colspan="2">Observer: _____</td></tr>
<tr><td>Age/D.O.B.: _____</td><td colspan="2">Date(s): _____</td></tr>
<tr><td colspan="3">Behavior: _____</td></tr>
<tr><td colspan="3">Operational definition: _____</td></tr>
<tr><td colspan="3">Examples of behavior: _____</td></tr>
<tr><td colspan="3">Reason for observation: _____</td></tr>
<tr><td>**Day/date**</td><td>**Time (from–to)**</td><td>**Total in minutes**</td></tr>
<tr><td></td><td></td><td></td></tr>
</table>

This chart gives the observer a sense of the duration of the selected behavior, although no other explanation of the occurrences of behavior can be offered. The observer might find it advantageous to calculate average duration as well as to analyze the pattern of behavior examples.

Group samples

Event Sampling

Names: _____   Ages/D.O.B.: _____

_____   _____

_____   _____

_____   _____

_____   _____

_____   _____

Observer: _____   Date: _____

Context: _____

Behavior: _____

Operational definition: _____

_____

Examples of behavior: _____

_____

Reason for observation: _____

_____

Time	Antecedent	Behavior	Consequence

Recording information about more than one child at a time has its limitations for practical reasons. Here the observer can record a set of examples of a preselected category of behavior. It is wise to limit the breadth of categories in this method, or else there may be too many examples. Further variants can involve simple frequency counts, duration recordings, or, for the observer without direct involvement, a full ABC format.

Severity recording

Event Sampling

Child's name: _____ Observer: _____

Age/D.O.B.: _____ Date(s): _____

Behavior: _____

Operational definition: _____

Examples of behavior: _____

Reason for observation: _____

Inference Coding Rating Scale

1	3	5	7	9
Mild		Moderate		Severe

Date	Time	Behavior	Rating	Comments

This chart uses a combination of an event sampling technique and a rating scale. Charting the severity of behavior is more interpretive than some other sampling methods because the observer is required to evaluate the behavior's severity as it is recorded.

Complex behavior sampling

Event Sampling

Child's name: _____ Observer: _____

Age/D.O.B.: _____ Date(s): _____

Behavior: _____

Operational definition: _____

Examples of behavior: _____

Reason for observation: _____

Inference Coding Rating Scale

1	3	5	7	9
Mild		Moderate		Severe

Date	Antecedent event	Behavior example	Consequent event	Duration	Severity	Comments

*This chart can be too demanding for the caregiver of a medium or large group of children. Parents, student observers, and psychologists whose focus is on only one child at a time find this an appropriate method of recording detailed information. It is particularly useful for challenging behaviors where guidance strategies need to be developed for **behavior modification**, cognitive therapy, or other management or therapy technique.*

Time Sampling

Time sampling is a method of observing and recording selected behaviors during previously set time periods. These observations can be used for recording information about one or more children simultaneously. Time samplings are usually structured to record behaviors at regular intervals but may also be done at randomly chosen times. Examples of time samplings, recorded in two different ways, can be found on pages 143–44 and 145–48.

▶▶ Key Features: Time sampling

- focuses on behavior of one child
- records behavior at preset time intervals
- records behaviors on a chart
- aims to identify behavioral patterns
- naturalistic
- participatory or nonparticipatory
- interpretive method of recording

Time intervals for samplings

Time sampling observations need to be even more rigorously set up than event samples, because the interval at which the behaviors are to be sampled must be structured to give the required information. A sampling made across several days at 15-minute intervals may give information about an infant's pattern of sleep and wakefulness, but it may not give such useful insights into a 7-year-old's concentration.

Watch out!

If the time frequency is too short, you won't be able to record quickly enough; if it's too long, you might not see a pattern!

Using time sampling

Advantages

- This method provides frequency data about behaviors.
- Information can be recorded quickly.

- Time sampling is more likely to allow for a representative sample of behavior appropriate for students and researchers.
- Results tend to be reliable over time.
- Time sampling provides an overview of a wide range of behaviors.

Disadvantages

- Time sampling lacks qualitative information.
- The recordings may be misinterpreted because of the lack of contextual information.
- Behavior observed infrequently may not be recorded effectively.
- Sampling relies on the skill of the observer to structure observations appropriately to elicit significant information.

Method charts for time sampling

Interval recording

Time Sampling

Child's name: _____ Observer: _____

Age/D.O.B.: _____ Date(s): _____

Context: _____

Behavior: _____

_____

Reason for observation: _____

_____

Date	Time/interval	Behavior	Comments

This chart presents a standard format, which can be adapted to various uses by altering the time/interval designation as required. Here the behavior category could be open-ended or quite specific, if necessary. An observer may wish to see the general pattern of activity during the course of the day or look for types of behavior to see if they are present or absent in the sample period.

Group interval recording

Time Sampling			
Names: _____ Ages/D.O.B.: _____			
Observer: _____ Date: _____			
Context: _____			
Behavior category: _____			
Reason for observation: _____			
#	**Child**	**Behaviors** (Time/units/intervals)	**Comment (Total)**
1.			

A group of children can be observed in this time sampling. The detail of activity that can be recorded is quite limited.

How to Use Samplings

Deciding what sampling methodology to use

1. Become aware of the various techniques; know their advantages and disadvantages and what information they could give you.
2. Assess your need for a sampling: What do you need it for? These are some of the most obvious uses:
   - to help you learn about sequences of development
   - to support the understanding of an individual child's behavior
   - to look at the behaviors demonstrated by a group of children
   - for formal record keeping
   - to support communications with parents, colleagues, and other professionals
   - to help evaluate the program offered to an individual or group
   - to provide information for behavior modification plans or for learning prescriptions
3. Choose the method of preference, use it, and evaluate its usefulness for the purpose required.

4. Practice use of sampling techniques and build skills in the component parts of objectivity, clarity, and accuracy of recording, checking with others on their perceptions of the validity of your work.

Event sampling versus time sampling

Event sampling	Time sampling
• can be used to study any event or behavior	• can record any demonstrated behaviors
• is a little less likely to give information about frequency of behavior over longer periods of time	
• is more likely to give qualitative information	• may make it easier to quantify behavior
• may indicate causes of behavior	
• is often used by practitioners	• is often used by researchers
• includes every natural occurrence of focus behavior as sample	
• may offer information about duration of behavior	• may offer behavioral pattern
• may indicate severity of behavior	
• can be user-friendly and easily carried out by parents and para-professionals	• may require professional background in child development to structure behavior coding systems

How to record a time or event sample observation

1. Decide on your reason for sampling behavior.
2. Select the behavior category or time frequency that applies.
3. Prepare a method chart to meet specific requirements.
4. Write your operational definition of the behavior category, if necessary.
5. Record as soon as possible the precise details of the examples of behavior observed.
6. When sufficient examples are recorded for your purpose, take time to analyze your findings.

7. Write your objective **inferences** as clear statements—but support your statements.

8. Use the inference statements to devise a plan or learning prescription.

The analysis: Interpreting data collected from samplings

Remember that your inferences rely heavily on the **objectivity** of your recording. Before you start to analyze the data, evaluate its **validity** and **reliability**. You will also need to review the effectiveness of the sampling before you proceed to analyze the content. Some samplings require you to select specific behaviors. The decision to observe a particular behavior may be found ineffective because you didn't see the behavior you expected. The operational definition of the behavior category can also be a source of difficulty—you could perhaps have selected a suitable category but not defined it well to cover the samples you include.

Focus the **analysis** on some of these issues:

1. determining the frequency of the events
2. considering what prompted the events
3. measuring the duration of the events
4. examining the developmental significance of the events
5. evaluating the necessity of responding to the events
6. identifying the pattern of behaviors/events
7. determining further observation and assessment needs

The samplings on pages 136–40, 141–42, and 145–48 include analysis of the observations.

The frequency with which a behavior is observed can be charted. Event samplings may offer clues as to the cause of a behavior. A favorite toy offers some comfort at a time of insecurity.

Using inferences drawn from the analysis

Other than for purposes of dry record keeping, there is little point in recording copious numbers of observations without putting them to some use. There is a wide range of reasons to record samplings, and often more than one reason for each observation.

Having checked the inferences for their validity, reliability, general objectivity, and supporting argument and reference, you will be ready to make use of your analysis. The sampling on pages 143–44 includes an inference chart.

The inferences can be used in a similar way to those drawn from other methods of observation (see Chapter 1, pages 24–33). Samplings are frequently used as a forerunner to devising a learning prescription or individualized program plan for children. The way in which the methodology reveals causality of behavior means that it easily lends itself to specific teacher action.

Taking a Special Look: Reinforcement

- Melinda's family came on "meet the teacher" night. Melinda showed her parents around the room and introduced them to the teacher. Both her parents and the teacher thought that Melinda had behaved very well and praised her beautiful manners.

- Ellie was just past her second birthday, and her parents were concerned that she had not yet said a "real" word but tended to repeat the same string of sounds. Her caregiver saw Ellie point at the shelf above her crib and say "bo-bo" repeatedly. "That's your bunny rabbit, bunny rabbit," the caregiver said. Ellie later said "bun-bun," and the caregiver said, "Yes, your bunny rabbit," and gave it to her.

- Craig, at 6 months, liked to hold his own bottle. But he didn't like to hand back the bottle when it was empty. His mother played a game with Craig where they passed items back and forth. The next time his bottle was empty, he handed it to his mother.

These examples suggest that behaviors can be reinforced through positive feedback or some kind of reward. **Reinforcement** is also used for more structured behavior modification. Be aware that this method is not used everywhere, because some people are concerned about manipulating behavior. The following example illustrates how sampling can be used in a classroom situation where behavior modification is practiced.

Gareth, aged 7, has been diagnosed as having a social adaptation difficulty, based on detailed narrative observations, a psychological test, and meetings with his parents and teacher. Recently, Gareth has had some new challenges in sharing art materials. He snatched items from other children, and the scene disintegrated into a fight. He also took home a pair of scissors, which he used to cut up an album of family photographs. When Gareth met with the psychologist, his parents, and his teacher, they decided that he would be "rewarded" for behaving appropriately and "corrected" for behaving inappropriately. Gareth agreed that he wanted to "behave himself." In the following days, he demonstrated positive behavior, such as helping hand out snack, waiting in line for the washroom, and helping a younger child find his lost coat. Each time the teacher observed such behavior, she recorded it on a sampling chart and allowed Gareth to have "privileges" like staying outside for longer or being first to select afternoon activities. For each negative behavior, Gareth was asked to do a clean-up job, made to sit away from the other children, or denied his book choice at circle time. Gareth understood this plan, which seemed to reinforce some of the better behaviors; his behavior was being modified to what was considered socially acceptable.

Key Terms

analysis	inference
antecedent event	objectivity
behavior	operational definition
behavior modification	reinforcement
bias	reliability
causality	sampling
consequent event	severity
duration	tally
event	time sampling
event sampling	validity
frequency	

Observation Sample

This observational recording is a clear example of an ABC event sampling. The operational definition is clear, and the examples of behavior are specific. The analysis explains the behaviors in paragraph form. Note how the observer has outlined the assignment on the first page and included a signed permission form from the parents. The child's identity is kept confidential through the use of a pseudonym in the observation.

Observation Assignment

Front Page

Student name: _Donna Francisco_ Student number: _000-111-000_

Section number: _061_

Assignment method: _Event Sampling (ABC format)_

Date due: _October 24, 1998_ Date handed in: _October 24, 1998_

Child's name (pseudonym): _Margaret_

Child's age (years/months): _1 year, 11-1/2 months_

Date of observation: _Oct. 8 and Oct. 15_ Time of observation: _Throughout day_

Setting: _Toddler room at child-care center and main entrance hallway at the center_

Parent's name: _Wayne and Jane White_ Phone # if released: _(203) 987-6543_

Each assignment has specific criteria. Please check with the assignment description and direction given in class.

Declaration by student

I have followed the assignment description and instructions given in class about confidentiality and privacy. I confirm that appropriate processes for making this observation have been undertaken and that permission has been gained from the parents. A copy of this observation will be given to the parents if they desire.

Donna Francisco

Signature of Student

Permission Form

Child Observations, Case Studies, and Portfolios

Student and Parent Agreement

Without written permission I will not observe and record information about your child. Please sign in the space provided if you agree that I may make observations and study your child. It would be helpful if you could initial each of the boxes if you are willing for me to undertake any or all of the techniques of information gathering.

I _____Donna Francisco_____ *(student name)* will not refer to the child in any written manner by his or her real name. Information recorded will be written objectively, treated professionally, and kept confidential.

_____Donna Francisco_____   _____Oct. 1/98_____
(student's signature)   *(date)*

I _____Wayne White_____
(parent's name)

agree to have _____Jennifer White_____
           (child's name)

observed ☑   photographed ☑   audiotaped ☑   videotaped ☑

by _____Donna Francisco_____
(student's name above)

at _____Grenadier Child-Care Center_____
(agency/home)

for the purpose of study in child development at _____Northern College_____

(school/college) for a period of ___2 weeks___ *(weeks/months)* on the consideration that copies are made available to me, the parent, if I so request.

_____Wayne White_____   _____October 1/98_____
(parent's signature)   *(date)*

Event Sampling

Child's name: ___Margaret___ Observer: ___Donna Francisco___

Age/D.O.B.: ___1 yr, 11-1/2 mos/Oct.30/96___ Date(s): ___October 8 and 15, 1998___

Behavior: ___Autonomy___

Operational definition: ___This is a behavior in which the child displays initiative___ to perform tasks independently to help herself achieve something specific.

Examples of behavior: ___Self-help skills: for example, independent toileting or___ identifying her need to have her diaper changed/sit on toilet; feeding self; washing/drying own hands without help; dressing self

Reason for observation: ___To see if Margaret is succeeding in her attempts at___ autonomous behavior(s).

Time	Antecedent event	Behavior	Consequent event
(October 8)			
9:45 a.m.	Sitting on floor playing with "linking stars."	Turned to caregiver and said, "I need help with this one."	Caregiver showed Margaret how to attach the star and handed it back to her, and she tried to put the pieces together.
2:45 p.m.	Margaret sitting on floor pulling on her sock.	Said to caregiver, "I am fixing my sock."	Caregiver said, "You did it all by yourself, Margaret!"
3:45 p.m.	During gross motor activity in hall, Margaret went to her cubby and took out her hat.	Margaret pulled her hat onto her head.	Looked at caregiver and said, "Look, I put on my hat!"
3:50 p.m.	Children had just re-entered toddler room to find a place at the tables to sit for snack.	Margaret, sitting at her place at the table, said to caregiver, "I want juice please; I want milk please."	Caregiver poured a cup of milk for Margaret and put it in front of her. She picked it up with both hands and drank.
(October 15)			
11:10 a.m.	Margaret, while seated at the table at lunchtime, was sorting through the plastic bibs.	Margaret chose a green bib.	Margaret said, "I want this one," while she was trying to put it on for herself.

Time	Antecedent event	Behavior	Consequent event
11:20 a.m.	Margaret's lunch was placed in front of her.	Margaret picked up her spoon, scooped up some pasta, and put it in her mouth.	Margaret success-fully placed food in her mouth and ate it.
2:30 p.m.	Margaret had just awakened from her afternoon nap.	She walked to the caregiver standing at the door and said, "Change my diaper?"	Caregiver said, "Yes, Margaret, let's change your diaper."
2:40 p.m.	Margaret returned to the toddler room after having her diaper changed.	She walked to her cot and picked up her shoes.	Margaret sat on the floor and tried to put her shoes on, saying, "Put shoes on."
3:35 p.m.	Caregiver had just placed coats on the floor in preparation for going outside.	Margaret went to where her coat had been placed and picked it up.	She tried to put her coat on, putting her right arm into the sleeve of the coat. She looked at caregiver and said, "I need help."

Observation Analysis

This is the age of the drive for autonomy. Children at this age are often heard to say, "Me do it myself!" They are striving for independence, while still needing lots of support from caregivers and parents. They make many attempts throughout the day to do things for themselves, and it is impor-tant that caregivers recognize their attempts in a positive and supportive way. According to Erikson, this is the stage of a child's social/emotional development where the struggle for autonomy versus shame and doubt takes place (Barrett, 1995, p. 264). To avoid power struggles with toddlers, which may impede their ability to achieve autonomy, caregivers need to offer children "yes" choices instead of those requiring "yes or no" answers. Leading them to the choices one wants them to make in a positive manner (for example, "I bet you can put the blocks away all by yourself!") is much more effective than making direct demands. When children feel that they have made decisions to perform specific tasks on their own, it contributes to their ability to think for themselves.

Throughout the observation period, Margaret displays many attempts to make decisions and do things for herself. The observation was limited to observing "self-help" skills and there were many to see. Each of the behav-iors recorded shows that Margaret consistently tries to perform tasks for herself and that she is aware of the order and routine in her day. For example, she tries to put on her socks, her coat, and her shoes at different times in the day. Once she completes the toileting routine after nap, Margaret knows that it is time to put on her shoes, and she looks for them as soon as she re-enters the room. While she still requires the assis-tance of an adult in her dressing routine, she knows what to do and consis-tently practices the skills she needs to do these things for herself (October 8, 2:45; 3:45; October 15, 2:40; 3:35).

The caregivers in the room recognize the importance of facilitating and supporting the children's self-help skills. For example, coats are placed separately on the floor of the toddler room when it is time to go outside. This gives the children the opportunity to find their own coats and attempt to put them on. Words of encouragement are also given consistently throughout the day, as when Margaret is successful at pulling her own sock back up her foot when it is falling off (October 8, 2:45). In each behavior recorded, Margaret's attempts at independence are recognized and positively reinforced. As she makes her attempts to help herself, she often seeks the attention of a caregiver. Caregiver responses support her attempts, and she knows that her requests for support/help will receive a positive response resulting in the help she needs. For example, she asks for help with her coat; she receives milk at snack time as she requests; her need for a diaper change is acknowledged verbally and accommodated immediately; and her success with the sock is verbally acknowledged. At the same time, caregivers do not interfere with Margaret's attempts to help herself until she asks for the help. Margaret is consistent in her requests for help and asks immediately when she requires adult assistance (October 15, 2:30; 3:35).

Margaret's attempts at self-help skills are developmentally appropriate for her age (almost 2 years old): "Self-help skills improve during this time period (18 months to 2 years). As far as dressing is concerned, toddlers can do a few things for themselves, but for the most part, they require the assistance of an adult" (Barrett, 1995, p. 213). Finally, "Erikson believed that if toddlers are allowed to learn to do things for themselves, such as walking or dressing and feeding themselves, they gain a feeling of autonomy. If they are not allowed to do so, feelings of shame and self-doubt will haunt their sense of themselves, and they will have trouble with the next phase of development" (Barrett, 1995, p. 204). Margaret's positive approach to helping herself and her comfort level at asking an adult for help are indicators that she is achieving success in her drive for autonomy, paving the way for the next stage of development, "initiative versus guilt," which she is moving into on the eve of her second birthday.

References Cited

Barrett, K.C., et al. (1995). Child development. Westerville, OH: Glencoe.

Biracree, T., & Biracree, N. (1989). The parents' book of facts: Child development from birth to age five. New York: Facts on File.

Martin, Sue. (1994). Take a look: Observation and portfolio assessment in early childhood. Don Mills, ON: Addison-Wesley.

Woolfson, R.C. (1995). A to Z of child development: From birth to age five. Toronto: Stoddart.

Observation Sample

This excerpt from an event sampling documents a "negative" behavior. The analysis examines a behavioral pattern and offers a good rationale for the inferences made. However, these inferences are not further validated.

Event Sampling

Child's name: ___Kyle___   Observer: ___Damian___

Age/D.O.B.: ___3 years, 2 months___   Date(s): ___March 20, 1998___

Time of observation: ___9:50 a.m.–4:00 p.m.___

Behavior: ___Aggression___

Operational definition: ___This is a behavior in which inappropriate words or actions___ are displayed by the child himself as a result of his anger or frustration. These actions are harmful and usually hostile to those around him.

Examples of behavior: Hitting, kicking, pushing, spitting, pinching, destroying property

Setting: ___Preschool room at The Briars nursery school___

Time	Antecedent event	Behavior	Consequent event
9:51 a.m.	A peer comes to say hello. Kyle grunts at her. Adult says that he is "Mr. Grump."	Kyle hits the adult on the shoulder.	Adult moves away from Kyle and says good-bye to him.
9:55 a.m.	A child comes and tries to take Kyle's shovel from him.	Kyle attempts to hit the child with the shovel.	Teacher tells him not to hit and to keep his shovel down.
9:56 a.m.	Kyle is told not to hit with his shovel.	Kyle rakes the ground roughly and rapidly.	Kyle stops raking and walks over to another child.
9:57 a.m.	Kyle walks over to a boy after raking aggressively.	Kyle picks up sand in his shovel and throws it at the boy.	Teacher comes and takes the shovel away from him.
10:01 a.m.	Asks a child if he can play with him. The child says "no."	Kyle kicks the child's sandcastle over.	The child tells him not to do that. Teacher tells Kyle not to ruin the child's work.
10:05 a.m.	A student waves at Kyle through the window.	Kyle hits the window with his hand.	Teacher encourages Kyle to move on.
10:52 a.m.	Kyle is playing in the dramatic play area with a friend. The friend asks him not to pull the sink back.	Kyle hits his friend on the head.	Kyle makes the boy cry. Teacher comes over and sends both children out of that area.

Time	Antecedent event	Behavior	Consequent event
10:54 a.m.	Kyle walks to the door after being instructed by teacher to get his jacket.	Kyle hits his friend on the back on his way out the door.	Kyle's friend tells him not to do that.
11:12 a.m.	Kyle's friend gets his bicycle wheel caught on Kyle's scooter wheel, preventing Kyle from moving.	Kyle catches up to his friend after getting free and bangs into the back of the child's bike.	Kyle's friend turns around and tells Kyle that he didn't like that.

Observation Analysis

I chose to observe Kyle's aggressive behaviors because of my past encounters with him and because of recommendations from regular teachers. I hoped to find the cause of Kyle's aggression and the regular intervals of occurrence.

Through my observation, I discovered that Kyle tends to act aggressively when he doesn't have much to do and when he may be bored or bothered.

Upon Kyle's arrival, he began his aggressive behavior. This continued until later that morning when we went inside and some students did an activity with the children. During this time period between 10:05 a.m. and 10:52 a.m., Kyle was occupied with many things to do. He did not display any acts of aggression until he had done all of the activities and appeared to be getting bored. The cycle of aggressive behavior then began again.

Kyle's aggression is displayed physically rather than verbally. He mainly takes his anger out on other children and on his teachers. Instead of using words to express himself, he prefers to use actions involving his gross motor skills such as hitting and kicking.

Kyle appears to use his aggressions to get even with others. On occasions when a child does or says something that Kyle does not like, he acts back aggressively by kicking, hitting, or pushing. Kyle appears to have a difficult time expressing himself verbally.

Kyle appears to be one of the most aggressive children in his junior preschool room, with twenty-one acts of aggression displayed over the course of this particular day. Most of these behaviors were displayed through violent and harmful acts.

The cause of this child's aggressive behaviors appears to stem from boredom, upset, and frustration, as well as possibly a lack of confidence in his language skills. The transition from home to day care could also be having an effect on his behavior, but the first act of aggression was displayed to an adult from home, possibly suggesting that this behavior carries on at home as well.

Through my observations, I have come to the conclusion that Kyle is a child who requires a constant, fulfilling curriculum with cooperative and group play regularly involved to encourage constant cooperation and teamwork. I think that it would be ideal to encourage acceptable behavior by praising Kyle for using words instead of actions, instead of focusing on his aggressive behaviors. Kyle would also most likely benefit from a full curriculum to reduce the frustrations he feels from being bored and to enhance his social well-being.

I have concern about the frequency of these aggressive behaviors and the length of time it takes Kyle to get over his aggressive outbursts. I will continue to observe his behavior and talk with the teacher and his parents about what we can work on together to support Kyle in gaining more pro-social behaviors.

We cannot expect Kyle, at his age, to understand the perspectives of others; he does not yet have the cognitive skill to do this. However, he needs to know that his actions have consequences. I want to try to shift his behavior so that he can feel positive.

Observation Sample

The "snapshot" style of this time sampling can be useful to determine behavioral patterns. Further examples on other days might have offered more information. The brief analysis uses the flow chart outlined on page 24 in Chapter 1.

Time Sampling

Child's name: ___Cassidy___   Observer: ___Donald___

Age/D.O.B.: ___15 months___   Date(s): ___Sept. 25 and Oct. 1, 1998___

Context: __Toddler room, morning__

Behavior: __Infant development__

Reason for observation: __Cassidy has recently moved to the toddler room; we want to look at her gross motor skills and how she is fitting in.__

Date	Time/interval	Behavior	Comments
Sept. 25	10:48 a.m.	Plays with push-pop toy with other child	Engaged in parallel play.
Sept. 25	10:51 a.m.	Mouths a plastic bracelet	Other child moved off.
Sept. 25	10:54 a.m.	Mouths books	Crossed the room to quiet area.
Sept. 25	10:57 a.m.	Rubbing eyes and crying	ECE had said book not for mouth.
Sept. 25	11:00 a.m.	Throws telephone on the floor	Seems to be looking for reaction.
Sept. 25	11:03 a.m.	Pulls self up to stand and jumps	Holds on to house while jumping.
Sept. 25	11:06 a.m.	"AAAAA" touches ECE's face	Having her diaper changed.
Sept. 25	11:09 a.m.	Mouths an abstract colorful toy	ECE is holding her on lap.
Sept. 25	11:12 a.m.	Sucking thumb "AAAAA"	ECE is rocking her.
Sept. 25	11:15 a.m.	Thumb in mouth, eyes heavy	Thumb in mouth, but not sucking.
Sept. 25	11:18 a.m.	Eyes are closed, appears asleep	ECE moves her to crib.
Oct. 1	10:50 a.m.	Pulls self up to standing position	Holding on to windowsill.
Oct. 1	10:53 a.m.	Crawls across room and stops and sits	Seems to change her mind.
Oct. 1	10:56 a.m.	Banging two wooden puzzle pieces together	Seems frustrated that she can't put them together.
Oct. 1	10:59 a.m.	Same as above	Did not want help from ECE.
Oct. 1	11:02 a.m.	Throws puzzle and cries	Refused comforting from ECE (a).
Oct. 1	11:05 a.m.	Mouthing abstract colored toy	ECE (b) had given it to her to soothe her.
Oct. 1	11:08 a.m.	Puts face in ECE's chest and rubs	ECE holding her while sitting.
Oct. 1	11:11 a.m.	Sucks thumb and holds toy	Sitting on ECE's lap; seems to watch other children.
Oct. 1	11:14 a.m.	Sucking thumb "AAAAA"	Has her head on ECE's shoulder.
Oct. 1	11:17 a.m.	Eyes are closed and sucking thumb quickly	Seems still awake.
Oct. 1	11:20 a.m.	Eyes are closed; sucking has stopped	In her crib; seems asleep.

Making Inferences About Development

Behavior observed	Inference	Reasoning	Validation by theory	Validation by norms	Source	Bibliographic reference
The child would sing herself to sleep by singing "AAAAA" each time before falling asleep.	I infer that the child was soothing herself by saying a rhythmic "AAAAA" sound.	Because the sound was rhythmic and consistent and repeated each time before falling asleep, it appears to be a form of singing.		Child will use singing as a way of winding down before falling asleep.	K. Eileen Allen and Lynn Marotz	Developmental Profiles, 2nd ed., p. 75
The child mouthed the same colorful plastic toy before falling asleep.	I infer that the child had formed an attachment to the abstract colored toy.	Before falling asleep each day, the child would find her toy and mouth it to soothe herself to sleep.		Child will make requests for special bedtime items.	K. Eileen Allen and Lynn Marotz	Developmental Profiles, 2nd ed., p. 75
The child jumped up and down and threw things.	It seemed that, as the child became tired, her aggressive behavior increased.	As sleep approached each day, the child would bang and throw things. At times she also jumped up and down, perhaps to release tension as a way of preparing for sleep.	Children who have not burned off enough energy might find that their body won't let them sleep.		Susan Quilliam	Child Watching, p. 87
The child fell asleep at approximately the same time each day.	It seems that the child has formed regular sleeping patterns.	Regardless of activities, the child's internal clock caused her to fall asleep each day at the same time.	Children quickly develop regular patterns of sleep.		David Elkind	Sympathetic Understanding, p. 12
The child sucked her thumb while holding toy.	It seemed that the thumb sucking was a sign that she was becoming tired.	Each day, minutes before the child fell asleep, she would start to suck her thumb.		Thumb sucking is normal for an infant during sleep.	K. Eileen Allen and Lynn Marotz	Developmental Profiles, 2nd ed., p. 49
The child mouthed the abstract toy given to her by ECE.	It seemed that the child had formed an attachment to this toy and it soothed her.	Each day before the child fell asleep, she would seek out this toy. It also comforted her when she was crying.		Objects offer comfort when a baby is tired.	Eisenberg, Murkof, and Hathaway	What to Expect the First Year, p. 119

Observation Sample

This time sampling offers a narrative description rather than brief notes. This style is useful if the recorder wants more than a "snapshot." The analysis recognizes the significance of the behavioral patterns and tries to validate its statements.

TIME SAMPLING

Child's name: __Tyler__   Observer: ___Hana Nakagawa___

Age/D.O.B.: __11 months/March 29, 1997__   Date(s): __February 19 and 20, 1998__

Context: __The infant room. Tyler was sitting, mostly on the carpeted floor,__ __near toys and other kids.__

Behavior: __Whatever is observed.__

Reason for observation: __To discover behavioral patterns and what they reveal__ __about Tyler's development.__

Time	Behavior/comments

Feb.19

10:00 a.m. Tyler is sitting beside the padded mat on the floor, both feet extended in front of him. He is mouthing a small elephant car, taking turns holding it in each hand and looking at another infant sitting near him.
* Tyler appears content as he sits watching the other infants and mouthing a toy.

10:10 a.m. Tyler is still sitting beside the mat, and he smiles as he looks at the teething ring in his right hand. He throws the ring and murmurs as he reaches out his left hand to pick up the teething ring and places it in his mouth.
* Again, Tyler appears pleased with the teething ring and seems happy.

10:20 a.m. Now lying on his tummy, Tyler is kicking his feet in the air behind him and is crying slightly, as he seems to be stuck.
* Tyler's mood has changed slightly from seemingly happy to unsettled and restless.

10:30 a.m. Sitting on the mat now, Tyler has a push toy pulled up onto his lap and is playing with the balls and toys on the front of the push toy. During this, he is smiling and talking to himself.
* Tyler's mood has changed once again from unsettled to content.

10:40 a.m. Again, Tyler has managed to maneuver himself onto his tummy and is kicking his feet while reaching for a ball in front of him. After a few seconds without success, he starts to cry slightly again as he bangs at a nearby toy in an attempt to reach the ball.
* There has been another mood change as Tyler seems frustrated that he cannot reach his toy.

10:50 a.m. Sitting on the floor near the teacher, Tyler is mouthing another teething ring. He is trying to put the whole ring in his mouth.
* Tyler's mood is still unsettled. Although he seems more content with the teething ring, he is still crying slightly and has teary eyes.

Time	Behavior/comments

11:00 a.m.   Tyler is sitting on the floor and is still mouthing the teething ring as he watches the other infants around him. While watching the others, Tyler talks to himself and reaches out to a child with his left hand, almost pulling the child to him, smiling as the child laughs in response.
* Once again, Tyler has gone from unhappy to happy, and this seems to occur when he has a teething ring and is sitting up.

Feb. 20

10:00 a.m.   Tyler is sitting on the floor near the mat and the toys, where he is mouthing a teething ring and playing with a ball in his right hand. He puts the teething ring on the floor next to him and takes the toy from his right hand, with his left hand, and places it in his mouth. This seems to please him and he laughs to himself.
* Tyler seems to be experiencing some discomfort with his teeth, and he is trying to ease that pain by mouthing the toys and frozen rings.

10:10 a.m.   Tyler is crying as a teacher is hugging and trying to comfort him. The teacher offers him his teething ring, and Tyler takes it, rubbing it in his mouth.
* Again, Tyler seems to be unsettled and restless. He gets some relief from the teething ring but is still unhappy and crying slightly.

10:20 a.m.   Now sitting in a sit-in boat, Tyler is watching an infant in front of him. With a half-smile, Tyler plays with the steering wheel and the horn on the boat while pulling on the gearshift with his right hand.
* He appears to have calmed down and has moved on to something new.

10:30 a.m.   Still sitting in the boat, Tyler is watching the other infants in the room and is smiling at some of their actions, while talking away.
* Tyler appears to be enjoying himself playing in the boat and watching the others.

10:40 a.m.   Now sitting on the floor with a basket of toys in front of him, Tyler tries to reach for another toy that Beth is playing with. In doing so, he ends up on his tummy and begins to cry slightly. While crying, he tries to lift himself up by pushing with his arms and kicking his feet and legs.
* Here, Tyler becomes upset when he cannot reach a toy and then cannot get up from his tummy.

10:50 a.m.   Tyler is sitting on the floor and is playing with his teething ring. He is moving the ring back and forth between his hands and throwing it in front of him then retrieving it again.
* Tyler seeming content with himself again as he plays with his teething ring.

11:00 a.m.   Tyler is sitting on the floor, mouthing his teething ring. While doing so, he is talking to himself and smiling when he gets most of the ring in his mouth.
* Tyler still seems content as he plays with his teething ring.

Throughout the observations on both days, there are various recurring behaviors that outline examples of Tyler's development. The first behavior noted was the repeated mouthing of toys and objects.

Mouthing objects is normal for infants aged 8 to 12 months (Allen & Marotz, 1994, p. 62). This mouthing can be attributed to teething. From a note taken in class on February 12, 1998, the primary teeth start breaking through the bone of the jaw and the gums between the ages of 4 and 8 months. Allen and Marotz (1994, p. 134) state that the first two teeth to break through are the lower front, and the upper front follow those. The note taken on February 12 also states that between the ages of 9 and 12 months the surrounding teeth, on either side of the upper and lower front teeth, begin to break the skin as well. Although we may not remember this experience, we can imagine the pain and discomfort it can cause. Teeth breaking through the skin is known to cause flushness in the cheeks and, in extreme cases, a slight fever. Children who are teething are known to be unsettled and cranky. To alleviate the pain, children are often given frozen teething rings to soothe the swollen gums. Many children, whenever possible, will put whatever they have in their hands in their mouths to rub along the gum line. According to Laura Nathanson (1994, p. 132), "[Children] want to mouth everything and chew" when the teeth start coming through. Tyler was constantly putting toys in his mouth, and this seemed to comfort him. When given teething rings, Tyler would rub them along his gums and chew on them. Thus, Tyler's mouthing and discomfort can be attributed to the pain of the surrounding teeth breaking through, which is common in an infant aged 11 months based on the references stated above.

Another behavior observed was Tyler looking and watching the other children in the room. This behavior is typical of a child aged 11 months, based on data in Allen and Marotz (1994). This behavior is classified as <u>percep-tual—cognitive development</u>. An infant between the ages of 8 and 12 months typically "watches people, objects, and activities in the immediate environment" (Allen & Marotz, 1994, p. 62). Therefore, watching and looking at the infants in the center is normal for an 11-month-old infant.

The final behavior observed and noted was how Tyler became frustrated when he could not move around on the floor. This behavior was observed on several occasions. At 10:20 a.m. on February 19, Tyler was lying on his tummy and was unable to pull himself up from that position. According to Nathanson (1994), children between the ages of 9 and 12 months should be able to bear weight on their legs, and when on their bellies, "should be able to push way up and roll over in both directions. They should be able to get from lying down to sitting up. They should be trying to pull up to a standing position" (p. 130). Tyler showed that when he was lying down, after a few moments of trying to help himself, he would cry slightly for someone to help him sit up again. Tyler appears to be frustrated when he cannot move himself around like the other children; evidence of this is that he cries for help after trying to help himself. Not being able to creep, crawl, or walk at 11 months is atypical, according to Allen and Marotz (1994), but not necessarily a developmental alert. Nathanson (1994) states that it is okay that children do not walk at earlier ages, and that some children "don't [walk] until nearly 16 months" (p. 130). She goes on to say that some children don't ever crawl, but may pass this stage and "cruise" around the furniture, or use alternative methods of moving, eventually walking from there (p. 130). Allen and Marotz (1994) state that children between the ages of 8 and 12 months should be "creeping and crawling on their hands and knees, walking with adult support, beginning to pull self to a standing position, beginning to stand alone, leaning on furniture for support" (p. 62).

Although Tyler is not walking or completely mobile, he is trying and becomes frustrated when unable to do so. However slow Tyler may be at his mobile development, he is developing in accordance with some of Allen and Marotz's (1994) developmental norms; for example, Tyler has good balance when sitting and can shift positions without falling, which is stated as a profile of motor development (p. 62). Tyler is also able to "reach with one hand" (p. 61) and manipulate objects by moving them from one hand to the other (p. 62). Infants who are larger than average "may lack in motivation and delay motor skills" (Barrett, 1995, p. 145). This could be an explanation for Tyler's delay, since he is a large infant. Another explanation, according to _Child Development_, could be that Tyler is the second child born in the family, since "firstborn children tend to develop motor skills at an earlier age than their younger siblings" (p. 147).

Therefore, although Tyler is slow in his motor skills, such as crawling and walking, he is developing according to the other norms stated as references in the above paragraphs. There is no need for immediate alert as far as his motor development is concerned; however, observations and involvement on the part of the parents and caregivers is necessary to watch for possible problems in the future.

SELF-ASSESSMENT

This was a difficult assignment, in my opinion. I feel that I have met all the required components of the Time Sampling Observation; however, I am unsure if I did them correctly. Tyler's behaviors seemed to be those of any late-starting infant, and I found that it was difficult to describe those behaviors in this manner. Stating and validating inferences was not the hard part. I found the hardest part of the assignment to be the "pulling" of behaviors from the observations recorded. Although the assignment was difficult to put together, now that it is complete, I am able to see the relevance of the observations and the inferences made regarding the infant's development.

BIBLIOGRAPHY

Allen, K.E., & Marotz, L.R. (1994). _Development profiles: Pre-birth through eight_ (2nd ed.). Albany, NY: Delmar.

Barrett, K.C., et al. (1995). _Child development_. Westerville, OH: Glencoe.

Nathanson, L.W. (1994). _The portable pediatrician for parents_. New York: Viking.

Checklists

5

Contemporary assessment approaches ask teachers to use checklists to enhance the process of observation and make it more reliable.

Samuel J. Meisels (1993)

Checklists are closed, because they reduce raw data to a tally that indicates the presence or absence of a specified behavior.

Warren R. Bentzen (1993)

Checklists allow observers to make quick records of a child's behaviors and skills. This boy's outdoor play could lead to checklist observations related to his gross motor skills and personality.

Focus Questions

1. How could you record behaviors quickly when you are looking to see whether a child exhibits a particular skill?

2. If you listed some behaviors, how could you determine if they were in an appropriate developmental order?

3. Using the list of behaviors you have written and checking them off when you see them might be a good idea, but what could it tell you?

4. If you had to observe and record using a ready-made checklist comprising gross motor and fine motor skills, how would you know if the checklist was any good?

5. If checklist results are not what you expected, what might be the problem?

6. Would you have any concerns about comparing one child's behavior with what other children can do?

Learning Outcome

Learners will develop checklist criteria, use prepared checklists as tools to identify developmental characteristics of young children, and evaluate the validity and reliability of these methods.

History Notes

The testing of children became common in the 1920s. Many testing procedures have been modified over the years to enable the untrained to use them. **Checklists**, in their simplest form, allowed users to check off items on a predetermined list as they were observed. Items were identified as checklist criteria from the sequences of skills that formed the basis of earlier tests.

After World War II, a more scientific approach to child rearing focused on the new postwar baby boom. This approach fostered a need to measure and quantify children's **behaviors** whenever possible. Risking questionable methodologies, teachers, psychologists, and parents sought systems to evaluate children. Checklists easily fulfilled the need; both **norm-referenced** and **criterion-referenced assessment** systems were made easily accessible and usable.

During the 1960s and 1970s, a less competitive approach to child rearing and a more **child-centered** focus in learning developed. Some parents and teachers moved away from the more obviously measurable forms of observation and those that they considered to be too subjective or reliant on appropriate inferences. Checklists were, and are, still used, but you should be aware of their limitations as well as their strengths.

Types of Checklists

Definition: Checklists

Checklists record the presence or absence of particular predetermined behaviors such as skills, attributes, competencies, traits, reactions, achievements, or stages of development.

The items on a checklist may be chosen by the observer for a certain purpose, may be from a prepared checklist by a well-known authority, or may be written by a group of users who have a common reason for observing.

In this interpretive style of observing, the observer records a demonstrated **behavior** by checking off the item on the checklist. This may be done at the time it was demonstrated or a short time afterward.

Child Development Focus

Checklists may help the observation and recording of
* physical skills (gross and fine motor)
* self-help and social skills
* emotions and temperamental style
* cognitive skills
* language and communication

A knowledge of the **patterns of development** is essential for observers using checklists. These recordings can be only as useful as the items in them are sound; reference to recognized authorities on child development will support the writing of the checklist criteria. The items in the checklist must be **developmentally appropriate** and designed to give the information sought.

The homemade checklist

The homemade checklist is a useful tool for teachers or students to record developmental information about one or more children in a quick and efficient manner. Observers may want information about the children's **skills** in particular areas such as **language, fine** or **gross motor skills**, or shape recognition. A list of such skills, if developmentally appropriate and complete, will give the observer some insights into a child's **skill acquisition**. These results may be used as part of a program planning change if teachers think that new activities or experiences might enable the child to gain the skill.

Parents might want to keep a record of the sequence in which or dates by which their children achieve particular milestones. In this case, a checklist can be prepared to indicate key achievements; these can be checked off when they occur, and should also be dated.

▶▶ **Key Features: Homemade checklist**

- designed to record developmental information about an individual child
- lists expected behaviors
- used to check off observed behaviors
- interpretive method of recording behaviors
- naturalistic or "set up"
- participatory or nonparticipatory

Developmental Checklist

Child's name: _____   Observer: _____

Age/D.O.B.: _____   Date: _____

Context: _____

Source of checklist: _____

Age/stage designation: _____

Age/level	Behavior	Date	Evidence

Prepare the checklist before you need to record the evidence. You might want to use a developmental profile to select items. Make sure that you state the source of the checklist items.

The prepared checklist

Many well-designed checklists are available for use with young children. For ready-made observational tools, the same criteria for appropriate categories apply. If the items are not developmentally appropriate or do not fit the job you need done, then they will not give useful information.

Teachers, psychologists, caregivers, students, or parents may wish to carry out checklist observations for different reasons, but find that a part of a prepared checklist might be sufficient for their purposes; the whole schedule does not have to be used.

In addition to using a specifically prepared checklist, you can look for sources of checklist criteria in a variety of resources. An annotated list of prepared checklists and sources of checklist items appears on pages 161–62. Developmental profiles or schedules can also be used for this purpose.

▶▶ Key Features: Prepared checklist

- uses a standardized list of behaviors to record information about an individual child
- behaviors listed have been checked for their validity and reliability
- interpretive method of recording behaviors

Teacher Observation Form and Checklist for Identifying Children Who May Require Additional Services

Child's name: _____   Recording teacher's name: _____

Birth date: _____   Date: _____

LANGUAGE   Yes   No   Sometimes
Does the child
1. use two- and three-word phrases to ask for what he or she wants?   ☐   ☐   ☐
2. use complete sentences to tell you what happened?   ☐   ☐   ☐
3. when asked to describe something, use at least two or more sentences
   to talk about it?   ☐   ☐   ☐
4. ask questions?
5. seem to have difficulty following directions?   ☐   ☐   ☐
6. respond to questions with appropriate answers?   ☐   ☐   ☐
7. seem to talk too softly or too loudly?   ☐   ☐   ☐
8. Are you able to understand the child?   ☐   ☐   ☐

PREACADEMICS Yes No Sometimes

Does the child

9. seem to take at least twice as long as the other children to learn preacademic concepts? ☐ ☐ ☐

10. seem to take the time needed by other children to learn preacademic concepts? ☐ ☐ ☐

11. have difficulty attending to group activities for more than five minutes at a time? ☐ ☐ ☐

12. appear extremely shy in group activities (for instance, not volunteering answers or answering questions when asked, even though you think the child knows the answers)? ☐ ☐ ☐

MOTOR Yes No Sometimes

Does the child

13. continually switch a crayon back and forth from one hand to the other when coloring? ☐ ☐ ☐

14. appear clumsy or shaky when using one or both hands? ☐ ☐ ☐

15. when coloring with a crayon, appear to tense the hand not being used (for instance, clench it into a fist)? ☐ ☐ ☐

16. when walking or running, appear to move one side of the body differently from the other side? For instance, does the child seem to have better control of the leg and arm on one side than on the other? ☐ ☐ ☐

17. lean or tilt to one side when walking or running? ☐ ☐ ☐

18. seem to fear or not be able to use stairs, climbing equipment, or tricycles? ☐ ☐ ☐

19. stumble often or appear awkward when moving about? ☐ ☐ ☐

20. appear capable of dressing self except for tying shoes? ☐ ☐ ☐

SOCIAL Yes No Sometimes

Does the child

21. engage in more than two disruptive behaviors a day (tantrums, fighting, screaming, etc.)? ☐ ☐ ☐

22. appear withdrawn from the outside world (fiddling with pieces of string, staring into space, rocking)? ☐ ☐ ☐

23. play alone and seldom talk to the other children? ☐ ☐ ☐

24. spend most of the time trying to get attention from adults? ☐ ☐ ☐

25. have toileting problems (wet or soiled) once a week or more often? ☐ ☐ ☐

VISUAL OR HEARING Yes No Sometimes

Does the child

26. appear to have eye movements that are jerky or uncoordinated? ☐ ☐ ☐

27. seem to have difficulty seeing objects? For instance, does the child
- tilt head to look at things? ☐ ☐ ☐
- hold objects close to eyes? ☐ ☐ ☐
- squint? ☐ ☐ ☐
- show sensitivity to bright lights? ☐ ☐ ☐
- have uncontrolled eye rolling? ☐ ☐ ☐
- complain that eyes hurt? ☐ ☐ ☐

28. appear awkward in tasks requiring eye–hand coordination such as pegs, puzzles, coloring, etc.? ☐ ☐ ☐

29. seem to have difficulty hearing? For instance, does the child
- consistently favor one ear by turning the same side of the head in the direction of the sound? □ □ □
- ignore, confuse, or not follow directions? □ □ □
- pull on ears or rub ears frequently, or complain of earaches? □ □ □
- complain of head noises or dizziness? □ □ □
- have a very high, very low, or monotonous tone of voice? □ □ □

GENERAL HEALTH	Yes	No	Sometimes
Does the child			
30. seem to have an excessive number of colds?	□	□	□
31. have frequent absences because of illness?	□	□	□
32. have eyes that water?	□	□	□
33. have frequent discharge from			
• eyes?	□	□	□
• ears?	□	□	□
• nose?	□	□	□
34. have sores on body or head?	□	□	□
35. have periods of unusual movements (such as eye blinking) or "blank spells" that seem to appear and disappear without relationship to the social situation?	□	□	□
36. have hives or rashes?	□	□	□
wheeze?	□	□	□
37. have a persistent cough?	□	□	□
38. seem to be excessively thirsty?	□	□	□
seem to be ravenously hungry?	□	□	□
39. Have you noticed any of the following conditions:			
• constant fatigue?	□	□	□
• irritability?	□	□	□
• restlessness?	□	□	□
• tenseness?	□	□	□
• feverish cheeks or forehead?	□	□	□
40. Is the child overweight?	□	□	□
41. Is the child physically or mentally lethargic?	□	□	□
42. Has the child lost noticeable weight without being on a diet?	□	□	□

Source: K. Eileen Allen et al., *Exceptional Children: Inclusion in Early Childhood Programs* (1998). Reprinted with permission of ITP Nelson.

Features of a Checklist

A checklist can give you worthwhile information if the items it indicates are appropriate. To work out the usefulness of a checklist, you will need to assess its appropriateness, **validity**, and **reliability**.

Appropriateness

To judge the suitability of a prepared checklist, you will need to determine the following:

1. The checklist covers the areas of behavior you wish to record.
2. The items included cover a suitable developmental span of behaviors in the selected domain.
3. There will be a sufficient blend of behaviors demonstrated to show a pattern, rather than simply whether a behavior is absent or present.
4. The checklist will fit your purpose—for example, reports, record keeping, program planning, identification of a concern, and so on.

Watch out!

If you have checked off more than about 80 percent of the checklist, all it will tell you is that the child has progressed beyond it!

Validity

Checklist items must be effective in measuring the behaviors that they intend to assess. You may at first look at a checklist's broad categories and consider how they will provide information in those areas. There needs to be a sufficient number of subcategories, graduated in their level of difficulty. Without these, the criteria will likely not, in fact, measure what you desire.

Behaviors itemized in a checklist must be validated through an assessment of their theoretical basis and underlying foundation of accepted sequences of development. (Refer also to Chapter 1, page 20, and Chapter 10 to examine the notion of validity.)

Reliability

Prepared checklists have usually been tested for reliability, but you should not assume this. These standardized measures may be useful in many situations but the reliability may be affected by a built-in **bias** not easily seen. Most significant, but least easily detected, is a cultural bias that can lead an observer to believe that a child is either more advanced or less skilled than he or she actually is. Even supposedly "standardized" measures may not have eliminated these biases. For example, if you were to assess self-help skills as part of competence, you could find that a child lacks experience dressing himself because this is not considered a desirable early skill in his culture. Similarly, when a child's first language is not English, it is unfair to evaluate her communication skills in English. She may be far more competent in her own language; consequently, her cognitive skills may also be more advanced than your observations might suggest.

To be reliable, a checklist should evaluate a child's behavior in a way that does not fluctuate from one observation situation to the next. Some short-term consistency should exist among outcomes of the checklist recordings. Results should be consistent among observers recording information about a child.

Watch out!

The fact that a checklist has been printed doesn't mean it is valid and reliable!

Checklist Observations

Recording observations

Observers need to interpret the checklist criteria and match the observed behavior to the item. Observers mark the presence or absence of the behavior; often, only check marks, not comments, are used when the item has been demonstrated. This recording may not be done all at one time, but over a period of a few days, if a wide variety of behaviors is sought. Sample checklist observations can be found on pages 164–67, 168–71, and 172–74.

Watch out!

Date all checked-off items. You may forget later!

Items are usually checked off as a result of the child's spontaneous activity. On occasion, some desired behaviors will not have been demonstrated, so an observer may set up a situation in which the behavior may occur or organize a more formal "testing" situation to elicit the desired response. In any situation, the observer should record the contextual information that might have had an impact on the behavior.

Checklists are frequently used to evaluate information gathered from informal observations, but they may be compiled from a narrative recording or from other documentation. The direct method is more likely to give accurate results.

How to record a checklist observation

1. Decide on the purpose for using the checklist method.
2. Choose a prepared checklist or devise a list of behaviors that fits your purpose.
3. Assess the checklist for its developmental appropriateness, validity, and reliability.
4. Prepare the checklist and place it where you can record the behaviors as they occur or soon afterward.
5. Check off the items you see demonstrated and about which you are certain.
6. Make note of any areas about which you are uncertain because of difficulty in interpreting the criteria or because the behavior is just emerging.
7. When behaviors are not demonstrated, set up experiences so they may be seen. Document the results.
8. Make appropriate, validated **inferences**, remembering that the absence of a behavior does not necessarily indicate that the child is incapable of performing the behavior.

Using checklists

Advantages

- Recording is quick and efficient.
- This method can be used in a variety of settings.
- All details need not be recorded.
- A clear picture of the presence or absence of behavior is given.
- The observer can choose criteria to observe.
- The observer can record observations while responsible for children's care.
- The observer can choose to record information about more than one child at a time.

- Coverage of a range of developmental aspects may offer an overview of the whole child.
- Information can be used for program planning.
- Prepared checklists that are valid and reliable may be available.
- This method can identify concerns where an individual is not performing as per the norm.

Disadvantages

- Recording is so simple that errors are not easily seen. The detail and context of the observed behavior are lost.
- Recording may require a degree of inference or interpretation.
- Criteria can easily be inappropriate, invalid, or unreliable.
- Interpretation typically focuses on what the child cannot do rather than on skills mastered.
- The checklist requires prior evaluation and preparation.
- A checklist tends to represent a selection of isolated fragments of behavior.
- Information about a child's skill development does not necessarily translate into appropriate goal setting/planning.
- Checklist criteria may be difficult to validate for developmental appropriateness.
- This method typically relies on norm referencing, which is considered a dubious tool by some educators.
- Recorded behaviors may require a qualitative description in addition to a statement of presence or absence.
- The absence of a behavior does not necessarily indicate an inability to perform the behavior.
- Recording might be affected by emotional conditions or illness that might not be evident.
- Teachers and parents tend to "remember" behaviors and record them as present from previous occasions; these may be expectations rather than objectively recorded examples.

Watch out!

Check the checklist's source and accompanying data to help with your checklist findings!

The analysis: Interpreting the data collected from checklists

Inferences should not be drawn from the information unless the checklist has been assessed for its suitability and the recording has been made with **objectivity**. A typical **analysis** might cover the following areas:

1. Draw deductions from the pattern of skills present on or absent from the checklist. Highlight the strengths demonstrated.
2. Make inferences about the child's skill level using comparisons with expected performance. This **norm-referenced assessment** needs to make clear supporting statements that have thorough validity.
3. Depending on the reason for the observation, evaluate the effectiveness of the checklist and examine its outcome.
   a. Look at the supposed "lack" of skill development; ask yourself whether the skill has not been acquired or perhaps is present but was not demonstrated.
   b. Verify the checklist with information from others.
   c. Follow up with a variety of other observation methods and attempt to match the outcomes.
   d. Develop an **individual program plan** that devises activities and experiences to enhance skills.
   e. Ask the parents, school, or other interested party to offer insights or other informal observations to help explain the behavioral pattern.
   f. If the child demonstrates all the criteria, little information about the stage of development can be elicited. Use another checklist that is more developmentally appropriate.

Watch out!

Checklists may be "normed" in ways that are culturally inappropriate. Avoid judgments based on such checklists!

Prepared Checklists and Sources of Checklist Items

Allen, K.E., & Marotz, L.R. (1994). *Developmental profiles: Pre-birth through eight* (2nd ed.). Albany, NY: Delmar.

Six one-page developmental checklists for children at 12 months, 2 years, 3 years, 4 years, 5 years, and 6 years. Each contains broad categories of behaviors—good for an overview but not very refined. The emphasis is on easily observable skills rather than cognitive activity that requires more interpretation. The text of the book covers more detailed profiles of growth and development in each developmental domain, offering age/stage divisions. These could be adapted for use as checklists.

Beaty, J.J. (1998). *Observing development of the young child* (4th ed.). Upper Saddle River, NJ: Prentice-Hall.

Textbook written around a developmental checklist called "Child Skills Checklist," appropriate for 3- to 5-year-olds in any setting. Each developmental area is included (twelve categories) with eight items in each category. Broad categories may not reveal specific information, but the checklist is useful for any observer. The book identifies how each skill may be developed by appropriate curriculum planning.

Furuno, S., et al. (1995). *HELP [Hawaii early learning profile] checklist (0–3)* (revised). Palo Alto, CA: VORT Corp.

VORT Corp. (1995). *HELP for preschoolers checklist (3–6)*. Palo Alto, CA: VORT Corp.

Two detailed checklists covering hundreds of behaviors. Supporting resources include *HELP Activity Guide* and *Help at Home*, which give those working with children practical suggestions for supporting skill development. HELP charts enable checklist information to be presented in an easy-to-interpret format. Both checklists are intended for the majority of children who fall within the age ranges—not necessarily those with developmental concerns.

Herr, J. (1998). *Working with young children: The observation guide*. Tinley Park, IL: Goodheart–Willcox.

Several prepared age-related (birth to 5 years) or developmental-domain-itemized checklists designed for students learning about children's development. They could also be used by practicing teachers, caregivers, and parents.

Ireton, H. (1995). *Child development inventory*. Minneapolis, MN: Behavior Science Systems.

A brief overview of developmental domains in the age ranges 1–2 years, 2–3 years, 3–4 years, 4–5 years, and 5–6 years. An observational checklist is supplemented by parent questionnaires. There is an open-ended "other skills" section and the identification of possible "problems."

Norris, D., & Boucher, J. (1980). *Observing children through their formative years*. Toronto Observation Project. Toronto: Board of Education for the City of Toronto.

A guide to observing children in the age ranges 2–5 years, 5–7 years, 7–9 years, 9–11 years, and 11–13 years. Categories of skill development are identified. The school-age profiles are particularly useful and could be used as checklist items.

Schirmer, G.J. (Ed.). (1974). *Performance objectives for pre-school children*. Sioux Falls, SD: Adapt Press.

A developmental checklist covering a wide range of developmental domains. Each age category and domain has several identified categorized skills.

Sheridan, M.D. (1975). *The developmental progress of infants and young children* (3rd ed.). London: Her Majesty's Stationery Office.

Sheridan, M.D. (1974). *Children's developmental progress from birth to five years: The Stycar sequences*. Windsor, England: National Foundation for Educational Research.

A detailed listing of emerging behaviors identified in closely defined age ranges. Intended for developmental pediatric use, the book lends itself to formulating theoretically sound checklists that might be used by any caregiver, teacher, or informed parent.

Key Terms

analysis

behavior

bias

checklist

child-centered

criterion-referenced
assessment

developmentally
appropriate

fine motor skills

gross motor skills

individual program
plan

inference

language

norm-referenced
assessment

objectivity

pattern of develop-
ment

reliability

skill acquisition

validity

A developmentally appropriate checklist will reveal both the skills that a child has mastered and those that have not yet been attained. Playing together on a climber, these children will demonstrate not only their gross motor development but also their social and language skills.

Observation Sample

This sample is an excerpt from a toddler checklist that was used to review each developmental domain. Some evidence is offered for each item observed. A front page giving background information and a signed parental permission form should be part of every assignment, and a pseudonym for the child should be used in the observation.

Observation Assignment

Front Page

Student name: <u>Carla Laws</u>   Student number: <u>00 777 000</u>

Section number: <u>CY 106-063</u>

Assignment method: <u>Checklist--self-selected items from Infants and Toddlers</u>

Date due: <u>18/04/98</u>   Date handed in: <u>18/04/98</u>

Child's name (pseudonym): <u>Sasha</u>

Child's age (years/months): <u>21 months</u>

Date of observation: <u>05/04/98, 12/04/98</u>   Time of observation: <u>9:00-11:30 a.m.</u>

Setting: <u>Toddler Room, Busy Bee Child Care Center. Children engage in free play.</u>

Parent's name: <u>Sandy Peters</u>   Phone # if released: <u>n/a</u>

Each assignment has specific criteria. Please check with the assignment description and direction given in class.

Declaration by student

I have followed the assignment description and instructions given in class about confidentiality and privacy. I confirm that appropriate processes for making this observation have been undertaken and that permission has been gained from the parents. A copy of this observation will be given to the parents if they desire.

Carla Laws

Signature of Student

Permission Form

Child Observations, Case Studies, and Portfolios

Student and Parent Agreement

Without written permission I will not observe and record information about your child. Please sign in the space provided if you agree that I may make observations and study your child. It would be helpful if you could initial each of the boxes if you are willing for me to undertake any or all of the techniques of information gathering.

I ___*Carla Laws*___ *(student name)* will not refer to the child in any written manner by his or her real name. Information recorded will be written objectively, treated professionally, and kept confidential.

___*Carla Laws*___   ___*March 29, 1998*___
(student's signature)   *(date)*

I ___*Sandy Peters*___
(parent's name)

agree to have ___*Amelia Peters*___
      (child's name)

observed ☑   photographed ☑   audiotaped ☐   videotaped ☐

by ___*Carla Laws*___
(student's name above)

at ___*Busy Bee Child Care Center*___
(agency/home)

for the purpose of study in child development at ___*Harlow College*___
(school/college) for a period of ___*4 weeks*___ *(weeks/months)* on the consideration that copies are made available to me, the parent, if I so request.

___*Sandy Peters*___   ___*April 5/98*___
(parent's signature)   *(date)*

Source: <u>Infants and Toddlers</u>
Age range: 18-30 months identified for checklist
Physical characteristics: fair-skinned, light-brown curly hair, brown eyes, ears pierced, green cotton pants, green flowered sweater, running shoes

Legend: ✓ -if seen present
   ✓₂ -if reported to be present by qualified teacher or parent

PHYSICAL DEVELOPMENT
Muscular Control
Locomotion
✓ Walks forward *when walking*
✓ Walks backward *displayed in a game led by one of the teachers*
✓ Walks sideways *displayed in a game led by one of the teachers*
✓ Runs with stops and starts *when running outside on the playground*
✓ Jumps with both feet *gross motor play—jumping to a song*
✓ Kicks object *gross motor play—kicks balls (attempts to)*
___ Walks up stairs holding railing
___ Walks down stairs holding railing
✓ Pushes and pulls objects while walking *pushes and pulls doll stroller*
✓ Climbs *climbs the slide on the playground*
✓ Pedals cycle *rides Fisher-Price tricycle*
Arm
___ Throws object at target
Hand
✓ Grasps and releases with developing finger muscles *when handling small toys*
✓ Pulls zippers *zipping down zipper to take off coat*
✓ Helps dress and undress self *getting dressed and undressed from outside*
✓ Scribbles *displayed in her drawings/artwork*
✓ Increases wrist flexibility, turns wrist to turn object *when attempting to turn handle on door*
✓ Establishing right- or left-handedness *handles utensils (cups, paintbrush) mostly with right hand*
✓ Turns book pages *when handling books, she turns various pages at a time*
✓ Digs with tools *using the shovel at the sensory bin to dig oatmeal*
✓ Makes individual marks with crayon or pen *a drawing she made with a pen*

Sleeping
✓₂ May move from crib to bed or cot *adjusted from home to day care with relative ease*

Eating
✓₂ Controls cup and spoon better *noticed by teacher*
✓₂ May eat anything, then change to picky eating *noticed by teacher during lunchtime*

Teeth
✓ Has most baby teeth *apparent*
✓₂ Uses toothbrush *mom says that she attempts to*

Elimination
✓ May show interest in and readiness for toilet training *says "pee-pee" and "doo-doo" when she needs to go to the washroom*

EMOTIONAL DEVELOPMENT

Types of Emotions/Feelings

___ Views internal feelings and external behavior as same

___ Shows one or more emotions at same time

___ Continues to develop feelings about self

___ Changes feelings about self

✓ Seeks approval *likes to show her accomplishments, e.g., washing her hands*

___ May develop new fears

___ Increases fantasy

✓ May increase aggressiveness *pulls another child's arm when he takes her toy*

___ Seeks security in routines

✓ May become shy again *when she comes into day care in the morning*

___ Sometimes rejects parent or caregiver

Control of Emotions/Feelings

✓ Uses reactions of others as a controller of own behavior *when teacher raises voice, she stops and looks at the teacher*

___ May resist change

✓ Moves to extremes, from lovable to demanding and stubborn *frequently when she doesn't get her own way*

SOCIAL DEVELOPMENT

Self

✓ Is egocentric, sees things from own point of view *sometimes throws tantrums if she doesn't get her way*

___ May change identity of self from day to day

✓ Identifies materials as belonging to self *"my book," "my mommy," "my ball"*

✓ Uses I, mine, me, you *often says "mine, mine, me, me"*

Others

✓ Demands attention *frequently calls teacher by name for attention*

✓ Begins to be aware of others' feelings *tells teacher someone is crying*

___ Believes people have changes in identity

✓ Expands social relationships *will approach other children*

✓ Looks to others for help *will approach teacher for help*

✓ Imitates tasks of others *wipes the table after seeing teacher do it*

✓ Wants to help, assists with tasks *voluntarily assists teacher with tasks*

___ May do opposite of what is requested

✓ Difficulty sharing *she doesn't like to share toys*

✓ Engages in parallel play *frequently seen during free play*

Source: <u>Infants and Toddlers</u>, 3rd ed., by LaVisa Cam Wilson, Linda Douville-Watson, and Michael A. Watson. Delmar Publishers, Albany, New York. Copyright 1995. Reproduced by permission.

Observation Sample

The recorder has selected an appropriate checklist for the developmental level of the child. The prepared checklist allows room for supporting evidence when items are observed. This sample shows excerpts from the complete checklist.

Child Skills Checklist for Preschoolers

Child's name: Jimmy   Observer: Cody

Age: 5 years, 9 months   Dates: 25 and 30 June and 2 July, 1998

Setting: Laboratory School

Key: **A–agree** **D–disagree** **N–not observed**

* Observation of day-care teachers   ** Observation of mother

Item	Evidence	Date
1. Self-identity		
A Separates from parents without difficulty	Mother tells him good-bye; he says bye and continues to play.*	30 June
A Does not cling to classroom staff excessively	Plays at the assigned areas on his own	30 June
A Makes eye contact with adults	Looks teacher in the eye as she explains how to stop the tricycle	30 June
A Makes activity choices without teacher's help	Hollers out, "I want to paint!" after the teacher explains their options for play	25 June
D Seeks other children to play with	Will seek out an activity, not a playmate	25 & 30 June
N Plays roles confidently in dramatic play		
A Stands up for own rights	Teachers say he often expresses anger if he does not get his way.*	30 June
A Displays enthusiasm about doing things for self	Holds up his artwork to show another student	30 June
2. Emotional development		
A Allows self to be comforted during stressful time	During play, when Jimmy is running around wildly not listening to the teachers, he allows an instructor to pull him onto her lap. He remains there until he is more settled.	25 June
A Eats, sleeps, toilets without fuss away from home	Uses the bathroom and eats lunch at the day-care center with no fuss	25 June
N Handles sudden changes/startling situations with control		
D Can express anger in words rather than actions	Jimmy has hit teachers and peers when he is angry or is not getting his way.*	30 June
D Allows aggressive behavior to be redirected	Teachers say it is difficult to redirect his anger and aggressive behavior when he is upset.*	30 June

Item	Evidence	Date
A Does not withdraw from others excessively	Eager to do activities even when they involve the entire group	25 June
A Shows interest/attention in classroom activities	Asks teacher to read a story again that involves imitation	25 June
A Smiles, seems happy much of the time	Often smiles while playing	30 June

3. Social play

Item	Evidence	Date
A Plays by self with or without objects	Plays with a paper airplane while other children are around or alone	2 July
A Plays by self in pretend-type activities	Pretends his tricycle is an automobile	30 June
N Plays parallel to others with or without objects		
A Plays parallel to others in pretend-type activities	Pretends his tricycle is an automobile; other children are present	30 June
A Plays parallel to others constructing or creating something	Coloring and cutting out a picture at a table with other children	30 June
A Plays with a group with or without objects	Pretends to dig in sand with a shovel during a circle reading activity	25 June
N Plays with a group constructing or creating something		

7. Cognitive development: classification and seriation

Item	Evidence	Date
A Recognizes basic geometric shapes	Can identify triangles, squares, and circles**	30 June
A Recognizes colors	Can identify the main colors	2 July
A Recognizes differences in size	Will tell his mother he wants a big cup not a small cup**	30 June
N Recognizes differences in musical tones		
D Reproduces musical tones with voice	Will sing a song but does not noticeably change his tone**	30 June
N Sorts objects by appearance		
N Arranges events in sequences from first to last		
N Arranges objects in series according to rule		

8. Cognitive development: number, time, space, memory

Item	Evidence	Date
A Counts by rote to ten	Counts by rote up to one hundred**	30 June
A Counts objects to ten	Can count at least up to ten with a one-to-one ratio**	30 June
A Knows the daily schedule in sequence	Has to make his bed and brush his teeth after breakfast so that he can play before he goes to school**	30 June
N Can build a block enclosure	Child has never tried to build one. He builds bridges and airplanes with Lego.**	30 June

Item	Evidence	Date
A Knows what happened yesterday	Can recount events of days that have passed**	30 June
A Can locate an object behind or beside something	Finds the Slinky that is behind a bigger toy	25 June
A Recalls words to song, chant	Can repeat/sing popular country songs that he hears frequently**	30 June
A Can recollect and act on directions of singing	Participates in a group activity that involves singing and acting out parts of the song	25 June

9. Spoken language

Item	Evidence	Date
A Speaks confidently in classroom	When the teacher asks the group a question about a story she is reading, he answers the question with, "It's a wave."	25 June
A Speaks clearly enough for adults to understand	Same as above	25 June
A Speaks in expanded sentences	Tells his mother, "I have an airplane. Ben made it for me."	2 July
A Takes part in conversations with other children	Talks to a child sitting next to him while he is coloring a picture	30 June
A Asks questions with proper word order	Asks the teacher, "Can we go in this room to play now?"	2 July
N Makes "no" responses with proper word order		
A Uses past tense verbs correctly	Tells the teacher, "I used my feet to stop the bike."	30 June
N Plays with rhyming words		

10. Written language

Item	Evidence	Date
N Pretends to write by scribbling horizontally		
N Includes features of real letters in scribbling		
A Identifies his own name	Can point to things that have his name and recognize his name written**	30 June
N Identifies classroom labels		
A Knows some of the alphabet letters	Knows the entire alphabet and can recognize most of the letters**	30 June
A Prints real letters	Can print his first name**	30 June
A Prints letters of name	Can print his first name**	30 June
A Prints name correctly in linear manner	Can print his first name**	30 June

Item	Evidence	Date
12. Imagination		
N Pretends by replaying familiar routines		
N Needs particular props to do pretend play		
N Assigns roles or takes assigned roles		
N May switch roles without warning		
D Uses language for creating and sustaining a plot	Mother says she's never heard him make up stories about an event.**	30 June
N Uses exciting, danger-packed themes		
A Takes on characteristics and actions related to a role	Makes sounds like a car while riding a tricycle	30 June
D Uses elaborate and creative themes, ideas, and details	Mother says she's never heard him make up stories about an event.**	30 June

Source: *Observing Development of the Young Child,* 4th ed., by Janice Beaty.
© 1994. Adapted by permission of Prentice-Hall, Inc., Upper Saddle River, NJ.

Observation Sample

This school-age child has been observed using a checklist developed from a normative profile. The recording contains quotations in the child's (and recorder's) first language.

DEVELOPMENTAL CHECKLIST

Observer: Ki Wan A Yau

Child's name: Mei Lin
Age/D.O.B.: 8 years, 8 months (June 10, 1989)

Date of observation: March 2–16, 1998
Time of observation: throughout day
Setting: March 2–16 at her home and her aunt's home; March 4, 9:25–11:30 a.m. in her classroom and gym

Source of checklist items: Allen, K.E., & Marotz, L.R. (1994). Developmental profile and growth pattern (Appendix 2). In *Development profiles: Pre-birth through eight* (2nd ed., p. 171). Albany, NY: Delmar.

Designated age/stage of checklist items: 8 and 9 years

Key: ✓ Observed

  ✓$_2$ Observed by caregiver or parent

  N No opportunity to observe

  ✗ Behavior not yet demonstrated

Behaviors	Key	Date	Evidence
1. a. Have energy to play	✓	March 4	She showed she had energy to play in gym. She climbed a rope, walked across a balance beam, jumped up and bent her knees on a boxhorse, turned somersaults.
b. Continuing growth	✓	March 2	Now, her height is 51.5". Since last June, her height has increased 1.5".
c. Few illnesses	✓	March 6	Last winter, she only had one cold.
2. Use pencil in a deliberate and controlled manner	✓	March 4	She can hold a pencil and marker using a tripod grasp. I saw this when she was drawing pictures in her journal.

Behaviors	Key	Date	Evidence
3. Express relatively complex thoughts in a clear and logical fashion	✓	March 2	She used macaroni to make a bracelet and talked at the same time. Quote: Chinese language: 地對媽說：「我用這條繩去度手腕的長度。」(她再度橡筋，然後將通心粉串上)又說：「陣間我會沰上顏色。」媽說：「你串好，十分難上色。」地說：「我要知道用幾多，然後拿出來再上色。」 Translation: She said to her mom, "I use this string to measure the length around my hand." After she had done, she cut a rubber band and threaded macaroni one by one. She said, "I will paint them later on." Mom said, "If you thread them all, you will find it difficult to paint afterward." She said, "I want to know how many I will use, then I will let them out and paint them."
4. Carry out multiple (4-5) step instructions	✓	March 13	Quote: Chinese language: 媽對她說：「Tracy，去廚櫃拿一個碗和碟放在枱上。然後去雪櫃，取兩隻蛋，兩塊HAM。打蛋於碗內，至起泡，用剪刀把HAM剪絲。做完後，話我知，我會教妳煮菜。」 Translation: Mom said, "Mei Lin, get one bowl and one small plate from the cupboard and put them on the table. Then, get two eggs and two pieces of ham from the refrigerator. Break the eggs into the bowl and stir them with a fork until bubbles appear. Cut the ham into stick-size pieces on the plate with scissors. After you finish, tell me. I will teach you how to cook it."
5. Become less easily frustrated with own performance	✕	March 5	She was frustrated with her own performance when she did paper folding to make a turtle because she didn't remember exactly the steps.
6. Interact and play cooperatively with other children	✓	March 14	She talked to her cousins when they played games together. They played Monopoly cooperatively. She waited for her turn patiently.

Behaviors	Key	Date	Evidence
7. Use eating utensils with ease	✓	March 4	She can use her right hand to grasp chop-sticks and left hand to grasp a bowl at the same time to eat food. She uses her right hand to grasp a knife and left hand to grasp a fork at the same time to cut food.
8. a. Have a good appetite	X	March 5-16	She could eat half a bowl of rice, lots of vegetables and meats.
b. Show interest in trying new foods		March 15	Mom mixed salad and tuna fish. She did not want to eat it.
9. Know how to tell time	✓	March 4	Quote: Chinese language: 在校裏，我问她：「recess 幾時完?」她說評束十。 Translation: I asked her when she finished recess in her school. She said "10 to 11."
10. Have control of bowel and bladder func-tions	✓	March 2-16	She has control of bowel and bladder func-tions. I saw this when she went to the wash-room regularly and independently without any problem.
11. Participate in some group activities a. Sports	✓	March 4	In gym, she participated in the group routines.
b. Plays	✓₂	March 4	Every Monday, she joins the folk-dance club after school.
c. Games	✓	March 17	She played games with her cousins.
12. Demonstrate beginning skills in a. Reading	✓	March 6	She read a book to her baby sister. Sometimes she reads books borrowed from the school library.
b. Writing	✓	March 12	I saw this when she wrote letters to her classmates using handwriting.
c. Math	N		
13. a. Want to go to school	X		
b. Seem disap-pointed if must miss a day	X		

Charts, Scales, and Pictorial Representations

6

Mapping the children's movements on a floor plan of my room helped me to reorganize my space a bit better. The older children watched me watching them—they decided to record my movements so I gave them a copy of the floor plan.

ECE student (1993)

Plotting on the chart shows a steady upward curve for each child. When this ascent either slows down abnormally, dips or flattens out, it tells the caregiver something is happening to that particular child.

Veronica Rose (1985)

Understanding a child's family and social context can help an observer interpret the child's behavior. Family trees and other social maps can be used to chart the child's relationships.

Focus Questions

1. How might you devise a quick and efficient method of recording information about a child's daily routine?

2. How might a map of a room, outdoor play space, or other children's area be used to benefit the program or an individual child?

3. What inferences might you draw from a pattern of behavior that you have charted?

4. How could you tell if a prepared rating scale was appropriate for evaluating personality attributes?

5. After interpreting data from observations of a whole class, the teacher wants to present the findings in a graphic manner. In what ways could this be done?

6. What information represented on a family tree could be useful to a child-care worker?

Learning Outcome

Learners will use a variety of techniques to record and interpret observational data as scales and diagrams.

History Notes

Visual depictions of observational information use mathematical-style representations. Some of these forms have been used for hundreds of years. They usually rely on quantitative evaluation, which is presented as **numerical scales**, graphs, and scale diagrams.

The idea that social topics could be subjected to quantitative analysis acquired prominence in the first part of the seventeenth century. This analysis concerned demographic enumeration (counting people) rather than the types of quantification needed by teachers and psychologists today. In 1886, August Meitzen, a professor at the University of Berlin, published a book on statistics that described the usefulness of collecting, tabulating, and interpreting demographic and social data. The move toward data collection was occurring in North America as well as in Europe.

Family trees are a form of social data collection. Some date back before the eleventh century. An interest in tracing ancestry has re-established itself, perhaps because of the mobility of families and the need to search for roots. Family, cultural, religious, or ethnic attitudes and beliefs may be under threat as people move about. Appreciation of the importance of the child's background has led professionals and parents to seek this documentation.

Mappings and trackings predate the emphasis on the learning environment, which evolved from the educational theories of the 1960s. But the 1960s and 1970s were times of change in educational and caregiving agencies. New understandings about how children learn led to different styles of constructing children's environments to allow for choices, self-direction, free movement, open planning, and, in some instances, mixed age groups. The environments needed to be planned and evaluated in use. Mappings and trackings became ways of maximizing learning potential in space and activity planning.

Observation charts evolved out of the need to find quick and efficient ways of recording information. Many come from charts used by the medical and nursing profession. Growth, medical, and infant information most easily fits the chart methods, which offer clear-cut, rather than qualitative, ways of recording.

The earliest rating scales were in use in the 1920s and 1930s. The *Twenty-Eighth Yearbook of the National Society for the Study of Education* (1929) cites types of personality and social rating scales. Further scales were published by other authors in 1930 (Irwin & Bushnell, 1980).

Social relationships were not commonly represented in diagrammatic forms until the late 1960s and 1970s. Sociometry became popular in the 1970s because it offered a way of depicting the dynamics of relationships. At this time, there was a rising awareness of the necessity for individuals to be evaluated in their naturalistic setting rather than in a test situation. Also, new insights encouraged the observation of both individual and group behavior; sociometry allowed for both simultaneously. For similar reasons, at much the same time, the genogram evolved from family systems theory. Murray Bowen's (1978) work provided the conceptual framework for analyzing genogram patterns.

The ecomap is a more recent model than other social mappings, coming into frequent use in the 1980s. It offers a simple diagrammatic representation of the ecological influences on the child's development, allowing for a clearer understanding of those influences. Ecomaps have gained popularity with social workers and psychologists interested in the sociological and contextual aspects of the child's experience.

Features of Charts, Scales, and Pictorial Representations

Definition: Chart

A **chart** is observed information that is recorded onto a prepared format or map according to specified criteria.

Definition: Scale

A **scale** is a form of measuring information that uses lists of behaviors or other items and rates them according to predetermined values.

Definition: Pictorial representation

A **pictorial representation** is any form of recording or interpretation that uses visual presentation to demonstrate collected data.

Charts, scales, and pictorial representations are all interpretive methods of recording observational data. They enable the observer to write down information quickly and efficiently as it is perceived. These methods are heavily dependent on the **objectivity** of the recorder; frequently there is little way of validating the accuracy of the recording. Practicing teachers may have to observe while engaged in activity with the children. These forms of recording may enable them to collect information that might be impossible to record using more time-consuming methods.

Some charts and many pictorial representations and scales are completed soon after the activity is over. Again, their easy use enables teachers to record some of the essence of what was observed without writing all the details. This recording requires professional skill in deciding what is relevant and what is not. Almost any untrained person could complete a rating scale or chart; some of the information might be useful and accurate, but it may not all be reliable. The outcome may look fine but lack the objectivity of a professional's work. These observations should not be used alone to determine a child's program plan. They can be used in addition to other observation methods, as they may be helpful in providing a fuller picture.

Child Development Focus

Visual representation may assist in determining
- social relationships
- typical patterns of behavior
- contextual influences on development
- mobility
- personal preferences

Useful recording methods

Charts, scales, and pictorial representations are methods for recording observational data or ways in which information is presented after analysis. They have in common the use of visual representation of information. The following are the most useful categories for the observer.

1. **Observation charts** (pages 180–88): These are prepared blank forms with labeled and sectioned categories to be used for charting behaviors, relationship dyads (connections/interactions between two individuals), routine events, and other significant information as it is observed.

2. **Observation scales** (pages 188–92): Commonly called rating scales, these are listings of behaviors or traits prepared in advance for scoring at the time of or after observation. These can be open to subjective recording. They may include forced choices, semantic differentials, numerical scales, or graphic scales.

3. **Social maps** (pages 193–99): Pictorial presentations of the family composition, history, social relationships, or life experiences are all helpful to the observer. These may include sociograms, ecomaps, genograms, family trees, and flow diagrams or pictorial profiles. Information is gathered from the child, family members, or those in other social relationships and is presented as a chart or diagram.

4. **Mappings** (pages 199–201): Trackings or mappings are observations of a child's movement or activity within a specified room zone or space. By recording the path of movement on a prepared map of that space, the teacher has evidence of the child's mobility, interests, and attention span. Mappings may support a teacher's evaluation of the use of space.

5. **Interpretive graphic representations** (pages 202–203): In analyzing quantities of observations, observers might wish to explain their findings in visual ways. Graphs, block charts, and pie charts are simple methods designed to make evaluative comparisons.

- visual representations of observational data
- interpretive methods of recording information
- may focus on one or more children
- usually naturalistic
- mostly nonparticipatory

Observation Charts

Recording behavior on a wide variety of **observation charts** has been an observation method of choice for many teachers because it is quick and efficient and can be done while the teacher continues to participate in the children's program. Routines and sequences of a child's day may be recorded to help indicate the child's personal rhythms and adaptation to a changing environment, and to assist a caregiver in being responsive to the child's needs. Using a prepared form or chart, the caregiver can check off when particular events have occurred, such as sleep, rest, feeding, periods of activity, diaper changing, or bowel or bladder elimination. The pattern of feeding, wakefulness, sleep, and toileting can give clues to the child's health and well-being. These charts have often been used for infants, but their use should not be underestimated with toddlers and older children in circumstances where identification of behavioral patterns could help the caregiver appreciate the child's needs in a holistic sense. A sample infant chart can be found on page 205.

The effectiveness of charting observations relies on the philosophy on which the chart is based, the appropriateness of the chart in its inclusion of a range of predictable categories, the accuracy of the recording as the observer interprets what is seen, and the consistency of interpretation among adults using the chart.

Watch out!

Charts record interpreted data, so make sure they are correct before you draw any conclusions!

An obvious limitation of charts lies in their simplicity, which offers little opportunity for explanations of behavior. It is tempting to make efficient use of a chart and to avoid analyzing the resulting patterns and identifying any need for intervention. As records, they need to be used, not just stored. While it is necessary to observe indicators of individual needs, health, well-being, and disease in order to be responsive, it is also important to see this information within its familial and social context, and to understand its impact on the interrelated aspects of the child's growth and development.

Watch out!

The inferences made on a chart may be helpful but should not stand alone in making evaluations of any child.

Participation charts can give teachers a good indication of the interests, motivation, and focus of individual children or groups. They frequently quantify involvements, but their weakness can be that they offer little opportunity to describe the quality of activity. Some charts allow for recording the number of children involved in a specified activity; others count activity in predesignated time slots or enable the teacher to determine who has participated. Charts may be designed to increase the children's responsibility for their activity by having the children themselves check off what they have done.

Charts may be designed to increase parent–teacher communication or facilitate the exchange of information among caregivers. Separate charts for each child may be useful for focusing on an individual; group charts can be helpful for program planning. In the latter case, caution should be taken in making assumptions about the "average" or "majority" responses, and in planning curriculum on that basis. "Averages" may in fact apply to nobody; the groups of children may have levels of competence and participation above or below that average, and your programming may not suit anybody. Similarly, focusing on the "majority" may leave out children who are in need.

Observations of health indicators and symptoms may be made by caregivers, social workers, or teachers, who can then offer information to health professionals. Charting symptoms can only be done where the non–health professional is trained in what to look for. Children with a variety of special medical conditions—such as asthma, anemia, cystic fibrosis, diabetes, eczema, epilepsy, or allergies—may be in mainstream settings but need close observation and appropriate intervention when particular symptoms are demonstrated. Many of these children may have mild conditions, others much more severe; in all cases, observational information should be passed between parents and caregivers, with a further connection to the health professionals involved.

Baseline observations should be done every day. These informal observations act as a base for measuring a child's change of behavior or appearance later in the day and are particularly useful for children with special conditions that need to be monitored. They can be recorded as anecdotal records but are more often unwritten observations.

Using observation charts

Advantages

- Charts may enable observers to record behaviors quickly and efficiently.
- Behavior may be recorded during or after observation.
- Charts may include routine information as well as behaviors—for example, feeding, diapering.
- The format is pleasant and user-friendly.
- Observations are usually easy to interpret.
- Charts may identify behavioral patterns.
- The format is useful for information exchange between caregivers and parents.
- Charts frequently offer health as well as developmental areas for observation.

Disadvantages

- This method requires a prepared chart that includes all predictable categories.
- Charts often require inferences to be drawn at the time of recording.
- The format may encourage observers to concentrate on domestic routines rather than on responses and learning.
- This method may be used for efficiency rather than depth.
- Charts tend to offer only superficial information, limited to observation categories that are expected.
- The format may encourage simplification of developmental issues.
- Charts should not be relied on as the sole source of observational information.

Types of observation charts

The following pages show several types of charts that can be used to document such observations as general behavior, social relationships, and health.

		Mon.	Tues.	Wed.	Thurs.	Fri.
Caregiver – Parent Information Chart for Infants						
Child's name: _____						
Week of: _____						
Age/D.O.B.: _____						
Caregiver(s): _____						

		Mon.	Tues.	Wed.	Thurs.	Fri.
Liquid intake	a.m.					
	p.m.					
Solid intake	a.m.					
	p.m.					
Sleep	a.m.					
	p.m.					
Activity	a.m.					
	p.m.					
Urination	a.m.					
	p.m.					
Bowel movements	a.m.					
	p.m.					
Behavior notes	a.m.					
	p.m.					
Comments/ messages	a.m.					
	p.m.					

This chart offers essential information to parents. The caregiver keeps an ongoing record of observations of the infant's day. The format allows for a changeover of caregiver while sustaining the information flow. However brief, the notes can form the basis of a log, which over weeks can show developmental changes. The chart may also aid the caregiver's memory, prompting some verbal anecdotal accounts to support the information. A sample information chart for a single day can be found on page 205.

Daily Program Implementation Chart

Children's names: _____ Age/D.O.B.: _____

_____ _____

Date: _____

Observer(s): _____

Activity area	Materials	Objectives	Observation
Creative			
Language			
Sensory			

This chart underlines the notion of a dynamic, ongoing process of observation and activity planning. The activity area would always be a response to the previous day's observations; the following day, these observations would be used to determine the new plan.

Activity Response Chart

Observer(s): _____ Date.: _____

	Children's names				
Zone, activity, or room area	1_____	2_____	3_____	4_____	5_____

The activity response chart shares some features with event sampling but uses only a tally or check mark to identify each child's involvement in an activity. An alternative is to have separate charts at each activity or learning center and check off the name as a child participates.

Activity/Routine Chart for Infants

Name: _____

Age/D.O.B.: _____

Date: _____

Context: _____

Observer: _____

Time	Activity/routine	Imposed (I)/Choice (C)	Feeding	Personal care	Rest/sleep	Outdoor activity	Play	Other
6:00 a.m.								
6:30 a.m.								
7:00 a.m.								
7:30 a.m.								
8:00 a.m.								
8:30 a.m.								
9:00 a.m.								
9:30 a.m.								
10:00 a.m.								
10:30 a.m.								
11:00 a.m.								
11:30 a.m.								
12:00 p.m.								
12:30 p.m.								
1:00 p.m.								
1:30 p.m.								
2:00 p.m.								

The pattern or rhythm of a child's day needs to be considered with reference to the context and any imposed routine. Infant schedules may be structured or responsive; if flexible, the pattern will reveal the child's natural rhythm and may help indicate the child's personal style. This chart includes a column to indicate whether an activity is imposed or chosen by the child. Older children continue to have their own patterns; if accommodated, they may be happier and more able to maximize their learning opportunities. This chart is a form of time sampling.

Immunization Record

Immmunization type	Date	Reaction	Given by

Parents may keep an immunization record card for their own benefit, to be aware of immunization needs. Agencies may wish to see the record with verification of the information.

Patterns of Relationships Within a Group

Date(s)/times: _____

Context: _____
_____

Observer(s): _____

Children's names: Ages/D.O.B.:

A:_____ _____

B:_____ _____

C:_____ _____

D:_____ _____

E:_____ _____

F:_____ _____

G:_____

Child	A	B	C	D	E	F	G	H	I	J
A	■									
B		■								
C			■							
D				■						
E					■					
F						■				
G							■			

To use this chart, observe the children in various activities where they are free to choose their companions. Record interactions between children with a tally mark in the appropriate box. When two children interact for longer than five minutes, put another mark. Patterns of interactions will enable you to identify isolated children and those who have made social relationships. This chart could also focus on initiating and responding to invitations to play. For example, if C initiates play with F, record "CF," but if F invites C to play, record "FC." You can classify positive, negative, or neutral interactions (with a color-coded tally) to add a further dimension. This practice requires further interpretation, which has to be recorded in-process.

Components of Participation Chart

Children's names: _____ Ages/D.O.B.:_____
_____ _____

Observer: _____

Activity: _____

Names	Physically involved	Follows instructions	Attempts to solve problems	Cooperates in action/ verbally	Creative/ constructive	Keeps on task

This chart can be used to record participatory information about an activity for a group of children. Do not assume that each component of participation is, of itself, always positive. Appropriate and valid participation may involve solitary activity, experimentation, and even destruction! Chart results can be useful if analyzed without prejudgments and assumptions.

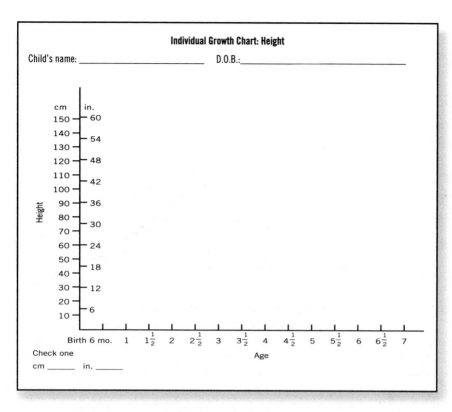

Individual Growth Chart: Height

Child's name: _____ D.O.B.: _____

Height

cm	in.
150	60
140	54
130	
120	48
110	42
100	
90	36
80	30
70	
60	24
50	18
40	
30	12
20	
10	6

Birth 6 mo. 1 1½ 2 2½ 3 3½ 4 4½ 5 5½ 6 6½ 7

Age

Check one

cm _____ in. _____

A child's height can be plotted on this chart. A pattern of growth is a useful consideration when evaluating aspects of gross motor skill development.

A similar chart can be used for weight. Plotting a child's weight gain can help parents and professionals determine the pattern of change. Comparisons with norms can be helpful if there is an understanding of the range of what constitutes an average; undue emphasis should not be placed on slight variations from a norm.

Taking a Special Look: Children born prematurely or at low birth weight

Many babies, with expert pediatric assistance, survive premature birth, and some of them are extremely small. Other babies have low birth weight for other reasons. But not only their size presents a challenge; many of these babies also have a range of medical and developmental difficulties. You will need to consider birth size and developmental history when you are interpreting your observations of infants, toddlers, and also older children. For example, some children may be developing at an appropriate rate, but their actual skill performance will match that of the norm for a younger child.

Symptom Chart for Chronic or Special Medical Conditions

Child's name: _____ Age/D.O.B.: _____

Observer(s): _____

Diagnosed condition: _____

Date(s) from: _____ to: _____

Reporting line: _____

Date	Behavior symptom	Number of times observed	Severity	Comment

The parent, caregiver, or teacher may need to record observations of a child's specific behaviors or symptoms as they occur. If a child with a special medical condition is integrated into a mainstream setting, the caregivers should be taught to identify the behaviors that are important to record for that child, and they should ensure that such information is reported appropriately.

Observation Scales

Rating observed information according to the degree to which a quality, trait, skill, or competence is demonstrated can take a variety of forms. The simplest **rating scale** may involve the use of a checklist-style inventory of items accompanied by a scale that elaborates a yes/no response. The scale may contain opposites on a continuum, numerical ratings, choices of levels of behavior, or pictorial or graphic representations. More complex rating scales may have established criteria for grading a performance or demonstration of skill. Each type of scale is scored at, or soon after, the time of observation. Some require evidence to help validate the scoring.

All rating scales require **inferences** to be made at the time of recording. The complex inferences required in identifying a behavior, labeling it, and evaluating the quality of performance require considerable skill on the part of the user. The components of the inventory itself, coupled with the form of evaluation that goes with it, may be insufficiently valid. It can be challenging to assess the **validity** and reliability of a rating scale; too often, a scale is chosen because of its apparent ease of use rather than its technical merit or appropriateness. A scale can be only as good as the philosophy, theory, and research on which it is based. Allocating a grading or scale to a checklist may alter its intrinsic reliability if it was not designed to be used that way. Also be aware that evaluating skills based on a preset scale presumes that the performance will fall into the stated grading system. The sample scale on page 206 is accompanied by an assessment of the scale.

Watch out!

Rating scales are often skewed without the creator realizing it. Check before use!

Using observation scales

Advantages

- Scales can be used to record information about a wide range of behaviors.
- Recording is efficient.
- Little training is required to use scales at a basic level of implementation.
- This method can be used to measure behaviors not easily measured in other ways.
- Scales may be used to record information at the time of observation or shortly afterward and allow for the continued participation of the observer in the program.
- Scales may offer a large amount of information about children quickly.

Disadvantages

- The validity of items may be questionable.
- The format offers little contextual information.
- For effective choice and use, thorough training is necessary to evaluate behavior.
- The rater needs to make qualitative judgments of behavior.
- The position of items on the inventory may affect scoring.
- Inferences must be made rapidly and without full validation.
- A scale may have wording inconsistency or lead to assumptions about "**positive**" and "**negative**" **behaviors**.
- Scoring may not be consistent over time.

- Scoring may depend on the observer's interpretation of an item.
- Evaluation should not stand alone as the sole information-gathering technique.
- Observer **bias** is not easily detected.
- Observer bias may take a variety of forms.
- There may be a tendency to rate well-known, liked, or attractive children higher.
- There may be a tendency to overcompensate for known and recognized biases.
- There may be a tendency to avoid extreme scores.
- Results may be affected by the positioning of inventory items.

Types of observation scales

1. **Forced choice scales:** Observers choose between predetermined ranges of behavior to identify levels of functioning.

Example

handwriting (Circle the category most applicable.)

messy, ——	some ——	some ——	words ——	phrases ——	clear, ——
illegible most	letters	words	legible,	legible, tidy	legible
of the time	readable but	readable but	varying	most of the	sentences
	untidy most	quite untidy	tidiness most	time	most of the
	of the time	most of the	of the time		time
		time			

2. **Semantic differential scales:** The observer's choice with a semantic differential scale is between two extremes or opposites, or at one of three, five, seven, or nine points between them. Typically seven categories are used between the extremes. The categories may be numbered or there may be an open continuum. A sample semantic differential scale can be found on pages 206–207.

Example

a.	cooperative	☐☐☐☐☐☐☐	uncooperative
b.	sociable	☐☐☐☐☐☐☐	unsociable
c.	honest	☐☐☐☐☐☐☐	dishonest
d.	skilled	☐☐☐☐☐☐☐	unskilled
e.	extrovert	☐☐☐☐☐☐☐	introvert

3. **Numerical scales:** Rating the inventory items may take the form of a number system. The item is graded with reference to a predetermined set of criteria. Assigning a number to a skill can indicate the level at which it is performed. Pre-assigning the grading can help in ensuring objectivity in the structure of the scale but does not ensure objectivity in grading.

Example A
How well does the child dress herself/himself? (Choose one of the categories.)

1. Competent in all respects, including doing up buttons, laces, zippers.
2. Puts on clothes, tries to close fasteners, but lacks sufficient skill to complete task.
3. Attempts to put on clothes, cannot do fasteners, and needs help.
4. Does not attempt dressing.

Example B
Preschool physical skills (Circle the number as appropriate.)

1 = poor skill —————————————— 5 = highly defined skill

runs	1	2	3	4	5
skips	1	2	3	4	5
hops	1	2	3	4	5
climbs stairs	1	2	3	4	5

Example C
Communicates wishes and needs verbally.

1. Clear articulation in full sentences.
2. Makes self understood with phrases and gestures.
3. Attempts to make self understood with some success.
4. Attempts infrequently to make self understood.
5. Does not attempt to communicate wishes and needs.

    Circle one: 1   2   3   4   5

Example D
Obeys simple instructions
Scoring
5   Clearly follows a series of instructions in order they are given.
4   Follows instructions/does not keep to sequence requested.
3   Attempts to follow instructions but makes some mistakes.
2   Makes limited attempts to follow instructions but makes many mistakes.
1   Makes erratic effort to obey instructions but follows them incorrectly.
0   Does not attempt to obey instructions.

4. **Graphic scales:** Points along a line indicate the degree to which the item is applicable. This evaluation form is frequently seen as a scale between "always" and "never." Descriptions may also be used for clearer evaluation.

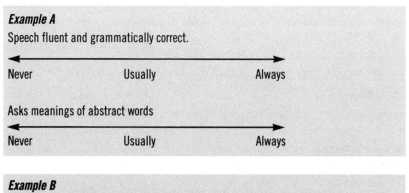

Example A
Speech fluent and grammatically correct.

Never   Usually   Always

Asks meanings of abstract words

Never   Usually   Always

Example B
Response to new activities:

| positive, inquiring, and exploratory approach, long attention span | —— | erratic, inconsistent, varying attention, relatively easily distracted | —— | negative, disinterested, does not respond to stimulation |

Taking a Special Look: Temperamental differences

Children respond to the same situations in different ways. The style of response particular to an individual is called his or her **temperament**. Although you may see fairly typical patterns of responses from a child, sometimes you will be surprised when a child acts "out of character." Observing what is typical and also what is unusual for a child helps you determine environmental influences and how the child is coping with the situation.

Chess and Thomas (1996) review nine categories of temperament and three temperament "constellations." These categories can be scored on a rating scale—mild, medium, high—to develop an individual child's profile. The child is rated on activity level, rhythmicity (regularity), approach or withdrawal, adaptability, threshold of responsiveness, intensity of reaction, quality of mood, distractibility, and attention span and persistence.

Social Maps

The complexities of a child's social context can make professionals very wary of delving into the child's background. It is wise to acknowledge that quickly drawn conclusions can lead to quite inappropriate judgments and assumptions. Nothing can replace the sensitive observations and recording of the observer who has taken time to delve into the home life and social backdrop of a child in order to understand who the child is and appreciate the range of factors that affect the child's growth and development. Social maps can offer a backdrop against which you can increase your understanding of what you observe directly.

Watch out!

Social maps cannot account for complex relationships, so avoid their overuse!

The child's social context can be represented in various ways. These maps are not intended to replace a more detailed study, but they may help support an in-depth study. They can offer, in a diagrammatic form, key life experiences, family trees, social relationships, or factors affecting the child's world, providing a structure to help make sense of the whole. In themselves, they offer little detail of the child's life, but they may provide some basic hooks on which to hang observational information.

Family trees

Sentimental interest is often the prime motivation for an individual to research a **family tree**. Such research, however, may also offer the possibility of understanding a child's genetic inheritance, life patterns, and history, which can help medical professionals, social workers, caregivers, and teachers, as well as the child. A family tree provides historical background information gained through interviews, diaries, and archives. Name searches can be part of the research; surnames can help in tracking family members but should not be relied on in determining complete ancestry.

The mobility of families has increased considerably since the last century. Immigration has frequently complicated research, but information recorded in passenger ship lists and diaries has assisted in tracing ancestors. Adoption, multiple partners and offspring, name changes, wars, changes of location, inadequate local record keeping, translations, and individuals trying to cover up their ancestry are some of the common challenges in formulating a family tree. A typical family tree may look like this:

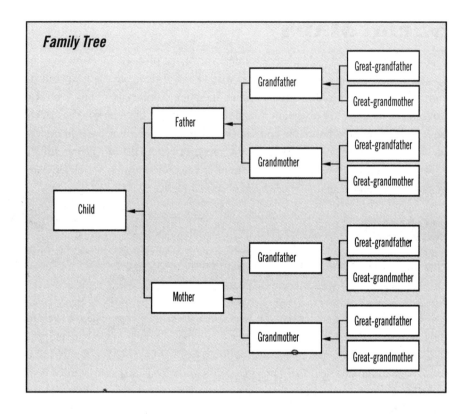

Family Tree

Ecomaps

An **ecomap** is a diagrammatic representation of a child's world—the significant people, activities, and organizations in that world and the relationships between the child and those elements of her environment. For social workers, an ecomap might facilitate an understanding of how the family's demands and resources compare. Teachers, caregivers, and parents might find the exploration of the child's ecosystem enlightening in understanding how the immediate social setting (the family) and the more remote social settings (such as child care, school, media, clubs, and so on) influence the child's development. A sample ecomap can be found on page 210.

Urie Bronfenbrenner's (1979) **ecological systems model** of child development can help determine the components of a child's environment. He describes four systems that influence the child's development. These can offer an ecological model on which to base a study of the child's environment. It is, perhaps, impossible to include all environmental components and to determine their effects on the child. The ecomap makes an attempt, but we need to acknowledge its limitations.

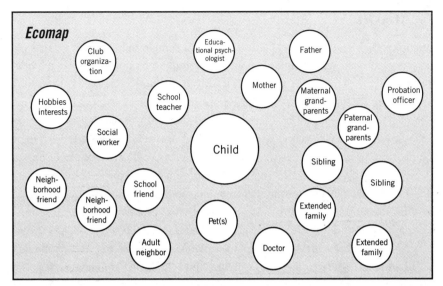

Source: Department of Health, Great Britain, *Protecting Children: A Guide for Social Workers Undertaking a Comprehensive Assessment* (1988).

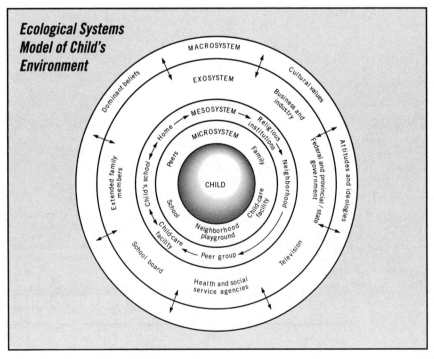

Source: Based on Urie Bronfenbrenner, *The Ecology of Human Development: Experiments by Nature and Design* (1979).

Genograms

According to McGoldrick and Gerson (1985), "a **genogram** is a format for drawing a family tree that records information about family members and their relationships over at least three generations." It is arrived at through interviews, discussion, and research with family members. Family structure and composition may be depicted in a variety of forms, there being no "standard" format. A genogram may include critical family events, dates of birth, marriages, adoptions, custody arrangements, partnerships, separations, divorces, and deaths, and details of places of residence, occupations, and other significant information. It provides a clear view of complex family scenarios, family patterns, and lifestyles. It is not intended to detail the day-to-day interactions or be a "snapshot" that evaluates the family's functioning. Social workers will find the genogram a valuable tool.

The process of collecting the data with family members may be as important as the product. Adults in the child's life may find the genogram enlightening as it enables them to look at the connectedness of the family members and identify possible stressors. Sensitivity to the privacy and range of styles and practice of families is essential when undertaking a genogram. Symbols for representing birth order, individuals, relationships, and living arrangements need to be agreed on before a genogram can be drawn.

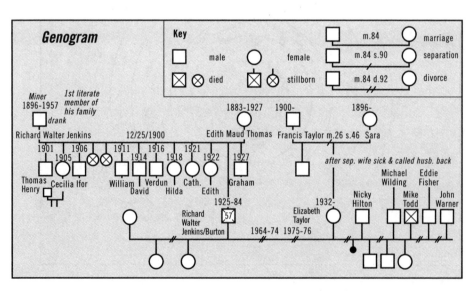

Source: Monica McGoldrick and Randy Gerson, *Genograms in Family Assessment* (1985).

Sociograms

Sociometry is a research technique used to identify the acceptance of children by their peers and to explore their social status. A **sociogram** is the visual representation of the child's perceptions of acceptance within the group. Children in an organized setting may be asked to name the child who is their "best friend" or "person they do not especially like" or "like best" or "admire most." Results depend on the phrasing of the question and may be influenced by what the child thinks the adult wishes to hear. Information gathered from group members is pieced together and presented diagrammatically. Popular children and those who are solitary or isolated may be identified quickly; some unexpected connections may come to light, leading the teacher to observe interactions more closely. Over a period of time, the sociogram may change quite radically. It may be interesting to use a sociogram at designated times during the year to assess the dynamics of the group. Children must be old enough to understand the question posed, be able to give a clear answer, and be of sufficient maturity to have formed social relationships within the group. The interactions or "friendships" of younger children tend to be transitory because the children are not yet able to communicate, appreciate the perspectives of others, or form social attachments with peers. For these children, a sociogram would reveal little.

Watch out!

Social relationships are fluid in young children. They may change daily!

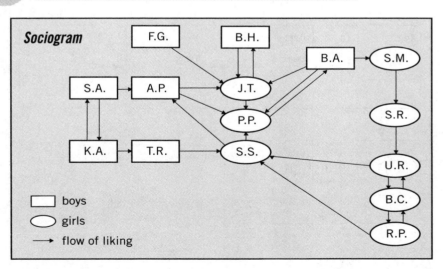

Information collected from a class of 8-year-olds (seven boys, eight girls). The children were asked, "Who are your two best friends?" The sociogram may indicate whether some of the children are isolated.

Life experience flow charts

A person's significant life experiences can be reduced to a list of dates that offer a structure for understanding chronology but provide no contextual information to explain why the events occurred. A **life experience flow chart** explores the context, identifying key experiences and labeling and sequencing the events. The flow chart can reveal structure and patterns in a child's life. Teachers and caregivers can use such charts to help them appreciate the child's cultural identity, traumas, life stages, and joyous experiences. As a result, they may have a greater sensitivity to the child's needs and an increased understanding of the child's perception of reality.

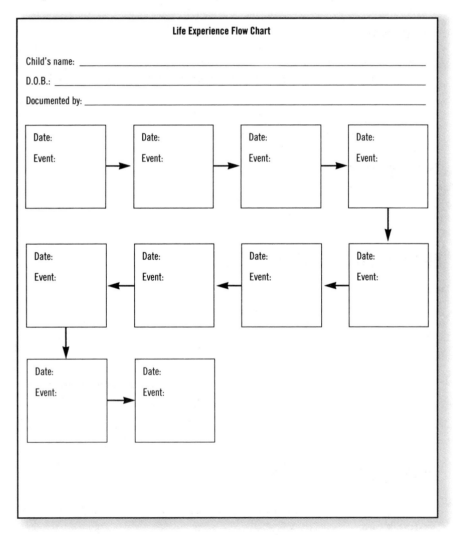

Using social maps

Advantages

- Social maps are relatively easy to create.
- Social maps give a visual overview of the situation/context/environment.
- Families are usually helpful in supporting access to information.
- Social maps may appear clear and concise.
- The information is easily accessible.
- The format may enable individual and group contexts to be examined.
- The child may be involved.
- The process of drawing up maps may have a therapeutic purpose.

Disadvantages

- Social maps are heavily dependent on professional sensitivity.
- The format can be simplistic and insufficiently supported by contextual information.
- Social maps rely on the accuracy of information collected.
- Objectivity of recording is required.
- Inferences may be difficult to draw.
- Training may be needed to analyze family patterns.
- Inaccurate assumptions may be made by unqualified people.
- If support is not available, the child may be unnecessarily vulnerable.

Mappings

Sensitivity to the planning, set-up, and use of the children's environment leads educators and caregivers to evaluate what they provide (see Chapter 11). Part of a qualitative assessment of the use of space will be to create a **mapping** of the room or outdoor space to see how well it meets the needs of the children. The evaluation might consider the effectiveness of the learning environment, the aesthetics of the space for children and adults, the contrasts of activities in different areas, the degree to which the space allows for appropriate mobility and safety, the flexibility of use, and the construction of the environment based on an agreed philosophy of care and education.

Watch out!

Mappings can indicate what space is used but not the quality of the activity!

Trackings can allow the movement of groups of children to be observed to see how they interact, move, and use the different parts of the environment. By tracking individual children, you might be able to notice what interests them, their mobility, their concentration span, and their range of movements between activities. Caregivers' roles within the room or play space can be evaluated by tracking their movements within the available space.

A simple line on a map can follow the movement of a child. Arrows can explain the direction in which the movement occurs. Movement back and forth in the same place can be represented by arrows in both directions (< >) showing the number of times the space was traveled. A circle containing the number of minutes or seconds can show how long a child stayed at a particular activity. More than one child can be tracked on the same map if the observer has sufficient skill and uses a different color of line for each child.

A narrative description of the details of a tracking can help to explain what is recorded. This dual technique offers the possibility of elaborating the "tracks" so that a more qualitative evaluation can be made. The sample tracking on pages 208–209 includes a narrative account.

Using mappings

Advantages

- Mappings are easy and efficient to record.
- The tracking can focus on an individual child or group action.
- Mappings may be used to analyze traffic, use of space, or safety considerations.
- Analysis can help to identify
  - mobility
  - attention span
  - interests/motivation

  - child–child interactions
  - child–adult interactions
  - participation in specific areas of the program
- Maps can be layered to show evidence of change, compare activity levels, or identify traffic problems.

Disadvantages

- The space/room needs to be mapped beforehand.
- It is difficult to record the action of more than one child at a time.
- Qualitative evaluation is difficult without an accompanying narrative.
- Reasons for behavior may not be revealed.
- Inferences must be drawn on little data.
- Participants in a program may find it difficult to make an accurate tracking.

Mapping templates

A mapping can show both the physical layout and the use for which each area is intended. Such blank maps can be used for observation or environmental evaluation. A sample observational tracking of a child's movements can be found on pages 208–209.

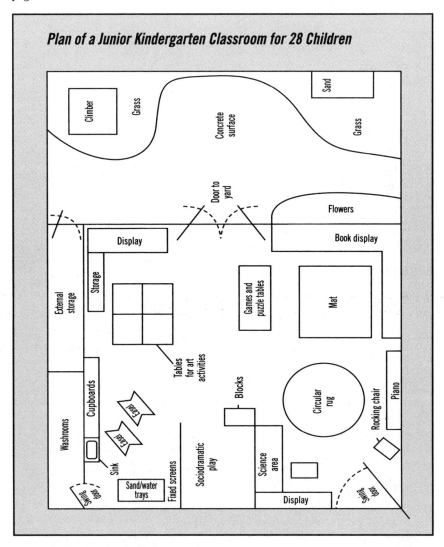

Plan of a Junior Kindergarten Classroom for 28 Children

This mapping could be used by a teacher to evaluate the use of space—for example, to consider whether all curriculum areas have been included or whether activities are allotted appropriate space. The plan could also be copied and used to track the movements of individual children.

Interpretive Graphic Representations

Rather than recording direct observational material, **interpretive graphic representations** are concerned with demonstrating numerical results, percentages, comparisons, variables, proportions, or other quantifiable outcomes from observation or evaluation. Pictorial representations are used to understand and analyze the content of assessment **data**. While there can be a danger of oversimplifying such information without appreciating its context, the intention is to support the conceptualizing of large amounts of information.

Graphic representations are generally mathematical and statistical ways of presenting data in a clear and objective way. Often easier to understand than to create, they may require some practice before being relied on for accuracy.

A wide variety of techniques might be used. Charted tally marks can form simple graphic representations. Block graphs, **bar charts**, flow diagrams, **pie charts**, graphs, picture diagrams, genetic maps, percentile charts, and picture symbols can all be used to present data. A sample graphic representation can be found on page 210.

Using graphic representations

Advantages

- Graphic representations can offer simple, easy-to-understand information.
- Certain formats may offer trends and comparisons.
- Mathematical data analysis may be more objective than anecdotal reports.
- Information from various sources can be put together.

Disadvantages

- Graphic representations rely on valid and reliable data collection.
- Users may need an understanding of statistics to interpret the information.
- Results are quantitative rather than qualitative.
- Graphic representations may encourage comparisons with other children rather than an analysis of changes in the child's own performance.
- Results can be used for unwise program planning.
- Comparisons may foster unnecessary parental anxiety.
- Trends may be analyzed without contextual information.
- Graphs may be more usable for research psychologists than practitioners.

Types of graphic representations

The following examples show two of the most common types of graphic representations and suggest the types of data for which such graphs can be useful.

Bar chart

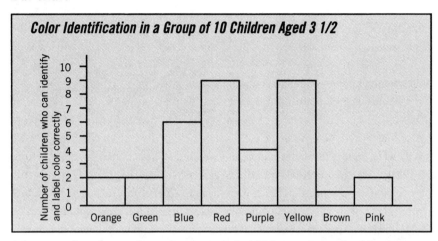

Color Identification in a Group of 10 Children Aged 3 1/2

Information charted is not designed to show which child knows which colors; the intention is to determine the number of children who can identify each color. The bar chart can be used to present a variety of data.

Pie chart

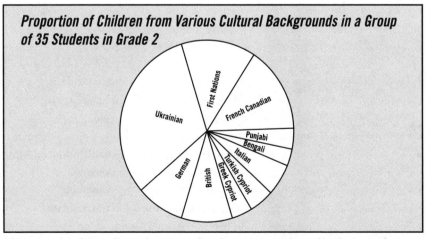

Proportion of Children from Various Cultural Backgrounds in a Group of 35 Students in Grade 2

This particular chart indicates heritage rather than origin or place of birth. A pie chart may need a key to explain the items. The "whole" must be identified; otherwise, the proportions of the whole are meaningless. Percentages can be written into the pie for extra clarity.

Observation scales can be used to record information about a child's behavior or to evaluate her skills in a particular area.

Key Terms

bar chart	numerical scale
bias	objectivity
chart	observation chart
data	pictorial representa-
ecological systems	tion
model	pie chart
ecomap	positive behavior
family tree	rating scale
forced choice scale	reliability
genogram	scale
graphic scale	semantic differential
inference	scale
interpretive graphic	sociogram
representation	sociometry
life experience flow	temperament
chart	tracking
mapping	validity
negative behavior	

Observation Sample

This information chart provides daily information for parents and caregivers. A comparison of these charts as the weeks pass will also provide information about the infant's development.

Information Chart for Infants

Child's name: Adrienne
Age: 9 months
Parents: Lynn and Malcolm
Other caregivers and students: Michelle P., Jennifer, Carolie, Darlene, Michelle C.
Who brought the child to the center? Malcolm

Date: January 18, 1998
Observer: Scott
Time: 8:10 a.m.

Liquid intake	a.m.	Formula: 8:30 – 4 oz; 9:15 – 2 oz; 11:15 – 1/4 cup
	p.m.	Formula: 1:00 – 6 oz; 4:35 – 4.5 oz Water: 4:15
Solid intake	a.m.	8:30 – Cheerios; 11:15 – macaroni and cheese, breadstick, 2 oz. peas, 1/4 banana
	p.m.	2:50 – 4 oz. peaches mixed with 1 tbsp. of cereal
Sleep	a.m.	9:30–10:25
	p.m.	1:32–2:56
Health indicators	a.m.	Diaper rash, runny nose
	p.m.	Diaper rash, runny nose
Urination/diaper change	a.m.	10:30 wet; 11:55 wet
	p.m.	1:00 wet; 2:38 wet; 4:10 wet
Bowel movements/diaper change	a.m.	None
	p.m.	None
Behavior notes	a.m.	Very happy (11:15 lunch – all smiles)
	p.m.	Happy *on walk Adrienne became slightly upset – carried rest of the way
Play activities	a.m.	Gross motor room, different types of boxes, floor toys – crawling
	p.m.	Jello cube play on the floor
Climate/environment	a.m.	20°C room
	p.m.	7°C walk, partly cloudy, mild; 20°C room

Who picked up the child? Malcolm
Time: 5:45 p.m.

*NOTE: Only three infants in today

Observation Sample

This semantic differential scale is used to record observations on a child's personality. The attached personality profile comments on the validity and reliability of the rating scale and elaborates on the results.

Personality Attributes Rating Scale

Child's name: _Tasha_   Observer: _Salma_

D.O.B.: _5-5-90_   Age: _7 years, 8 months_

Circle the number that describes the degree of the attribute:

Outgoing	3	②	1	0	1	2	3		Reserved
Sensitive	3	②	1	0	1	2	3		Insensitive
Confident	3	②	1	0	1	2	3		Lacking confidence
Aggressive	3	2	①	0	1	2	3		Passive
Dominant	③	2	1	0	1	2	3		Submissive
Flexible	3	②	1	0	1	2	3		Inflexible
Patient	3	2	1	⓪	1	2	3		Impatient
Responsible	3	2	①	0	1	2	3		Irresponsible
Dependent	3	2	1	0	①	2	3		Independent
Imaginative	③	2	1	0	1	2	3		Unimaginative
Relaxed	3	②	1	0	1	2	3		Tense
Responsive	3	②	1	0	1	2	3		Unresponsive
Introverted	3	2	1	0	1	②	3		Extroverted
Generous	3	②	1	0	1	2	3		Mean
Trusting	3	②	1	0	1	2	3		Suspicious
Controlled	3	2	①	0	1	2	3		Uncontrolled
Serious	3	2	1	0	①	2	3		Easygoing
Courageous	3	2	①	0	1	2	3		Timid
Intelligent	③	2	1	0	1	2	3		Less intelligent
Emotionally stable	③	2	1	0	1	2	3		Emotionally unstable

Signature _Salma Ahmad_   Relationship _Student teacher_

Validity of the rating scale: There are more "positive" attributes on one side of the scale than the other. This makes me think that my responses may have been skewed a little. Also, a few of the items are presented as opposites when they are not, according to my own definitions. I am not entirely confident that the scale can measure what it is meant to measure.

Reliability of the rating scale: I think that there needs to be a way of indicating what exposure to the child is necessary before undertaking the rating. I might have been influenced by the fact that I have known Tasha for only a short time. If her mother or teachers scored Tasha's personality with this scale, they might come up with different responses.

Strengths of the rating scale: The rating scale prompts me to evaluate some elements of personality that I might not have considered otherwise. I see it as a kind of checklist with a way of stating to what degree the attribute "fits." This kind of rating scale is very quick to do and could be replicated by other adults to determine common perceptions.

Weaknesses of the rating scale: There may be some bias in my scoring because the items are not effectively random. Also, my results cannot be validated on their own. My current positive outlook on life may bias me to see Tasha more positively than I would at another time. A few items are not typical of most personality inventories; for example, intelligence seems inappropriate as a dimension of personality.

My profile of Tasha's personality: Personality is a matter of relatively enduring behavioral characteristics. These are difficult for me to determine in Tasha because I have not observed her with her family or anywhere outside her class. I have seen patterns of behavior that have repeated themselves. Some are sufficiently predictable that I have to alter my teaching strategies so that she cannot always be the leader of an activity! I think that Tasha tends to be warm and receptive to new ideas, but this wasn't scored on the rating scale. Her warmth may be seen as pro-social behavior that is developmentally significant, as well as part of her personal style. Focusing on what the scale did indicate, I see Tasha to be very imaginative in her artwork and sociodramatic play. She frequently has ideas for new dramas that she initiates and draws her peers into. She is willing to cooperate with others, but she is persistent in wanting the play to go her way. Tasha leaps into new situations without being daunted and appears confident in approaching unfamiliar people. Her trusting nature could be potentially worrisome, so she needs close supervision. Curriculum challenges may allow Tasha to use some of her dispositions in new areas. I am hopeful that she will soon expand her artwork into storytelling because the necessary pre-reading skills are emerging. We are using a lot of stories in the classroom; she responds and acts out some of them in her play.

Observation Sample

This mapping tracks a child's movements in order to assess his participation in a program. The accompanying narrative provides details that will help the observer draw inferences from the mapping.

Tracking in School-Age Program

Child's name: _Peter D._____   Observer: _____Rena_____

Age/D.O.B: _7 years, 2 months_____

Context: _Peter has recently come, with his sister Kate (6 years),_ to an after-school program in a housing complex. Both started the program less than three weeks ago. Mom and Dad have recently separated and there is now nobody at home until approximately 6:00 p.m., when Mom returns from work.

Reason for observations: _We tracked Peter's movement to help us deter-_ mine the level of his interaction in the program. There were concerns about Peter remaining in an onlooker role while other children were playing.

Narrative account of tracking

Peter came out of the room just after 4:00 p.m., a few minutes after arriving from school. Standing at the door, he looked around outside at the children. Walking to the storage room, he said "Hi!" to his sister, who was talking to some girls. After a moment, Peter came out of the storage room carrying a ball, bouncing the ball as he walked. Peter looked up to see where everyone was and dropped the ball. Standing momentarily, he watched a girl playing catch by herself against the wall. When she finished, only a moment later, Peter took over her position and bounced his ball against the wall. A boy called to him from a swing. He went over to the swing and had a conversation about school until the other swing became available. Snack arrived a few moments later, so Peter left the swing in response to the caregiver's request. Walking slowly to the picnic table, he sat down, but was sent in to wash his hands. Following instructions, Peter came back after a few moments, ate a snack that was offered to him, but declined the drink. Walking around the backs of three seated children, he went to sit under a tree for some minutes as he watched the others staying at the picnic table. Another boy came up to him. They talked and walked together to the baseball diamond.

Peter's movements are tracked on the attached map.

Outdoor Space for School-Age Child-Care Program

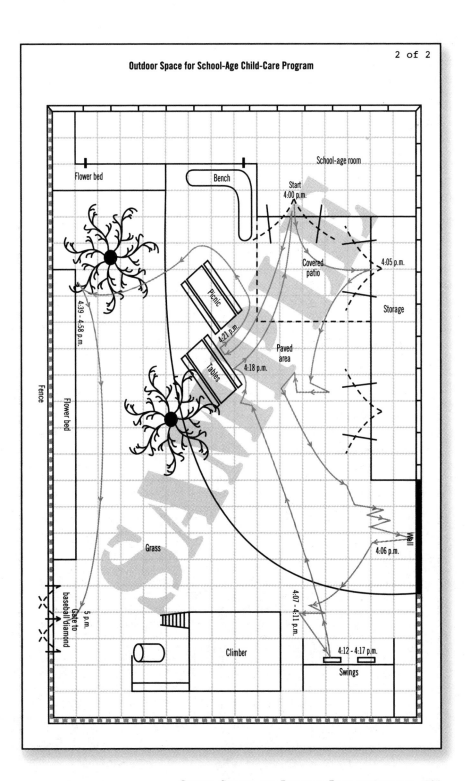

Observation Sample

This sample ecomap represents the people and organizations that make up a child's world. The annotations provide further information to help the observer understand the child's relationships and their influence on his development.

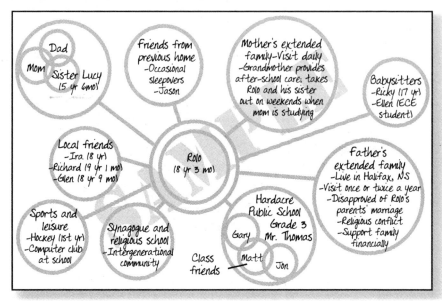

Observation Sample

This bar line graph does not identify particular children or order the results. Such a graphic representation allows observers to make comparisons and consider trends without commenting on specific children.

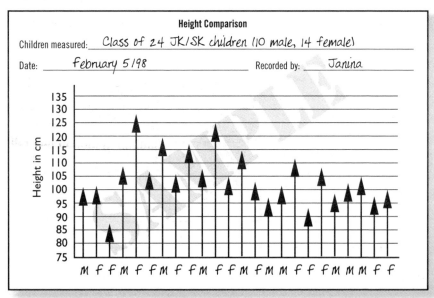

Media Techniques

We think we remember the growth of our children, and we remember the high spots. The triumphs and minor tragedies. But how much we miss with the camera of our memory. For the life of a child is a kaleidoscope of changing moods, aptitudes, activities and developing personality and physical growth. Photographs help us capture these facets to enjoy ourselves and to pass on to our children and our children's children. But we must realize that the pictures we can chortle or sigh over tomorrow we have to take today.

George Hornby (1977)

Oral reading tapes (audio recordings) provide excellent records of children's development in reading. A teacher or parent will find it more informative and interesting to listen to a tape of a child reading a story than to review reading scores.

Brenda S. Engel (1990)

A video recorder can be unobtrusive and help students in learning to observe. Here, an in-class observation opportunity is recorded so that replay can assist in making accurate inferences.

Focus Questions

1. What benefits might you have from using tape recordings of a child's language rather than writing down what the child says?

2. What kinds of photographs of children are useful to the educator and parent?

3. How could you reduce the possibility of children acting to the camera when videotaping or taking photographs?

4. What special issues of confidentiality must be recognized in using the newer technologies for recording observations?

5. Can you think of suitable ways of storing videotapes, audiotapes, and photographs that contain observational data?

6. If you record observations on videotape, how might you use them to help you understand the child and to program successfully?

Learning Outcome

Learners will select and use a variety of technologies to record observational information.

History Notes

Peeking through the lens of a camera can make you see the subject in focus rather differently than you might without the camera. Having a recording device pointed at you may also make a difference to your behavior. Bearing these two points in mind, we will look at how these **media techniques** have changed how we see.

Technological advancements in the last few decades have been only slowly adopted by those working with children. Typically, the resources have not been available or their application for record keeping has not been appreciated. In many instances, the only photographs taken at school have been the annual class pictures done by a professional photographer. Staff may take photographs from time to time, but more for sentimental than educational purposes. Systematic record keeping using photographs has been used by some for child identification systems and as an addition to written observations. But few agencies incorporate photography into their organization of information collection.

Films were first used for educational purposes as a research and learning tool. In the 1930s, René Spitz (1965) filmed children as part of a study of infants raised without attention and affection. Similarly, James and Joyce Robertson (1967–71) used films to record the separation of children from their parents. These old films have now been transferred to video format, and they can offer us insight as their content may still be valid. The methods of these pioneers, however, would not be recreated today; babies would not be recorded for such studies if intervention could avoid potential neglect or distress. Ethical considerations are of great importance in all media-supported recordings.

The video camera is much easier to use than the older movie camera. A gradual increase in its use for observational purposes has been evident, but this use is still by researchers more than practitioners. Relatively few agencies have organized systems for video-recorded observations. Where they exist, they have been used successfully for working with parents and sharing information about the child's development.

Observational use of the tape recorder has been common among language researchers. Its obvious application allows language samples to be gathered and replayed for analysis. Teachers and caregivers record segments of children's language and music either for record keeping or for the children to replay to increase their awareness of their own sound production. Language pathologists and speech therapists have used tape recordings for thirty years or more as a diagnostic tool or support for their therapy.

Educators are beginning to realize the usefulness of technically assisted recordings. As costs are reduced, these techniques are becoming a viable alternative to pen and paper, and they offer some advantages in speed, efficiency, and replay.

Features of Media Techniques

Definition: Media technique

A **media technique** is any method of recording or storing observational data that is achieved by mechanical, electronic, or technical means.

An ever-widening range of methods of observing and recording information is becoming accessible to those working with young children. If used properly, these techniques offer the possibility of gathering information more quickly or effectively. They require the same degree of sensitive perception as traditional methods because the choice of who is observed and what is recorded remains the decision of the observer. Varying amounts of skill are necessary for the use of the different media techniques. For example, the automatic functions of many cameras or video cameras can mean that little training is necessary to start; practice is the most effective way of improving the quality of productions.

Media techniques can provide a quicker, more efficient, more accurate, more detailed, more readily replayable, and possibly longer-lasting and more meaningful record of the child. These benefits, however, are not always present, and it should not be assumed that technically assisted observations are, of themselves, preferable to narratives or samplings. They are a useful addition to our range of information-gathering tools.

Child Development Focus

Media techniques may assist with observing and recording
- complex social interactions
- long sequences of conversation
- detail of posture, expression, and gestures
- physical skill acquisition

It is tempting to let a videotaped observation "speak for itself." Even if the observation was self-explanatory when recorded, it will become increasingly meaningless if not labeled, dated, explained, summarized, and analyzed as any other significant data would be. Appreciating the usefulness of the media techniques while acknowledging their limitations will mean that we can choose the most effective method for observing and recording.

▶▶ **Key Features: Media techniques**

- use various technologies to assist recording
- provide efficient way of documenting behaviors
- may provide comprehensive information that requires analysis
- usually naturalistic
- participatory or nonparticipatory

Overview of recording devices

The most frequently used aids to observation are cameras, video cameras (or "camcorders"), and tape recorders. In time, these will be enhanced or superseded by a range of other devices with additional abilities. Although not a recording device in itself, the photo CD system, which allows developed photographs to be transferred onto a compact disc for replay on a computer, could be used as a major information storage and retrieval system.

Computer software enables teachers to keep academic and other records. To date, programs for child-care agencies have tended to focus on administration and formalized record keeping. Software can also be designed to accommodate educators' specific needs in recording observational information.

Linkages between the different recording devices such as camcorders and computers are quite possible but can be expensive. Voice-responsive devices are used with children with special needs, but a wider use, particularly as an observation-recording device, is again hindered by high cost. Many of us would delight in the possibility of recording our observations on a portable machine, like a tape recorder, that would have the additional feature of providing a record in print.

To be realistic, most of us consider ourselves fortunate to be able to use tools for observing and recording that are more sophisticated than pen and paper. This chapter will concentrate on working with the camera, camcorder, and audiotape recorder, as these are the media you are most likely to use to support your educational purposes.

Using media techniques

Advantages

- These methods offer detailed information not possible with traditional methods.
- The observations recorded may show more **objectivity** than those requiring observer description.
- A quantity of information can be recorded quickly.
- The recordings can be analyzed by many professionals individually and collectively after the event.
- The observations can supplement and validate other traditionally recorded observations.

Disadvantages

- The costs can be high.
- The availability can be limited.
- Training is required.
- These methods can encourage quantity recording at the expense of well-analyzed quality recording.
- Knowledge of the recording may influence the child and alter behavior.
- **Confidentiality** issues are challenging to resolve.
- Storage and retrieval systems need to be established.

Photography
Uses for recording information

You will need to consider your intentions and the possibilities associated with the use of photographs. You can likely use photography in one or more of the following ways to help you perform your responsibilities or support your learning about children:

- as part of a **life book** to support a child's appreciation of his or her own "story"
- as evidence of a child's growth and changes in physical appearance
- to record significant life experiences and rites of passage
- to support traditionally recorded observations
- as part of a child's developmental **portfolio**
- to record episodes of a child's activity
- to keep information about the products of a child's activity
- for file identification
- as a safety measure to ensure security
- to aid a child's memory of situations

General principles

Some basic guidelines might be helpful if you choose to use photography to support your child observations.

1. Choose a camera that fits your level of competence and your purpose.
2. Keep the camera loaded with film, stored safely but close to the place it will be needed.
3. Always have spare film ready.

4. Choose your film and adjust your camera according to the lighting available.
5. Get lots of practice in taking pictures.
6. Have the children become familiar with you taking photographs.
7. Be aware of your reasons for taking a photograph and ensure that you avoid subjectivity.
8. Design and use a format for labeling and storing the photographs.
9. Ensure that every photograph is considered a confidential document.

Watch out!

Although the camera doesn't lie, it may not tell the whole truth!

The basics of photography

Taking photos for use in child care and education is not substantially different from family photography. Your family shots will be regarded as records of significant events or stages in life, as are the professionally used photographs. The essentials of recording are that you manage to capture what you believe to be pertinent in a way that is accurate and easily understandable. Some people have a natural flair for photography, while for others even the "point and shoot" camera presents challenges!

Here are some suggestions for increasing your skill and artistry.

Choice of camera

Watch out!

An expensive camera may not be the best for observational recording. Consider how quickly you can use it.

Many good pictures have been "lost" because of the time it took to set up a complex camera's speed, angle, and focus. The gifted and skilled photographer will get some marvelous results using expensive paraphernalia and lots of time, but adults working with children want to capture the moment spontaneously. They may prefer a camera that is relatively small in size, has automatic functions, has a built-in flash, and is loaded with a film likely to be suitable both indoors and out.

With an automatic pocket camera, you can often take an adequate photograph that might have been missed if you had to fiddle with the attachments. A camera that meets the following specifications is ideal and usable by any member of the work team:

- small, pocket-size with firmly attached cord for wearing around neck or tying to something
- automatic loading and automatic wind
- automatic shutter/exposure and automatic flash
- clear indicator for number on roll of film
- battery tester buzzer
- clear and accurate indicator of image through lens
- relatively inexpensive

Film facts

These points will help you with film choice:

- "Professional" film is very similar to "amateur," but it may be fresher.
- Exposed but unprocessed film is open to image decay.
- Slight temperature variations may damage film.
- High-speed films (above ASA 250) permit shutter speeds that enable you to take pictures with a hand-held camera even under dim light.
- Slow films have the finest grain and produce negatives of the highest contrast but may require the use of a tripod.

The importance of lighting

Adjust your technique to the lighting available. Ensure that there is sufficient light or supplement it with the flash if necessary. Avoid taking photographs while looking toward the sun. If evident, the sun should be behind you, preferably not casting long, sharp shadows. The degree of light can be deceptive: light in snow and evening sun are particularly difficult to evaluate without a light meter. Indoor lighting can seem stronger than it actually is and can also make your photograph turn strange, unpredictable colors. You may not know this until you have your pictures processed.

Instant cameras

Instant cameras are frequently called Land cameras—after Edwin Land, who invented them—or Polaroid cameras—after the company that developed, manufactured, and marketed them.

A photograph that depicts a part of an activity can be a helpful addition to written observations.

Instant photographs have some obvious advantages. They enable you to

- tell immediately if you have taken an appropriate photograph without waiting for processing
- avoid waiting for film processing and sending, delivering, or collecting film
- date and label the photograph immediately, and more accurately and rapidly share information with the subject of the picture, parents, and other professionals.

Against these points there are a few negative considerations:

- The cost per photograph is increased.
- The quality of the picture may not be as good.
- The photograph is thicker than a regular photo.
- The photograph may not resist fading as well as a traditionally processed film.

Photographic processing

If you have a dark room and the appropriate equipment, you might want to develop and print your own film. More likely, you will use a commercial processing service.

The cost of service varies considerably. In many instances, it relates to the time you have to wait for the process: the faster the service, the higher the charge. Although photography experts may argue about the types of process and their results, your choice may be more a matter of personal preference than objective choice. Size of photograph, finish, and number of copies will be further choices for you to make. It is a good idea to log the details of your photographs as you take them, because processing can cause a time lag in receiving the photographs.

Taking photographs for observational purposes

When to take a picture (being natural)

Your purpose is likely to "capture a moment" of child in action, to record interests, skills, relationships, learning, reactions, or some other educational consideration. Be patient; try not to attract the child's attention or disturb the activity in any way. The child's play and learning experience is always more important than the photograph. Recording the essence of the action is challenging but will not be achieved by trying to direct what the children are doing for the sake of the camera. If you start to interfere, you may be intrusive and contradict the professed philosophy of early childhood education.

To achieve naturalness, to record a child's interactions within a naturalistic setting, there is a longer list of what *not* to do than *what* to do. It may be helpful for the children to access "play" cameras or even to have opportunities for their own photography. This familiarity may help them accept the adult's use of the camera.

Watch out!

If the children are used to seeing cameras in use, they will be less likely to pose.

Capturing natural expressions

Getting down to the child's level is very important in understanding what the child is doing. The child's eye level is exactly where you need to be; the angle allows you the most open access to the child's expression and allows personal eye contact, which can help to personalize the moment, if that is what you wish. Less appealing is an angle that looks down at the child and distorts the action as the child sees it. You may have to lie on the floor, squat, kneel, sit on a child's chair, or adopt some other uncomfortable position.

When children try to pose, they tend to overact. If you take several pictures within a short period of time, you are more likely to get a useful shot. At moments of discovery and engrossment, the children are less likely to be influenced by your presence, and the result should be more successful.

Recording child development

To record child development, you should take regular and deliberate, rather than occasional or random, photographs of each child in your care. You might like to keep a chart record of your photographs so that you can check whether you have selected each child at regular intervals.

Early use of photography by child-care professionals frequently employed a static, impersonal, and posed technique. There are more effective ways of recording growth information than standing the child against a marked and measured wall like a police shot—a tape measure or scale can do that. What you want to do is take photographs of the child involved in typical activities.

Using photographs to supplement other observational recordings can be helpful because they can give a more real sense of "who" the child is when you review the data.

Photographs for record keeping

You may wish to establish a photographic record system that uses a predetermined labeling system. Information should include the child's name and age, the date of the photograph, the names of other children/adults in the photograph, and the situation depicted. For observational purposes, it is often helpful to have the photograph mounted on an accompanying form with additional information on the **context**. Writing directly on the back is seldom successful because the photo suffers from being handled and the writing may rub off or show through to the front. Self-adhesive labels can be used if you wish to cut down the bulk of paperwork, but even a preprinted label does not keep the picture from being lost in a file folder with other information. Photographs can be kept in albums for each child, with labels below each picture, although albums take up a lot of space. Box files designed for file index cards can also be used and form a wonderful gift to parents when the child leaves the agency.

A sample photographic observation with contextual information can be found on page 235.

Watch out!

Label and date all photos—it's amazing how quickly you can forget!

Video Recording

Uses for recording information

There are a number of purposes for videotaping the child's activities or environment:

- to replay when time allows for greater analysis
- to share information about the child's development with parents
- as a long-term record of a child's progress
- to assist in observing groups of children so that attention can be directed to each child's involvement and interactions
- for research purposes
- to record significant happenings or rites of passage in the child's life so that the child can review significant parts of his or her own life story
- to support observations recorded in a traditional way
- to recreate the activities and interactions of the child to facilitate a multidisciplinary evaluation
- to assist in evaluating the child's **environment**

The complexity of some play activity can be a challenge to record. These school-age children play a game involving rules. Video recordings can capture such activity better than any other method.

General principles

Skill can be gained quite quickly once you get started.

1. Survey the market of available recording equipment, identify the features you need, and consider your finances.
2. Familiarize yourself with your recording device and its functions.
3. Allow plenty of time and tape for practice.
4. Extend your vocabulary to include video terminology.
5. Desensitize your subjects before making recordings you intend to keep. You might have the children actively participate in videomaking.
6. Determine your purpose for recording.
7. Avoid **subjective** shooting that centers on what is "cute" or on children "acting up" to the camera.
8. Investigate possibilities for editing your video recordings.
9. Design and use a format for labeling and storing the videotapes.
10. Ensure that every videotape is considered a confidential document.

The basics of video recording

To get started, you need some beginner's tips:

- Read and use the owner's manual so that you can appreciate the camcorder's features.
- Try using a tripod to hold the camera, or brace yourself against a firm object to avoid a bouncing effect.
- Use an autofocus or practice focusing manually. Be aware that the camcorder set on autofocus will focus on the nearest object.
- Practice your use of the zoom to prevent the feeling that you are lurching back and forth, but do not overuse it.
- Compose your videotaping so that the context or background is clear before you go into close-up.
- Set or move the camera at different angles to the subject for more interesting images.
- Use your camcorder to record movement that cannot be captured by a still camera.
- Hold static shots, particularly at the beginning and end of a sequence.
- When panning across an area (left to right or right to left), go smoothly to direct the viewers' attention, but limit the angle of movement to 90 degrees.
- Follow the children's action at their level for a more insightful view of their world.

- The pause button is a form of in-process editing. Practice using it.
- Try to capture meaningful sequences of activity while being aware of the audio recording occurring simultaneously.

Videotapes

Blank tapes are not all the same. They vary in length, cost, quality, and type. Most of the guides to videotaping recommend using name brands sold by reputable dealers and buying them when the price is lowest. Alternatively, read a video magazine or consumer report for the "best buy."

Videotapes need to be handled carefully. Use fresh tapes, if possible, because the VCR tends to wear the tape. Tapes need to be protected from extreme temperatures and humidity. Tapes need to be kept clean, in their sleeves or cases, stored fully wound and vertical, and kept away from magnetic fields.

Video skills

To learn how to make video recordings, you may want to read "how to" manuals, but your starting point will probably be trial and error. Awareness of the most common mistakes will not necessarily help you avoid them, because you need to see how they occur before you can rectify them. Become familiar with the functions of the camcorder on a try-out basis. Short of dropping the camcorder or applying physical force to it, you are unlikely to do it any harm.

Watch out!

Practice may not make perfect, but it will lead to better recordings!

In *Learn to Make Videos in a Weekend*, Roland Lewis suggests that the fourteen basic skills of video can be learned in two days. He describes the sequence of skill development from holding and moving the camera through lighting and composition to editing, titles, and sound tracks. Another good reference is John Hedgecoe's *Complete Guide to Video: The Ultimate Manual of Video Techniques and Equipment*, which is easily understandable for the newcomer while providing helpful detail.

Additional camcorder features

- **Age subtitles:** It is possible to program some camcorders to memorize an individual's birth date so that his or her actual age can appear on the video.

- **Date/time:** Camcorders usually record the date and time of recording on the screen.
- **Title superimposer:** A memory function in the camcorder can record a title or picture over a scene.
- **Self-timer:** A timer allows the camera operator to "get into the action" for participant observation.
- **Insert edit:** New recordings can be put over the old with a sophisticated, dedicated insert edit facility that you can preset to the point where you want to add new material.
- **Macro close-up/zoom:** Camcorders allow for varying degrees of close-ups. On some, this function can be controlled automatically.
- **External mike socket:** This feature can help with sound pick-up when the fixed microphone is too far away to pick up language.
- **Audio dub:** The recorded sound can be replaced with a narrative on some models.
- **Auto exposure:** The iris diaphragm automatically adjusts the size of the aperture to suit the available lighting.

Making videotapes for observational purposes

When to make a video recording

As your skill begins to develop, you will start to see opportunities for recording the activities of the children in your care. Such a flow of action will make it difficult to decide when and what to record; the availability of your time may well dictate your choice. It can be a challenge to maintain your supervisory role, be a participant in the activity, and also manage to record what is happening. This problem can be resolved if you have systems of shared care, time designated for recording, or a small, undemanding group of children. However, educators who are committed to videotaping usually manage to do it.

Watch out!

Try to use the camcorder to capture group activities that are hard to record any other way!

You may want to record some of the more domestic and routine elements of the children's day. In only a short time, these routines evolve as the children develop, and mere memories of them can be lost. Recording typical behaviors may be as rewarding as seeking new advances in development. The dated record will help you see developmental changes over a period of time. Capturing children's **spontaneous play** activity can be the most revealing and meaningful element of videotaping. Having the camcorder available in the children's play area can mean that you can shoot what happens without any fuss. Indoors and out, you can record a variety of play sequences and social interactions.

Video recordings may center on the activity of one child. You will seldom record that child in isolation; she will usually be involved with others. If you make a videotape, you must decide how to pick out the individual child's behavior from the general flow. Editing facilities form the foundation of effective individual record keeping.

What video recordings can highlight

Here are some suggestions of the types of observations you could record on video-tape:

- any of the features of audio recordings (see pages 232–33)
- play patterns
- body language/eye contact
- program effectiveness
- use of space
- group interactions/behavior
- gross motor skills
- manipulative skills
- children's responses to activities
- discovery and curiosity
- experimentation with objects and materials
- mood changes
- independence skills/autonomy
- process of play and learning
- products of activity
- creative activity and artwork in process
- social groupings
- parenting styles
- separation or other anxieties
- any other aspect of development that could be revealed by other observation methods

Taking a Special Look: Observing and recording sign language

American Sign Language is the most common form of sign language used by people who are considered deaf (this does not always mean people who are completely nonhearing). Observing and recording the communication of children who use sign language is even more challenging than observing children who use spoken language!

The most obvious way to record sign language and other gestures is to videotape the child and transcribe the communication. Another alternative is to write a full narrative description that includes all the gestures as well as any facial expressions and postural changes; you would likely have to devise a coding mechanism in order to capture all the detail. Or, you could record the use of sign language in a narrative without a full description of the signing but with a commentary that included the meaning of the signing.

Videotapes for record keeping

Video recordings can form a history of the children's development, activities, or festivals. Videotapes can be labeled and stored vertically in chronological order.

An educator's videotapes that record the activity of groups of children may require editing, but they can be very useful for program planning for the group. These tapes can be stored fairly simply and accessed by staff when necessary. They may also provide very good teaching material for student educators and caregivers.

Most important is the record keeping done for the individual child. These recordings should be kept with, or alongside, an observation file or portfolio, and they should be considered an integral part of the observation and assessment system. To make these individual tapes, it is essential to have an effective editing facility.

Confidentiality and professionalism must apply to the use of videotaped observations. You may need to use a permission form that addresses video recordings specifically (see page 12).

Watch out!

You might need to prepare permission forms for video recordings. Specify what the parents are permitting!

Labeling and dating is a common difficulty with videotapes because they offer little space for detail. A reference card showing the same counter numbering as the tape itself can accompany the video in its sleeve or box.

Videotape Recording Log			
Name:		Group:	
Date	Counter #	Context	Comment

An information card can have predetermined categories of information.

Audio Recording

Uses for recording information

You may have any of the following purposes in making audio recordings:

- to support any traditionally recorded observation
- to record the educator's **narrative observation** of a child's behavior
- to record a child's/children's verbal communications
- to facilitate close analysis of a language sample
- to record a child's/children's explorations and production of sound and music
- to keep records of a child's language, music, or reading skill development
- to communicate with parents in sharing direct recordings or anecdotal observations
- as part of a child's developmental portfolio
- for the student teacher to learn about language, music, humor, and thinking skills of children

General principles

The following steps will help you get started with audio recording:

1. Consider your needs and purchase a tape recorder that is resilient and portable.
2. Set up the tape recorder in a convenient place, but use its portable feature to go where the children are when necessary.
3. Give yourself lots of time to practice tape recording.
4. Familiarize the children with tape recording and playback.
5. Organize time for replay and analysis.
6. Determine your purpose for recording.
7. Consider the possibilities of editing your recordings using specialized equipment.
8. Accept failures.
9. Design and use a format for labeling and storing the audio recordings.
10. Ensure that every audiotape is considered a confidential document.

The basics of audio recording

Here are some beginner's tips:

- Try using an extended microphone with a jack to pick up sounds more clearly —a pair of microphones at least 9 inches (23 cm) apart can be helpful.
- Avoid constant rewinding and re-recording because this may stretch and distort the tape.
- Use the pause button for in-process editing.
- Set up your recordings in an area that minimizes sounds of background activity.
- Use a Dolby noise reduction system if one is built into the recorder—it will give you a better, clearer replay.
- Keep tapes and recorders in a dry atmosphere, in moderate temperatures, and away from magnetic fields.
- If the tape becomes unraveled, you can try to rewind it with a hexagon-shaped pencil, but damaged tapes might jam in the recorder.
- If a tape gets jammed in the recorder, do not try to force it out. Take it to a dealer.
- For educators working in well-designed environments with sound systems, try linking a microphone with a recording device.

Choice of tape recorder

You may be familiar with a range of audio recording machines; reel-to-reel, cartridge, and cassette systems are available, but the cassette is the most popular. The cassette protects the tape and makes threading a simple process. Small portable cassette recorders are most suitable for an observer.

Here are some features to look for in a basic tape recorder:

- easy hook-up to microphones/sound system
- resilient, robust design
- battery/power cord operated
- simple operation
- a counter system
- Dolby noise reduction
- easy access to repair and servicing

Batteries can be expensive, so rechargeable batteries may be a good choice. If you have a machine that can operate on both batteries and a power cord, you can save battery power by using the cord when rewinding and replaying.

Choice of tape

Higher priced tapes are often the best, but try out a variety when they are offered at a discount. Avoid the cheaper copies of the well-known manufacturers' tapes. The brand-name tapes are usually superior because of their high frequency response, high output, consistency of magnetic characteristics, freedom from squeal, absence of stretching, and accuracy of sound reproduction. However, they do vary.

Set-up

The set-up of your recorder and microphones is important for success. You will sometimes miss opportunities for recordings because you are not ready, but you can limit these occasions if you are set up to record.

Laboratory schools and agencies with built-in sound systems that allow students and teachers to "listen in" will be at an advantage. Not all of these systems are built for recording, so you might want to check into this. A good sound system has microphones a little above the children's heads, fairly evenly spread across areas where the children are active. Observers listen from a distance, usually from a one-way mirrored observation booth with speakers or headphones. The system can allow observers to select which microphone they wish to use and therefore pick up the sounds they want. If there is an additional recording facility, a lot of useful information can be stored.

Dangling microphones can be used if you are doing straightforward recording. One mike might give you a "flat" sound recording, while two or more give a stereophonic reality and can record a group of children more effectively. A propped-up mike on a table usually picks up too much white noise. When the children move around, you might try the reporter's technique of following them with a hand-held microphone.

Watch out!

Background noise is the biggest problem with audio recording. Think about how you can reduce the noise!

Making audio recordings for observational purposes

When to make an audio recording

You will need to decide what to record according to your purpose. The children may become so familiar with the tape recorder that it does not bother them. Desensitizing them is often done by allowing the children to record and replay by themselves or, for younger children, by sharing your recordings with them. Squeals of delight are typical for the preschoolers but younger children may be confused when you replay their language.

You might like to make an audio recording at many times in a child's day. Try not to miss the normal, average, and domestic aspects as well as the more structured peak programming times. Be prepared to record spontaneously, and also acknowledge that you will have to be patient. Here are some suggestions for what to record:

- circle times
- greetings, separations, and reunions
- group singing
- experimentation with sounds/instruments
- book corner—conversation, reading, storytelling
- spontaneous play activities
- crib sounds
- interactions with adults
- sociodramatic play

- imitative play
- transitions
- bathroom routines
- individual singing or reciting rhymes
- music activities
- hearing children read
- bilingual children's conversation
- toddlers' emerging language
- problem-solving activities
- outdoor play
- outings, picnics
- at home with parents/siblings/friends
- formal assessments
- examples of school-agers' jokes
- portfolio assessment meetings

What audio recordings can highlight

This list is not comprehensive or ordered, but offers some ideas of what you might look for in analyzing recordings:

- pronunciation
- reading strategies
- MLUs (mean length of utterances)
- pitch discrimination
- experimentation with oral sound production
- rhythm of speech/length of phrase
- accent/cultural patterns
- phraseology/speech patterns
- use of parts of speech/grammatical errors
- communication difficulties
- egocentricity/egocentric speech
- expression of ideas
- overextensions
- misunderstandings
- social relationships
- humor and incongruities
- moral views/attitudes
- social role play
- developmental level of thinking skills

- demonstration of feelings
- solitary activity/isolation/talking to self
- memory
- sequencing of stories or events
- imagination
- use of rhyme
- musicality
- concentration length
- interests
- play level
- fantasy or realism
- logic
- friendships and peer interactions
- imitation or repetition
- conversation with adults
- sibling interactions

Audiotapes for record keeping

Like any other observational material, audio recordings must remain confidential. You may wish to have individual and group recordings. Remember that individual children's records are more effective in helping you determine developmental levels and program in response to needs and skills. Where you have recordings of a group, you will find it almost impossible to edit the tapes for individual files. Instead, you could write a narrative account from the tape. It may be difficult to get complex language down on paper, but the tape can be replayed many times, and the resulting document will capture all the detail.

If you can organize taping so that you put into the record the child's "own" tape, you will manage to gain some chronologically recorded bits of information for that one child. Use the counter and write down the numbers to keep track of where you are on the tape.

Tapes must always be labeled, dated, and accompanied by a numbered log. They should be kept at room temperature in their boxes, having been rewound. Tapes may be kept in the child's portfolio, or, because of their bulk, in a storage system near the portfolio.

Audiotape Recording Log

Child's name: _____ D.O.B.: _____

Date	Counter #	Sequence	Narrative documents		Comment
			Yes	No	

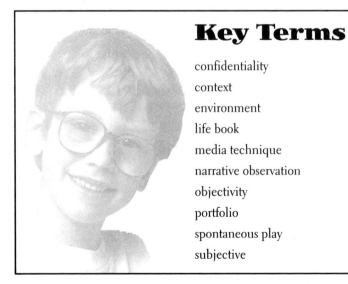

Key Terms

confidentiality

context

environment

life book

media technique

narrative observation

objectivity

portfolio

spontaneous play

subjective

Observation Sample

This photographic record could be put in a photo album or the child's portfolio. The comments provide a context to explain the significance of the picture.

Name: Ashley (second from right)   Age: 5 years, 7 months

Date: May 27, 1998

Others represented: (from left) Kayleigh, Elizabeth, Lashonda

Situation: On the bus on the way to an outing at the Museum of Science

Comments: Ashley tends to be a loner. Her home life is unsettled (her parents were recently divorced and her grandmother, whom she is very close to, is quite ill), and this seems to have contributed to her reluctance to form close relationships with the other children. Elizabeth, who lives next door to Ashley, sometimes invites Ashley to be part of her group. Perhaps because she was excited about the trip, Ashley let herself be drawn into the fun with the other girls on the bus, as seen in this photo. Observation of Ashley's interests may help her teachers find other activities to draw her into social interactions with other children.

Observer: Josh

Portfolios and Child Studies

8

Portfolios are powerful instructional tools. They offer children, teachers, parents, administrators and policy makers an opportunity to glimpse the sweep and power of children's growth and development. When carefully structured, portfolios display the range of a child's work. Above all they integrate instruction and assessment.

Samuel J. Meisels (1993)

When children take the lead in selecting the contents for their portfolio, their interests become vested and their motivation to learn more intrinsic.

Margaret B. Puckett (1994)

Portfolios document a child's development for the benefit of both educators and the family. A visual presentation of a child's portfolio can help parents understand the assessment, especially if they speak English as a second language.

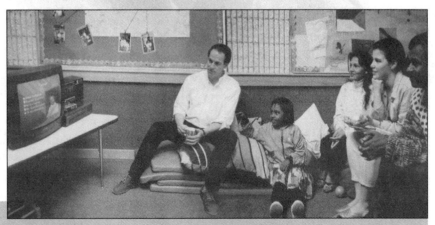

Focus Questions

1. How could you gather information about a child in a way that offers objective recording but does not rely on standardized tests?

2. What kind of contextual data can help you analyze observational information?

3. How could you ensure that your records about a child's development are as thorough and complete as possible?

4. What might a student learn from carrying out an in-depth child study?

5. On what basis would you choose to keep examples of a child's artwork for later appraisal?

6. When would a child be able to contribute to record keeping about his or her own experiences and learning?

Learning Outcome

Learners will demonstrate the philosophy of authentic assessment by compiling a range of observational, health, and contextual data about an individual child and analyzing this information holistically.

History Notes

Child studies and portfolios are both methods of collecting and making sense of information about individual children. They have evolved from the studies of John Locke and Jean-Jacques Rousseau in the seventeenth and eighteenth centuries. In their original form, they were collections of narrative descriptions of a child's behavior and perceived characteristics. Although fascinating, early examples would not meet today's standards of objectivity and analysis.

Granville Stanley Hall's contribution to the study of children was more systematic and changed the focus of study to a more scientific approach. In the late nineteenth century, he wrote *The Contents of Children's Minds*, which altered the way children were studied in the United States. A dominant part of his technique was to use questionnaires to get information directly from the children being studied, one of the methods used today for gathering data.

Baby biographies were a new methodology in the 1890s. Wilhelm Preyer, in Germany, devised an approach in which mothers studied their own children in an attempt to understand their thinking. He had spent several years studying his own son and became a master of narrative recordings in the child-study method. His influence spread to the United States, where he advanced interest in the newly emerging study of children.

Milicent Washburn Shinn (1900) also included mothers in the process of observing and recording. She carried out her own studies of a young relative and promoted this type of study. She believed that a biographical method allowed an understanding of the individual's unfolding development. Combining this method with an approach that checked the child's responses to particular stimuli, Shinn's studies contained elements of today's child study, which is done for the purposes of academic inquiry.

Other early approaches compared observed behavior with "typical" behavior, by means of set-up tests, recorded information on charts, and measures. The child study that is undertaken in our time tends to pick and choose from a range of these techniques, often employing several so that a better picture can be drawn.

Recordings used for study purposes, planning, or information exchange with parents and professionals have altered considerably in the light of changing understanding of how children develop. Forms of record keeping changed as teachers were trained to understand children's needs and appreciate the stages of development through which they progress. The importance of parental involvement was only slowly recognized.

School practices vary considerably today. Some schools provide term reports that offer little more than a vague percentage scoring and a brief comment like "satisfactory" for each curriculum area. The parents' need to know how their child is progressing cannot be met by this approach. An informed parent will want to know how the grade has been determined—by testing or by comparison with a class norm. The term "satisfactory" may indicate the teacher's feelings about a child's progress, but it does not offer anything more than that.

The developmental view, which requires a fuller appraisal of a child's skill development, has been picked up more seriously by child-care workers and kindergarten teachers than by others in the education system. Over the last thirty-five years, early childhood programs have been refined to meet children's individual developmental needs. A push for accountability within the education community has led teachers to support their philosophies and programs with concrete data in the form of developmental records. In the last fifteen years, the portfolio method has received the greatest praise for its breadth and effectiveness. This system enables a flow of information to parents about their child's development.

In spite of a growing confidence in the appropriateness of what is being done within the professional early childhood community, the demand from outside for clearer measurements of children's progress has also increased. We now have conditions that compel us to use portfolio evaluation and record keeping. These methods address the need for accountability for what we are doing with young children, while holding firm to the principles of developmentally appropriate practice.

Child studies and portfolios are both methods of collecting information. They focus on one child and represent data gathered in a variety of ways. Case studies, individual file records, **baby books**, journal recordings, **records of achievement**, profiles, and **life books** have some similar characteristics and can be included in this category of data collection.

Features of Child Studies and Portfolios

 Definition: Child study

A **child study** is a thorough analytical document in which a student or practitioner collects information about a child. It will contain observations and may include a variety of other information collected over a period of time. Typically, it is used more for the benefit of the student in his enquiry into child development than for the child herself.

 Definition: Portfolio

A **portfolio** is a record-keeping device in which observations, health and social information, test results, work samples, and other significant information about an individual child are stored. The system enables child-care professionals to keep records over a period of time, add items as necessary, evaluate the child's performance, evolve plans to meet the child's needs, and review progress.

While the child study is undertaken primarily to support a student's learning, the portfolio is done to help a practicing teacher find out more about the child, for the child's benefit. In spite of this difference, they have many features in common.

Contents of a portfolio or child study

Child Development Focus

Portfolios may assist in observing, recording, and analyzing
- holistic development
- the process and products of development
- a child's culture and context in which development is occurring
- a child's development in relation to the norm or goal achievement

Teachers and caregivers vary in their philosophies regarding record keeping. The portfolio approach is sufficiently flexible that all practitioners can adapt it to their needs.

The following list suggests items a portfolio might contain. Those using the system will want to choose those elements that suit them, their skills, the agency or school, and the child.

- health records (parent questionnaire, information from a physician)
- contextual information (parent questionnaire, objective notes, **genogram, ecomap, life experience flow chart**, etc.) (see Chapter 6)
- notes forwarded from previous caregiving agencies
- **anecdotal records** (see Chapter 3)
- **running records/specimen records** (see Chapter 3)
- development **checklists** (see Chapter 5)
- parental input in a variety of forms
- infant **charts** (see Chapter 6)
- **event/time samplings** (see Chapter 4)
- **rating scales** (see Chapter 6)
- assessment results from **standardized tests** (see Chapter 10)
- psychologist's reports
- social worker's notes
- photographs of the child (passive or in action) (see Chapter 7)
- photographs of special moments in the child's life
- photographs of things the child has made
- special items selected by the child

- artwork samples
- samples of the child's writing
- audiotapes of the child's language, reading, or music (see Chapter 7)
- videotapes of the child's activities (see Chapter 7)
- the child's own records-of-achievement journal
- a learning log of the child's lifetime experiences
- questionnaire responses

The portfolio philosophy

►► Key Features: Child study

- documents a child's development using observation and other information-gathering techniques
- may document development over an extended period of time
- analyzes a child's development in each domain
- naturalistic
- mostly nonparticipatory

►► Key Features: Portfolio

- contains a variety of observations, samples, and contextual information
- documents development over a period of time
- considers development as an individual and holistic process
- analyzes and assesses development sympathetically within the individual's context
- mostly naturalistic

A portfolio is much more than a collection of information; it is an attitude and a process. While it is relatively easy to describe the possible contents of a portfolio, it is more challenging to generate enthusiasm for the concept of portfolio evaluation and record keeping and to get each member of the team to participate in the process of data collection.

Several principles underlie the portfolio philosophy:

- The process of a child's experience is important and individual to that child.
- The most effective way to record information about a child's experience is to observe the child in a natural setting—that is, home, child-care center, or school.

- Information about a child is most usefully supplied by parents, teachers, caregivers, and other stakeholders in the child's life.
- Portfolios provide the opportunity to record data about the process of a child's experience and evidence of the products of a child's work.
- Portfolios enable the stakeholders in a child's life to be involved with both **formative** and **summative assessment** of the child's performance, skills, and competence, based on valid collection of data.
- Portfolios encourage teamwork and cooperation among the stakeholders, supporting the process of meeting the child's needs.
- Portfolios offer the possibility of recording family health and contextual information, which puts the behavioral data into a more meaningful framework.
- Portfolios encourage (in the long term) the child's involvement in the record-keeping process and selection of items for inclusion, a sense of responsibility and ownership for his or her behavior, and a sense of control in determining the educational experience.
- Portfolios are flexible in meeting the needs of the stakeholders as they can contain various types of information.
- Portfolios may include input from additional professionals, as desirable; psychologists, social workers, and others may add to the portfolio in ways that extend the information base and frequently validate the findings of the primary caregivers and parents.
- Portfolios encourage professional accountability by providing documentary evidence of evaluation processes and program planning.

Through practice, teachers and caregivers will see the value of the portfolio process. Those who say they observe all the time but do not record their observations will see that portfolios can help them do their job more effectively with only a little effort and time investment.

Watch out!

Students frequently focus on gathering information rather than analyzing it. Collecting observations is only the first part of the portfolio process!

Furnished with information from a variety of sources, the teacher may be better able to understand a child's needs and see how family and context should determine how the needs are met. Agencies that subscribe to the portfolio philosophy will usually find that the practice supports close work with parents and a cooperative style of teaching. At a time when parents, boards of education, and other administrative bodies are demanding greater professional accountability, the portfolio provides appropriate documentation of evaluation, planning, and practice.

Using child studies to learn about development

Advantages

- A child study provides an opportunity to study one child in depth.
- Each aspect of the child's development can be seen in relation to the others.
- Contextual information helps the observer make more valid inferences.
- Information gathered over a period of time enables the observer to appreciate the changing process of development.
- A variety of observations and accumulated information can give a more accurate picture of the child.
- The detail of analysis can surpass any other evaluation method.
- A child study provides a strong learning experience that supports the student later in carrying out portfolio assessments in practice.

Disadvantages

- A focus on one child is not the basis for generalizations about all children.
- The close connection with the child may mean that the inferences drawn are more subjective.
- The process is time consuming and cumbersome.
- The study may not lead to any direct benefit for the child studied.
- All children in the group cannot be studied in the same depth.
- The student may make inappropriate inferences that are not challenged.
- The large volume of material may not be evaluated in sufficient detail to offer adequate feedback.

Using portfolios for ongoing evaluation and record keeping

Advantages

- A portfolio provides for a comprehensive record-keeping process.
- A portfolio allows a variety of observations and information to be kept together.
- Professionals and parents can access records and make additions.
- The record can be used at any time.
- Information is stored over a long period of time and can be passed on from one agency or school to the next.

- The process includes deliberate parental involvement.
- A portfolio provides for the most rigorous, thorough, and developmentally appropriate assessment because its contents are so diverse.
- Informal and formal records may be kept alongside each other, which helps identify program intentions.
- A portfolio provides the opportunity for ongoing assessment. It allows for more immediate responses than some other assessment procedures.
- The system can be adapted whatever the child's needs or abilities.
- Both the process and the product of the child's experience can be recorded.
- The child values the portfolio assessment process, which validates the importance of her or his activity.
- A wide variety of teaching and caregiving philosophies can be accommodated.

Disadvantages

- A portfolio requires effort to keep updated and is time consuming.
- A portfolio can become more of a sentimental memory box than a valid assessment tool.
- A substantial amount of file space is required.
- The focus may be deflected from the process of the child's learning to overzealous record keeping.
- Information may be stored without having been evaluated on a regular basis.
- The criteria for inclusion of items in the record may not be clear.
- Teachers need training in what to look for when choosing samples.
- Meetings may be required for teamwork planning.

Types of Portfolios

Baby book

Perhaps the most commonly used portfolio is the **baby book** kept by parents. Parents can use a ready-prepared album or create their own to record the significant happenings in their child's life and to map out developmental milestones. Some parents may wish to keep up the book until the child reaches school age, or even until the child leaves home. These records might contain some of the following:

- a list of homes/accommodation
- a family tree
- copies of newspaper headlines on the day of birth

- a lock of hair
- hand/foot prints
- lists of favorite foods, toys, etc.
- feeding/sleeping records
- caregiver information
- developmental milestones
- photographs
- religious information
- lists of gifts
- name information, naming ceremonies record
- "firsts": first words, events at day care or school, first party, etc.
- artwork
- anecdotes, funny things the child said or did
- health and immunization records (dates of infectious diseases)

Some items might be included for sentimental reasons, to give parents a concrete reminder of the child's early years. The book might also serve as a way of keeping health or developmental information that may be required later.

Life book

A life book can be started at any stage of a child's life. It attempts to capture the individual nature of the child's own story. Initiated by a parent, guardian, social worker, adoption and fostering worker, or other child-care employee, the book can be passed on, with the child, from person to person involved in the child's care. The child can benefit directly from such documentation. Changes, both happy and sad, should be included so that the child can reflect on his or her own experiences and personal story. Agencies may use this kind of portfolio to support mental health, particularly when the child is undergoing transitions in parenting, home, or caregiving, or other potentially traumatic change.

A life book may contain some of the following:

- photographs of the parents/guardian
- a family tree
- pictures of significant people
- pictures of significant places/homes
- small sentimental objects
- lists of favorites, such as foods, games, objects
- birthday greetings
- mementos from outings/special occasions
- developmental charts

- health information, immunization schedules
- letters from friends and family members
- tape recordings of people, music, etc.
- religious affiliation records, initiations
- club membership cards, friendship souvenirs
- artwork

Learning log

While a **learning log** is not in itself a full portfolio, it can form part of a meaningful record documenting a child's learning. Written by a teacher or, later, by the child, the log keeps an account of the child's activity. There are two parts to this kind of log. One part records the program plan, curriculum activity, or experience as "provided"; the other records how the child responded to the experience—that is, what he or she "learned." The log system requires a teacher to be diligent in record keeping. It can provide a detailed analysis of what the child is doing. For the child who has a diagnosed special need, this type of record keeping can provide data to be interpreted as part of the planning process. For teachers with large numbers of children in their care, or for whom curriculum planning is more spontaneous, this method might not be as useful.

Older children capable of documenting their own experiences may keep a log, directed by the teacher, in which they record their responses to classroom or other activities. A more informal type of log, called a **record of achievement**, can be used by either the teacher or child to keep an anecdotal record of skill development and achievements.

Learning Log		
Date	**Curriculum experience**	**Response**

Child-care center/school individual records

An agency, with the support of parents, may choose what components of the portfolio the worker should use. A list of possibilities might be viewed and discussed so that the needs of the child, parent, and agency can be met.

Child study

The student's assignment may require certain components or focus on particular aspects of development. The child study enables the student to appreciate the complexity of the child's context and development. The student focuses on one child as objectively as possible, and also gets a more personal view of what that child's experience and development are like. Critics of the child-study approach say that it tends to be subjective and gives information that is not statistically significant. While this criticism may have some validity, child studies can offer educators important insights into the individuality of the developmental process.

Curriculum-based portfolio

Teachers' records can be based on formative evaluation of the children in particular curriculum areas. Formatted to record information about the curriculum experiences offered and the group and individual responses to the experiences, the curriculum portfolio provides documentation of the curriculum development process, evaluation of its effectiveness, and data on which to base further planning.

Curriculum-Based Class Portfolio			
Date	Curriculum area/activity	Group response (anecdotal record)	Individual outcomes

Learning assessment portfolio

An individual learning assessment portfolio can be kept by a teacher or, as the child matures, by the child, adolescent, or adult to detail her or his own learning. In this portfolio, general experiences as well as more formal learning situations are documented. Experience is described in terms of the **competencies** achieved as a result of that experience. These learning outcomes are then analyzed to establish what the experience has enabled the person to do.

The learning assessment portfolio is a useful device for teachers and learners in all stages of their education. The process of recording and examining experiences forces the individual into active learning and self-evaluation.

An early childhood educator may wish to log the experiences of a child day by day and evaluate the effectiveness of the program by determining and recording the newly acquired competence. Practice in recording behaviorial information is necessary, but, once mastered, the portfolio provides tracking of the child's learning.

Older children can, with help, log their own experiences and what they learned from them. Identifying what has been learned helps the child consolidate learning.

More mature individuals may want to explore their experiences to express the learning outcomes as acquired competencies. Evaluating experience and determining skills is becoming more widely accepted as a means to gaining credit and access to college and university programs, and may be useful in a job evaluation. To start this process in early childhood settings can only be helpful to the child growing up in a changing educational and work environment.

Portfolio Entries

Health records

Health information should be updated regularly. A child's health history is not a static record but a document that needs new additions as further health and growth information becomes evident. This type of data will not only help you know the child better, but also enable you to respond to her or his needs. Health conditions affect the child's development and are therefore an important part of the portfolio. A child health information questionnaire is best completed with the parent at an interview. Students should ask only those questions that help in understanding the child's development; a sample showing how to frame health questions can be found on page 267. An additional updating sheet can be used to make extra entries when new information becomes available. Because of the strong correlation among growth, health, and development, it may be a good idea to include measurements as the child grows. Refer to the chapter on charts (Chapter 6) for prepared formats for height, weight, immunization, feeding, and sleeping charts. A sample health questionnaire can be found on pages 268–69.

Taking a Special Look: Prenatal and neo-natal conditions

Some babies are born with fetal alcohol syndrome (FAS) or other prenatal and neo-natal conditions caused by the mother's exposure to alcohol, illegal or prescription drugs, or other chemicals. Teachers and caregivers working directly with such children may observe characteristic behaviors. Very young babies may be underweight, have poor breathing, and even suffer from withdrawal. More lasting effects may include diminished intelligence, learning disabilities, and social adaptation challenges.

Increasing numbers of children contract HIV from their mothers. Parents may decide to keep this information to themselves, fearing that the child will be excluded from an agency or school, or cut off socially. Caregivers may observe behavioral or appearance changes that might indicate illness, but cannot diagnose this or any other disease. They must always use "universal precautions" to ensure that infections of any type are not spread.

Menu plans should be provided for parents to review, and known allergies must be catered to. Adults must also observe and record any significant behavioral changes.

Child Health Information Questionnaire

Please take time to complete this form. The information will help us know your child better and respond appropriately to his/her needs.

Today's date: _____

Recorded by: _____

Family information

1. Child's name: _____
                               (first)   (last)

   "Pet" name, nickname: _____

2. Child's address: _____

   _____

   Home telephone number: (____) _____

3. Mother's name: _____

   Mother's home telephone number: _____

   Mother's home address (if different from above): _____

   _____

   Other contact during day: _____

   phone: _____

   fax: _____

4. Father's name: _____

   Father's home telephone number: _____

   Father's home address (if different from above): _____

   _____

   Other contact during day: _____

   phone: _____

   fax: _____

5. Child's sex (male or female): _____

6. Child's year of birth:_____
                                month   day   year

   Age (years/months): _____

7. Other family members living at the child's address (names and ages of children): _____
_____

8. Previous child-care agencies/schools attended: _____
_____
_____

Birth history

9. Child's weight at birth: _____

10. Length of pregnancy (premature/full term, # of months): _____

11. Were there any complications with the pregnancy or birth? If so, what? _____
_____

12. Did your child have any medical problems at or soon after birth? If so, what? _____
_____

13. Family physician's name: _____
Family physician's address: _____
_____
Family physician's phone number: _____

14. Pediatrician's name: _____
Pediatrician's address: _____
_____
Pediatrician's phone number: _____

15. Dentist's name: _____
Dentist's address: _____
_____
Dentist's phone number: _____

Health status

16. Please give a complete history of your child's immunization schedule (this may need to be verified by your doctor).

Immunization type   Date given
_____   _____
_____   _____
_____   _____

17. What infectious diseases has your child ever suffered from? (Circle Yes or No and add date if Yes.)

measles	Yes	No	Date: _____
rheumatic fever	Yes	No	Date: _____
chicken pox	Yes	No	Date: _____
pneumonia	Yes	No	Date: _____
mumps	Yes	No	Date: _____
meningitis	Yes	No	Date: _____
whooping cough	Yes	No	Date: _____
others: _____			Date: _____
_____			Date: _____

18. Has your child suffered any repeated infections? (cold, flu, tonsillitis, etc.) _____

_____

_____

19. Has your child ever received treatment in a hospital emergency room? If so, why? _____

_____

_____

20. Has your child ever been admitted to hospital as an in-patient? If so, why? _____

_____

_____

21. Does your child take any medication on a regular basis? If so, what? _____

_____

_____

22. Please offer any information about your child's health check-ups. Has your child recently been evaluated by any of the following? (Circle Yes or No and add result if Yes.)

dentist	Yes	No	Result: _____
eye doctor	Yes	No	Result: _____
hearing specialist	Yes	No	Result: _____
pediatrician	Yes	No	Result: _____
other specialist	Yes	No	Result: _____

23. Does your child have any known allergies?   Yes   No

To what? _____

Severity of reaction: _____

24. (a) Does your child have problems with any of the following? (Circle Yes or No and describe if Yes.)

asthma	Yes	No	Describe: _____
hayfever	Yes	No	Describe: _____
skin sensitivity	Yes	No	Describe: _____
reaction to the sun	Yes	No	Describe: _____
warts	Yes	No	Describe: _____
dairy products	Yes	No	Describe: _____
constipation	Yes	No	Describe: _____
easy bruising	Yes	No	Describe: _____
concentration	Yes	No	Describe: _____
mood swings	Yes	No	Describe: _____
sleep	Yes	No	Describe: _____
spasms, twitches, tics	Yes	No	Describe: _____
habits	Yes	No	Describe: _____
other			_____

(b) Are there any genetic diseases in the family? _____

25. Does your child behave in any way that concerns you? If so, what? _____

_____

26. Has your child ever been exposed to any significant traumatic event? (witnessed violence, divorce in family, moving home, death of relative, etc.)   Yes   No

Describe: _____

27. Does your child play in a way that you would expect?   Yes   No

Describe: _____

28. Do you have any concerns about your child's speech, communication, or understanding? If so, what?

_____

29. What is your child's height? _____

weight? _____

shoe size? _____

30. Describe your child's feeding/eating patterns. (number of meals, snacks, types of food/milk/formula, attitude to eating) _____

_____

Health Update

Name: _____ Age/D.O.B.: _____ Today's date: _____

New immunizations (cross-reference to immunization record card):

    Immunization type   Date given

    _____   _____

    _____   _____

Recent health conditions: _____

Medication: _____

Physician's reports (attach if appropriate): _____

Updates on growth information (also plot data on growth chart)

    height: _____

    weight: _____

    shoe size: _____

Identified health needs: _____

▶ Taking a Special Look: Prolonged illness ▶

> When children are sick for a long period of time, they may experience some regression in their development, particularly in the emotional domain. For example, a child with a chronic condition such as asthma may be hospitalized whenever he has a serious attack. Such children might have great intellectual potential, but they may need special intellectual stimulation to encourage their play activity.

Contextual information

A working portfolio makes much more sense and is likely to be interpreted more accurately if some **contextual information** is included. Some of the entries might come from observation, but you will probably have to rely on parental input for a large amount of background information. An initial interview in the child's home can help forge links between home and the agency you represent. There is a fine line between asking for information that is pertinent and asking questions that seem to be none of your business. These interviews are better conducted as an informal chat rather than a long question-and-answer-type questionnaire process.

"Why do you want to know that?" is a fairly typical and reasonable question. If you can explain why the information is helpful to you before you ask any questions, the parents' response is more likely to be favorable. Parents can decline to offer information. This decision must be respected.

The following background information form may help you know what to ask. Review the questions ahead of time. You may have to modify areas according to legal requirements, your understanding of the need to ask the questions, and the parents' comfort level. This questionnaire is not intended to be completed by parents, although they must be asked for input and allowed access to what has been recorded. Most jurisdictions have freedom of information and privacy provisions of which you should be aware, as your information-gathering processes must comply with such legislation. The sample background information form on page 270 uses questions the student found appropriate.

A full set of contextual information may also include a sociological survey of the child's home neighborhood.

Background Information

Recorded by: _____   Date: _____

1. Child's name: _____
                         last   first   middle   pet name

2. Current age: _____ D.O.B.: _____

---

3. Child's appearance: height: _____

    weight: _____ eye color: _____

    skin color, birth marks, texture: _____

    identifying features: _____

    hair color, style, condition: _____

4. What does the family see to be their nationality, race, citizenship, ethnic origin? (In some jurisdictions, this question may need to be altered or omitted.) _____

5. What is (are) the language(s) spoken in the home? _____

6. Family composition (mention all those living at the same address and their relationship): _____

_____

7. Extended family: _____

_____

8. Mother's occupation, if employed: _____

    Mother's hobbies/interests: _____

    Father's occupation, if employed: _____

    Father's hobbies/interests: _____

    Guardian (if not mother or father): _____

    Guardian's occupation, if employed: _____

    Is the child fostered, adopted, or in the care of adults who are not the child's parents? _____

9. Abilities/disabilities observable in nuclear family: _____

_____

10. Accommodations/residence type: _____

    # bedrooms: _____   # bathrooms: _____   # people living in home: _____

    living space: _____

11. Pets/animals living in home: _____

12. Locality of residence (urban/rural, industrial, residential, etc.): _____

13. Play space available to child: _____

14. Availability of playthings/books: _____

15. Child-care/educational/recreational programs where the child is registered: _____

    _____

16. Transportation access (bus, train, car, etc.): _____

17. Who are the significant adults in the child's life? _____

18. Does the family require welfare, social insurance, grants, etc.? _____

19. What changes in the family have occurred since the birth of this child? _____

    _____

20. Does the family practice a particular religion? _____

21. Can family members trace their family tree? _____

22. What is the parenting style? _____

23. What kind of lifestyle does the family enjoy? _____

24. Are there particular mealtimes/bedtimes or other rituals? _____

25. Does the family express or demonstrate particular attitudes, values, or beliefs? _____

    _____

Changing Circumstances – Portfolio Update

Child's name: _____   Date: _____

Age: _____   D.O.B.: _____

Entry made by : _____

Nature of change (move home, divorce, unemployment, etc.): _____

Identified need of the child: _____

Observations

Observations are an essential part of the portfolio. They are the core to which the other components are additions. Your observational methods will be chosen on the basis of the developmental information they can reveal. A variety of styles will be necessary, some being repeated. Refer to the chapters on different methods of observation to help you with your choices.

Unless you focus on what a child can do and observe behavior in a natural setting, you will not be able to make adequate evaluations. The central part of the portfolio will be observations from both home and the care agency or school. Those written by the professionals require **objectivity** and detail; parental contributions should be valued even if they are not written in the format and language of the teacher or in a completely objective fashion.

Not all your written observations will, or could, be included in the portfolio; selection of material will be necessary. Choose the observations that offer the most up-to-date or significant developmental information.

Copies of blank observation forms can be made available for parents to complete. Some parents may be more comfortable with giving you verbal anecdotes of what they have seen. You can record them on a parent sheet if that works best.

A parent's spontaneous comments may not always be the best record. A mother may tell you about her child's reaction to catching the parents in an intimate moment, or may tell you how exasperated she is about her child's irritating habit of nose picking. These comments may not be appropriate to keep in a formal record. From another perspective, you might see the validity of including accounts of how the child first slept through the night, rejected the breast, or became more cooperative in play with cousins. These professional decisions are based on understanding what is significant.

Parental input

On busy days, we sometimes think that we provide the most significant influences in a child's life. This is not true; parents are the center of the child's world, and our task is to support them. Parents can help us ensure the child's happy development by providing information about their child. They know their child well and are almost always in a better position to decide what is best. Accepting parents' opinions can be difficult when their values differ from our own, but we must keep a professional respect for their perspective on their task.

In addition to any forms, questionnaires, and reports filled out during or after communication with parents, it is useful to keep a log of meetings with parents, as a summary of dates, permissions granted, and topics discussed. A sample parent meeting log can be found on pages 271–72.

If parents have been part of the portfolio process for a while, they might give you information about how a guidance strategy is working, how they are implementing a learning plan, or what they have learned from a health professional or psychologist. While this information is second-hand, recording it can be useful. Notes must indicate the source of the comments.

A teacher–parent journal can aid both parties in communication. Some notes may focus on practical requests like "Please drop off more diapers," but a more analytical approach may include thoughtful comments about the child's mood, interests, or development. This record book can be included in the portfolio and provides an interesting picture of changes.

Watch out!

Parents are an important part of the portfolio process, but you may have to show them what you are doing and why you want their input.

Records from previous agencies

You will be fortunate if assessments, health records, and reports have been transferred to your agency. Treat the material with respect, but be cautious about believing everything you read. You will want to think that the records are accurate and objective, but without some verification of the findings, avoid making programming decisions based on them.

Legal requirements governing the transfer of this kind of information vary according to the jurisdiction. Be aware of the legalities and policies that pertain to your situation, whether they are by-laws, municipal guidelines, Board of Education policies, procedures agreed to by agencies, or local practices.

The contents of the record may be a useful prompt to ask questions of the parents; they may wish to see the record themselves and offer opinions on the contents. Their rights may include the possibility of removing items or including further items or comment on the information.

Use the records to prompt some informal observations as the child settles into the new environment. Records can be obsolete by the time they get passed on. You may note considerable development and life experience changes in the time between leaving one agency and starting at another.

Some supervisors choose to limit access to child histories because they do not want to color the attitudes of the teacher with direct responsibility for the child. Teachers are trained to be objective and professional and to be aware of inappropriate influences. They should usually evaluate for themselves the content of records that they receive.

Professional reports

Assessment records, reports, suggestions, and plans from professionals contributing to the child's health, education, and well-being may be included in the portfolio. When the caregiving agency requests a report from a specialist, the consent of the parents is usually required. Parents may also seek a specialist's help directly. The report that results from such intervention may not always be accessible to you, as caregiver or student, for personal reasons that you may never know. It may not be mistrust that leads to a lack of access, but you might feel that you could help better if you had as much information as possible.

In some situations, your input may be crucial to the assessment process. If you agree to offer input, you will, even then, not necessarily receive feedback.

If assessment results do not reinforce what you have already observed, it may not be that either is "wrong," but that you are evaluating the child from a different perspective. Because your observations are carried out in a naturalistic setting, they are more likely to represent what the child can do every day. When test results indicate a level of achievement below that which you have observed, the test was likely inappropriate or presented in a way that induced stress or elicited unexpected responses. If the results duplicate your findings, you can feel that your inferences are more likely to be valid. You could, though, both be wrong. Ideally, the team will work together, parents will be involved, and outcomes will be commonly agreed on.

 Taking a Special Look: Resource teachers and assistants

Some child-care facilities and schools have access to resource teachers and assistants. Resource teachers have specialized training to provide physical assistance, learning activities, emotional and social support, and other aid to children with special needs within a mainstream setting. Assistants are sometimes hired specifically to work with one or two particular children with diagnosed special needs, but they usually provide general support to the program rather than specific support for the child.

Artwork can be included in a portfolio to demonstrate a child's skills, emotions, and perceptions. The child may also choose a favorite piece of work as a personal contribution to the portfolio.

Products of learning and experience

Observations may enable you to glimpse the process of a child's learning, but examples of the products confirm achievements. In keeping products, such as artwork and writing samples, you will still value the process by which they were made. Concrete examples of the child's end products can help the professional to appreciate the stage of the child's development.

While you must remain cautious about making invalid, unsupported inferences, representative samples of a child's can help evaluate progress. With knowledge of the sequence of drawing skills and representation of the child's world in art, you can make pertinent comments about the child's feelings, skill level, and perception. Writing and math work can be analyzed on a similar basis. By looking at what the child can do, you can attempt to appreciate conceptual understandings and have a glimpse of the child's construction of knowledge.

Selecting items for the portfolio can be difficult when the child creates a large volume of products. You may be tempted to select "the best" according to your personal responses. More significant is the most typical of the child's work at this time.

Media techniques

Photographs, video and audio recordings, and other **media techniques** for gathering information can be helpful in the portfolio process. They enable you to put together a more comprehensive collection of items than would be possible by using only traditional observation techniques.

Video and audio recordings of the child supplement the portfolio by adding detail of the child's activity and language that is often superior to a narrative recording. Remember that recordings, of themselves, are not interpretive unless narrated by a teacher or analyzed in detail after the event. Review Chapter 7 to help you use media techniques.

We are accustomed to using photographs for identification and record keeping. Keeping a loaded camera near the children's activity will help you be ready to "snap" the children in action. A variety of action and posed pictures is a useful addition to the portfolio and brings it to life for readers.

Inclusions made by the child

The sense of involvement in and ownership of the educational process increases when the child has some control over the input to her or his own record. In choosing pieces for inclusion, the child can identify items of particular significance. If the item is too precious to be stored in the portfolio, it might be possible to photograph the item and include the photograph instead.

Assembling a Portfolio

Since a team approach, in which parents and practitioners work together, is desirable, it may be a good idea to decide collectively on the system to be used for record keeping.

Organizing the contents for storage

How the portfolios are kept will depend on the space available. File folders are used most commonly. They can, however, be too small to accommodate large pieces of artwork. To get around this problem, you might take photographs of the artwork instead of including flaking paint and unstuck macaroni! Box files can be expensive and may not give you the kind of privacy and storage space you need. A local manufacturer might be able to let you have boxes—shirt boxes or others of that size are useful. Pizza boxes (if clean) may provide an answer. Ring binders for each child allow items to be put in chronological order and removed when necessary. Another option is accordion files, which provide sections that would allow items to be organized by type. Whatever method is used, be aware that this kind of record keeping requires space that is accessible but secure.

The portfolio should be kept in an orderly fashion. It should be labeled on the outside, and each item inside must be labeled clearly and dated. You should develop a system to ensure that you remember to make additions.

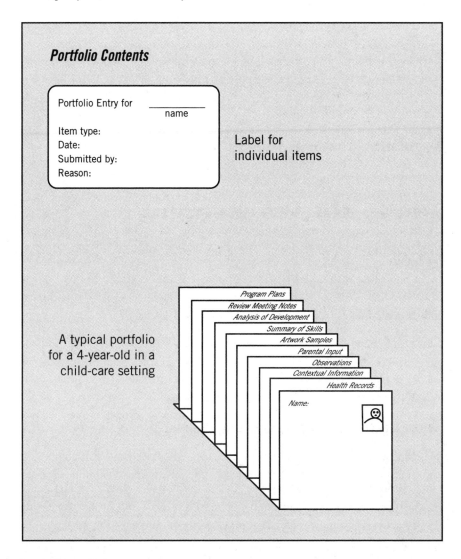

Choice of contents

What you put into the portfolio will depend on your philosophy and why you are keeping the records. Your team might like to discuss the following considerations to help decide on the contents:

- the purpose of each type of record
- the space available
- who will keep the portfolio up to date
- who will access the portfolio
- how the data can be analyzed
- the cost of keeping the system
- the philosophy of the agency (child-centered programs may have fewer standardized tests; some may focus on the process of learning and accentuate observations; others may want to have more products included)
- privacy and confidentiality
- the time available to collect and process information
- the attitude of staff and parents

Portfolio Assessment

After gathering all this material, we have to make sense of it. The use of portfolios for evaluation has been criticized as glorified work sampling rather than real assessment. However, a thorough assessment of a well-kept portfolio leads to a real understanding of the child. The following steps outline the process of careful **portfolio assessment**:

1. **Sort, date, and label all items:** Without a good labeling system, the portfolio will be a confusing collection of information.
2. **Organize the contents:** Items can be organized by date or by types of data. Add a contents page to show what is included and how it is organized.
3. **Write an introduction:** Explain the process you have used to create the portfolio. Ensure that you show you are celebrating an individual!
4. **Summarize the material:** Probably the best way to summarize is to scan the current material and categorize skill developments by developmental domain. A **summary** can help the assessor determine how the child is reaching any learning outcomes, expectations, or profile of learning. At this stage, sort objectively; do not explain. A sample portfolio summary can be found on pages 273–74.
5. **Make inferences about the child's skills:** Using clear statements, write an **analysis** of the child's development. Your **inferences** might be based on
   - applying theoretical models to explain a behavior, skill, or performance
   - matching the child's performance against an acceptable norm of development to see where the child is in relation to a specific age or stage (avoid inappropriate judgments)

- determining a pattern or cause of behavior

Validate or support all inferences using reasoned arguments and citing reliable sources. Be sure to reference all sources. A sample portfolio analysis can be found on pages 275–82.

6. **Write a portfolio review report for the parents and for your records:** Restate your inferences in a way that avoids jargon and that helps parents appreciate what you are trying to say. A sample report can be found on page 283.

7. **Present the parents with the portfolio:** Most parents are anxious to be part of the assessment process. Be prepared to adjust any inferences in your portfolio review report according to their perceptions. If a child is old enough to appreciate the portfolio collection process, he or she should be part of the process. At this time, an action plan can be developed by the teachers, parents, child, and other concerned parties (such as social workers or grandparents).

8. **Design an individual program plan (IPP) or individual education plan (IEP):** Create an **IPP** or **IEP** according to the skills that you see emerging. If you have documented learning in all developmental domains, you will be better prepared to design activities that support all domains. For children with special needs, it may be necessary to design a plan that has developmental or incremental stages. Sample program plans can be found on pages 38 and 39–40.

9. **Continue the portfolio collection and observations for future in-process assessment.**

Portfolio Review Meeting Report

Child's name: _____   Date: _____

Age/D.O.B.: _____   Meeting called by: _____

Those present: _____

Intention of meeting: _____

_____

Review of recent additions to portfolio: _____

_____

Changed context, social or family circumstances: _____

_____

Developmental summary given by: _____

Summary details: _____

_____

Cognition: _____

Personality: _____

Language and communication: _____

Emotional development: _____

Physical development: _____

Social skills: _____

Curriculum implications: _____

Program plan/strategies: _____

Key Terms

analysis
anecdotal record
baby book
chart
checklist
child study
competency
contextual informa-
    tion
ecomap
event sampling
formative assessment
genogram
individual education
    plan (IEP)
individual program
    plan (IPP)
inference
learning log

life book
life experience flow
    chart
media technique
objectivity
observation
portfolio
portfolio assessment
rating scale
record of achieve-
    ment
running record
specimen record
standardized test
summary
summative assess-
    ment
time sampling

Observation Sample

It is important for caregivers to ask health questions that will help them provide consistent care and assess development, and not to ask questions that are unnecessary or that infringe on the family's privacy. The process shown here will help students frame questions appropriate to their purposes.

FRAMING THE QUESTIONS FOR A HEALTH QUESTIONNAIRE

Student's name: Aaron   **Date:**   September 16, 1998

Component: Routines

Significance: I need to know the child's daily routines in order to help in the transition from home to group care. According to <u>Infants and Toddlers</u>, routines give the infant or toddler a sense of security. The infant learns to trust repetition and lack of change. Although the child may not <u>think</u> about the implemented routines, she or he <u>feels</u> the security of the familiar activities. Many daily routines nurture physical health, particularly those related to cleanliness, eating, and sleeping. Perhaps one of the most recognized and important routines is the child's need for rest and relaxation (in accordance with what is practiced at home). Infants follow their own individual rest schedules, which should be somewhat consistent with home. Opportunities for rest and relaxation, for example, are part of the development and individual needs of children. Therefore, I need to know the child's "normal" routines to fulfill the child's needs and optimize her or his well-being.

Questions I will ask:
1. Describe your child's sleeping patterns.
2. Does your child sleep with any security items? If yes, please specify.

Source: Wilson, L.C., Douville-Watson, L., & Watson, M.A. (1995). <u>Infants and Toddlers: Curriculum and Teaching</u> (3rd ed.). Albany, NY: Delmar.

Observation Sample

This health questionnaire was completed by interviewing the child's mother. The information will help the caregivers provide appropriate care, ease the transition from home to day care, and assess the child's development.

Health Questionnaire

Child's name: _Katie_   Date: _October 29/98_

Age/D.O.B.: _June 2/96_   Recorder: _Tanya_

BIRTH HISTORY

1. At birth, what was your child's length? _20.5 in._ and weight? _7 lb 11 oz_

2. What was the length of your pregnancy? _42 weeks_

3. Please describe any complications: _She was not positioned properly; her head was facing the wrong way at delivery._

4. What was the child's state of health at birth (jaundice)? _Born with Trachea Malacia (premature windpipe)-closing of windpipe. The cartilage in her windpipe wasn't formed, very soft. Her airway would close when she cried or fed._

5. Please describe your child's health after birth: _She was ill a lot, breathing complications. In and out of the hospital for her first year. She is much better now._

DEVELOPMENTAL PATTERNS

6. Do you think your child's growth is fairly steady? (YES)   NO

7. What is your child's approximate weight now? _36 lb_

BEHAVIORAL PATTERNS

8. Do you consider your child to be outgoing? (YES)   NO   SOMETIMES

9. Do you consider your child to be shy?   YES   NO   (SOMETIMES)

10. Are there people or objects that comfort your child when s/he's upset? _Mom, Elmo blanket, and her babies (dolls)_

DAILY ROUTINES

11. Does your child generally enjoy mealtime? (YES)   NO

12. Does your child have any diet restrictions? (cultural, religious, food allergy or sensitivity)   YES   (NO)
Although I do not allow her to have pop and chocolate (very rare)

13. Please describe an average day on the weekend for your child. Please include when s/he wakes up, feeding, sleeping, and play times until s/he goes to bed in the evening. _8-9 wake up, wash, change diaper, brush hair, teeth. 9:30 breakfast. 10-12 play, watch TV, go outside, on swings, games, neighbors come over. Use potty. 12:30 eat lunch, clean up. 1-5 have snacks, use potty, go visiting at Grandma's, stay home and play, clean together, out for walks 5:30-6:00 help get dinner prepared. 6:00 dinner._

6:30-7:00 brush teeth, use potty, bedtime story. 7:30 bed.

HEALTH STATUS

14. Do any family members have known allergies or chronic conditions? (YES) NO
    If YES, what: _____ *Allergies*

15. Has your child had any allergic reactions? (environmental, food, animals, or medications) (YES) NO
    Please explain which allergen and the severity: _*Grass, hayfever-aggravates asthma*_

16. Has your child ever been to a medical specialist? (YES) NO
    If YES, what was the ailment? _*Asthma and premature windpipe*_

17. Does your child take medication on a regular basis? (YES) NO
    If YES, which medication(s)? _*Vanceril (for asthma)*_

18. Please describe your child's general health. (e.g., recurrent ear infections, skin conditions, colds)
    *Health has improved over last few months; she does seem to catch colds quite often.*

19. Is your child ill on a fairly regular basis? YES (NO)

20. Which infectious diseases has your child had?

Mumps	YES	(NO)
Whooping cough	YES	(NO)
Measles	YES	(NO)
Chicken pox	YES	(NO)
Meningitis	YES	(NO)
Pneumonia	YES	(NO)

IMMUNIZATION RECORD

21. Please list your child's immunization schedule:

IMMUNIZATION TYPE	DATE RECEIVED	ANY REACTIONS
DPT	*August 2/96*	-
DPT	*October 25/96*	-
DPT	*January 30/97*	-
MM Rubella	*approx. 12 months old*	-
DPT	*January 24/98*	-

Observation Sample

These questions were put together by an ECE student to gather contextual information about a child. Rather than ask the parents to fill out a formal questionnaire, the student met with the child's mother to learn about the family through informal conversation.

Background Information

Recorded by: _Simon_   Date: _November 7, 1997_

Method of recording: _Interview with mother_

Child's name: _Robert_   Pet name: _Robbie_

What is the composition of your family? (# of adults/children) _Four adults and one child (Robbie). He lives with mom, dad, uncle, maternal grandma and grandpa. Grandpa works in the Middle East, and he sometimes lives there._

What links do you have with your extended family? (aunts, grandparents, etc.) _We are all very close. Robbie usually meets with his paternal grandparents, aunts, and uncles every weekend._

Are there any special activities that your family enjoys doing together? _Birthday parties, picnics, Christmas, Thanksgiving dinner, and we usually have a Halloween party at the house._

What kind of home do you have? _We live in a condominium townhouse with a small yard shared with neighbors._

Do you see yourself as belonging to any particular cultural, religious, national, or ethnic background or heritage? _We are a mix: Catholic, Islamic, and Trinidadian. Robbie goes to a Catholic church._

What languages are spoken in your home? _Creole, French, and English._

Is there any special information about your family? (e.g., particular talents, family experiences, interests, special needs, home moves, or stories) _We are all interested in sports. I play soccer in the Ontario Soccer Association. His uncle is a soccer player too._

Do you work outside the home? _No. I used to work at Consumers Gas as a clerk._

What are your current child-care arrangements? _Robbie attends the child-care center at Centennial College, where I am taking classes._

What were your previous arrangements for child care? _My grandma used to take care of him - that is, his great-grandma._

Do you have pets in your home? If so, what? _No, we used to have a cat, but when the baby was born we got rid of it._

In your family, do you have special words for things? (e.g., toilet = pee-pee) _In my family, we are used to calling the toilet a "potty."_

What do you hope for your child when s/he grows up? _To have a heart, be able to make good decisions, enjoy life to the fullest and all it has to offer. But most of all, to have an education, so that he will become somebody in the world. It might be hard, but I don't want him to give up ever!_

Observation Sample

This log is a simple record of all meetings and discussions with a child's parents. Such a log provides a quick summary of which permissions have been requested, which questionnaires have been completed, and what other discussions have taken place.

Parent Meeting Log for Portfolio

Child's name: Jean-Paul   **Student's name:** Cara

February 6, 1997: First formal approach to Jean-Paul's parents, Mr. and Mrs. Legore, re: observation of their son. Approached with the approval of toddler room supervisor, Christy. Introductions are made and I immediately describe the purpose of my observation. I receive written consent for the event sampling, informing them that further consent forms will be forthcoming for future observations. I now have to start recording.

February 21, 1997: Meet with the parents to discuss Jean-Paul's general routine as recorded in the format of a daily log. At this meeting, I inform Mrs. Legore of Jean-Paul's impressive oral skills and attempts at autonomous activity. We do discuss, however, Jean-Paul's tendency to become very agitated when a child takes his toy or a situation does not coincide with his immediate need for gratification. It is decided that the best way to deal with this typical behavior is to encourage verbal expression of Jean-Paul's thoughts and feelings, needs and wants. This is not inconceivable given Jean-Paul's strong oral skills.

March 13, 1997: Approach Mr. and Mrs. Legore in the morning to acquire permission to complete remaining elements of the port-folio assignment. I present two permission forms to be checked and validated--one to perform general observation for the purpose of a checklist observation, the second to take photographs of the child as a component of the portfolio. Permission is granted on both counts. Mr. Legore is also informed that a brief meeting will be needed for the purpose of acquiring contextual information. We agree to conduct this meeting the same day--March 13, 1997--at approximately 5:00 p.m., when Mr. Legore arrives back at the child care to pick up Jean-Paul.

Later that day, Mr. Legore arrives back at the child care and we conduct a short 10-15 minute meeting to fill out the contextual questionnaire. The interview is done in a direct, no-nonsense manner in order to keep the meeting short and to the point; both Jean-Paul and his older sister are waiting for Mr. Legore and me to finish in order to return home. At the end of our interview, I inform Mr. Legore that a similar meeting will have to be conducted for the purpose of obtaining information on Jean-Paul's medical history. We agree to set next Friday afternoon--March 21, 1997--as a tentative date for the next meeting to take place. I also receive verbal permission from Mr. Legore to obtain photocopies of Jean-Paul's immunization record from the center; we agree that this will save time at our future meeting.

March 21, 1997:   Mr. Legore arrives at the end of the day to inform me that he cannot meet at this time due to car problems. I ask him if next Thursday afternoon--March 27, 1997--would be an acceptable time for rescheduling. He agrees, and the meeting is temporarily postponed.

March 27, 1997:   Mr. Legore arrives shortly after 5:00 p.m., and we immediately sit down in the office to commence the meeting. Once again, we are both motivated to conduct the interview quickly; the children are waiting for their father and it is the beginning of Easter weekend. The questioning is fairly routine and Mr. Legore shows no reservations about answering the questions that I choose to ask. We get into an interesting discussion about blood type and why it is not a required component of child-care health questionnaires, nor a subject even mentioned in the Day Nurseries Act. The interview goes well. I opt to omit certain contextual details from my questioning in order to focus more on the child's health and to keep the meeting moving along at a good pace.

Observation Sample

This summary of skills was prepared as part of a portfolio assessment. The skills are categorized by domain, but they are not explained and no inferences are drawn.

SUMMARY OF SKILLS

Child's name: Kirsten   Recorder: Damian
Age/D.O.B.: 19 months   Date: June 4, 1998

Drawn from the following samples: running record, video recording, time sampling

Appearance
-girl
-dark brown hair
-ears pierced
-fair-skinned
-teeth in upper and lower front

Posture
-stands erect at water table with legs apart
-sits on carpet with back straight and legs extended in front

Mobility
-walks without assistance
-toddles quickly

Physical Skills
Gross motor:
-sitting
-walking/toddling

Fine motor:
-palmar grasp (picking up cup)
-pincer grasp (pinching sponges)
-eye-hand coordination (pouring water out of cup into bin)

Language/Communication
-puts words and sounds together
-squeals (apparently when excited)
-uses one word to signify whole thoughts
-"mine," "frog"

Sensory Explorations
-dips hands in water and moves them around
-creates splashes by raising hands in air and forcefully lowering them
 into water
-collects water in cup and then slowly pours it out
-feels sponges with her hands

Demonstration of Cognitive Function
-demonstrates understanding of function of a cup
-fills cup with water and then pours it out
-names objects: "frog"
-responds to experiences with some facial movement (smiling)

Demonstration of Emotions
-periodically squeals and laughs
-smiles while splashing water
-appears satisfied with her accomplishment
-screams and then hits another child
-at this time, apparently unwilling to share or co-operate

Social Interaction
-appears to be quite independent
-engages in solitary play at water table
-engages in associative play with three other children when playing with
 float

Observation Sample

This portfolio analysis provides a developmental profile of the child. Based on a variety of observations, including narrative recordings (see running record, pp. 112–14), charts, media recordings, and parental input, the student draws inferences about the child's development. The inferences are supported with theories and norms, which are detailed in the list of references.

PORTFOLIO ANALYSIS

Child's name: Mandy   Observer: Daisy
Age: 25 months   Date: December 2, 1998

The components of Mandy's portfolio were gathered from September 1998 to the present (December 2, 1998). She has reached some significant developmental milestones during this observation period, including the transition from emerging expressive language skills to acquisition of new vocabulary and quickly developing expressive language capabilities. The following analysis gives an overview of Mandy's developmental progress, skills, and behaviors in the following domains: physical, language and communication, emotional, social, cognitive, and temperament/personality.

Physical Development

Mandy's large muscle control appears good and is at a developmental level expected for a 2-year-old. As the checklist (for 2- and 3-year-olds) indicates, she has mastered the large motor skills identified as typical for a 2-year-old (walks alone, bends over and picks up toy without falling over, seats self in chair, walks up and down stairs with assistance) (Allen & Marotz, 1994, pp. 165–166). In fact, Mandy has shown competence in some physical skills identified as normal for 3-year-olds (runs well in forward direction, jumps in place with two feet together, throws ball, kicks ball forward) (Allen & Marotz, 1994, 165–166). The photographs of Mandy in the playground-- running, walking, climbing into and out of riding toys and on and off tricycles--also offer evidence that she is coordinated and able to use her body competently to participate in chosen physical activities. The running record observation offers many examples of Mandy's large muscle coordination, including use of a variety of riding toys, climbing stairs with ease, and climbing up the slide from the bottom.
    Her small muscle control is also typical for most 2-year-olds. The checklist indicates that Mandy has mastered use of a spoon; taking off her coat, socks, and shoes; holding and drinking from a cup; turning pages in a book; placing rings on a stick; and placing pegs in a pegboard. One area requiring more practice is the zipping and unzipping of zippers. The only zippers Mandy has experience with are on her coats, and they are

smaller than a "large practice zipper." Props in the environment to offer practice would be helpful here.

During the matching game identified in the anecdotal record (October 28), there was evidence that Mandy preferred to use large muscles rather than small muscles. Instead of using her hands and eyes to match the pictures, she chose to stand on the matching picture. This may simply mean that she found the game more fun this way, but may also be an indication that she is more comfortable using her body in this way. While she displays no difficulty with small motor activities undertaken, it may be that, while her visual acuity is maturing, she is more comfortable using larger muscles rather than hand/eye ("How Language Develops").

Language and Communication

Mandy's receptive language skills are excellent. She seems to understand what is said to her and is beginning to express herself verbally using sentences with correct grammatical structure (e.g., "I want to go outside"). The checklist indicates that she has mastered the language skills normal for a 2-year-old and has advanced in many areas to a 3-year-old level. During the anecdotal record done November 5, Mandy's mother was able to communicate to her that she had to leave and go to work. Mandy accepted this immediately and responded accordingly by saying good-bye and leaving her mother to join the group.

Evidence of good expressive language skills is apparent in the anecdotal record done November 19. Mandy was able to ask the caregiver what she was doing, and responded in a manner that showed understanding ("Can I help?"). She understood the question, "What color is this?" and responded correctly. Between the ages of 30 and 36 months, it is normal for toddlers to label objects (Wilson, Douville-Watson, & Watson, 1995, p. 348); answer questions appropriately (Allen & Marotz, 1994, p. 93); use pronouns and prepositions (Barrett et al, 1995, p. 235); and say many intelligible words (Sheridan, 1975). Mandy's language skills demonstrate all of these competencies, indicating a mastery of language and communication skills beyond expectations for a 2-year-old.

Mandy uses correct words, but sometimes mispronounces them. On the audiotape, she refers to the "sound" on the tape as "tound" and "yellow" as "lellow." As her muscle control matures and Mandy is exposed to appropriate modeling of the proper pronunciation, her next step in development will be to correctly pronounce vowel and consonant sounds. It is normal for children in the age range of 18 to 36 months to simplify the pronunciation of words they find difficult: "All of these implications show that your child is actively learning the sound patterns of language" (Skarakis-Doyle, 1988a).

The contextual questionnaire completed by Mandy's mother identifies language skills as "good for her age." She records that conflicts with Mandy are generally handled via verbal communication, and that this usually works. The same applies when Mandy reacts to new situations. These are also strong indicators that Mandy's language and communication abilities exceed the norm.

Emotional Development

Mandy appears to be well-adjusted emotionally to her routine at day care. The daily log chart indicates that she moves through routines and transitions well, and that she is able to anticipate what is coming next in her day (e.g., she finds her cot after lunch, and knows that after nap she needs to find her shoes and put them on). She displays a cheerful disposition consistently, exploring her environment and engaging caregivers with confidence. According to Allen and Marotz (1994), "the 2-year-old gradually begins to function more ably and amiably" (p. 78). The event sampling based on observations done October 8 and 15 indicates that Mandy displays autonomous behaviors as they relate to her self-help skills. She consistently tries to do things for herself, but does not hesitate to ask for help when she needs it: "Erikson has pointed to the struggle for autonomy as the big issue in the toddler's life. Autonomy means self-determination, independence. It is the ability to decide for oneself what one is going to do. Autonomy means, 'Me do it!' It means, 'no!'" ("Foundations"). Mandy is often heard saying both of these phrases; however, avoiding direct commands successfully avoids power struggles when caregivers need Mandy to move through a transition (e.g., leaving a play activity to prepare for lunch).

Another issue in toddlerhood affecting Mandy's emotional development is toilet training. Her mother has started leaving Mandy's diaper off at home and has asked for consistency at day care. The event sampling indicates that Mandy's attempts at toileting are positively supported and that she does not seem to be experiencing any stress in relation to this new routine. She accepts it as part of her day; however, this is a new skill. Sensitive and positive encouragement is very important to keep her from feeling that she is being pressured. Positive reinforcement (big fuss when successful!) results in pride-like behavior on Mandy's part.

Separation is an issue in toddlerhood, and Mandy appears to have successfully achieved the ability to separate from her parents. The anecdotal record done November 5 is evidence that she has formed a positive attachment and trusting relationship with her mother. This enables her to separate, knowing her mother is going to work and will return later. Wilson, Douville-Watson, and Watson (1995) suggest that "becoming a separate psychological being is one of the most complicated tasks a toddler has to face. During the two years starting from birth, the child establishes a very strong attachment to the mother" (p. 302). The more secure this relationship has been prior to 2, the easier the separation process.

Greenspan's (1985) theory of emotional development indicates that, by 24 months of age, children should be encouraged to express their feelings as emotional ideas rather than just act them out. Mandy is very successful at this and often chooses to play in the dramatic play area with dolls, dress-up clothes, toys, and materials from other parts of the room. She is also able to create images in her mind, pretending to be "mommy" while she cuddles a doll (Greenspan, 1985). Her excellent language skills enable her to express her role in play and to use items symbolically.

Mandy's ability to make independent choices throughout the day and her even, cheerful disposition are indicators that her emotional development is healthy for a 2-year-old. She is now entering Erikson's stage of initiative versus guilt, reflecting the "beginning of guilt-like behavior, pride-like behavior and shame-like behavior" (Barrett et al., 1995, p. 262). Her level of emotional development at 2 puts her on good footing to face this next phase of emotional development positively.

Social Development

Mandy is happy to play alongside the other children, engaging most often in parallel play. The running record observation and photographs give evidence that she likes to watch what others are doing, or likes to play alongside them. Her play behavior in the playground as she walks along with the children playing with the wagon is evidence of onlooker play. The daily log chart identifies pretend and symbolic play activity in which Mandy participates in solitary play or plays parallel to other children. While she may engage other children in play briefly, she prefers to play her own game. According to Barrett et al. (1995), Mildred Parten identified six categories of social play. Mandy's play activity best fits Parten's second, third, and fourth levels--solitary, onlooker, and parallel, respectively: "The second level in Parten's hierarchy, solitary play, involves a child playing independently and making no effort to interact with anyone else. The next level, onlooker play, occurs when a child watches other children play. At the fourth level, parallel play, a child plays in similar ways as another child with similar toys but does not interact with the other child" (Barrett et al., 1995, p. 326). The running record observation gives evidence of both solitary and onlooker play. The daily log chart gives evidence that Mandy, while engaged in pretend play, was playing alongside other children in dramatic play, but participating in her own activity.

Mandy likes to play with a variety of materials while in day care. Her mother identifies her favorite activities at home as "playing with dolls, reading, riding her bike, and helping mom with cleaning or laundry." Likewise, at day care, Mandy engages in a variety of play activities throughout the day. Her ability to move between different activities contributes to her ability to practice social skills with caregivers and other children in the room: "When toddlers play together, they talk to one another, and this gives them a chance to practice both their language and social skills" (Barrett et al., 1995, p. 238).

The checklist indicates that Mandy imitates adult behavior in play, as seen in her play behaviors identified in the daily log chart and by her mom in the health report. Although she is egocentric (see the incident in the running record where she is upset that another child is using the slide at the playground), Mandy's language skills contribute greatly to her ability to communicate with caregivers and other children. She is aware of her peers throughout the day; she screams with the other toddlers at the playground in response to their screaming. Still participating in her own play, she does not hesitate to "join the fun" with the others.

Mandy's social development is within the norm for a 2-year-old. She enjoys dressing up, imitates family activities, likes to be around other children, but tends to observe, sometimes imitating their actions (screaming), and explores everything, including other children. She is independent, but able to approach caregivers when she feels the need (Allen & Marotz, 1994, p. 83). In a photograph of Mandy in the playground, she is motioning that she would like to be picked up; the running record shows that she approached a caregiver for a cuddle.

Cognitive Development

Mandy loves to explore her environment and tries most materials and activities in it. When something new is introduced, she is eager to see what it is and make a decision about her level of participation. She prefers activities that do not involve "getting her hands dirty." As a result, a variety of sensory experiences must be available so that she gets the stimulation she needs as well as opportunities for creative expression through creative art activities.

Mandy's ability to expand symbolic thinking skills contributes greatly to her language development. Her ability to represent things with other things (e.g., she brings a toy car to the dramatic play center and uses it as a bus to take us to the store; she uses a large box in the room as a slide) indicates that she is moving into the first substage of Piaget's preoperational stage, called "preconceptual." For example, Mandy is able to keep track of time by understanding what is coming next (e.g., "We are going to eat lunch and then it is time for a nap"; understanding the routine, she knows that she is to go to her cot after lunch). She is beginning to classify and label objects (matching game, mittens and hats) and has some understanding of quantity (more, gone), number (more), space (up, down, behind, under, over), and time (soon, now). Wilson, Douville-Watson, and Watson (1995) identify these concepts as typical for Mandy's age.

Mandy's love of books positively contributes to her cognitive and language development. She is exposed to a variety of topics and information, facilitating her learning about the world around her. She loves to manipulate linking blocks, and enjoys making things out of them. For example, she loves to make a hat out of star linking blocks--linking them in a circle and putting them on her head!

Mandy also displays "deferred imitation" in her play activities. For example, during water play in which soap was added to make bubbles, Mandy went to the kitchen center and brought out some dishes. She identified her activity, "Washing dishes!"--clearly representing imitation of washing dishes at home. The developmental checklist used for this analysis identifies imitation of adult behaviors as within the norm for a 2-year-old.

Mandy's physical development is a factor in her cognitive development: "Toddlers learn with their whole bodies, not just their heads. They learn more through their hands than they do through their ears. They learn by doing, not only by just thinking. They learn by touching, mouthing, and trying out, not by being told" (Gonzalez-Mena, 1986). The use of her whole body rather than just her hands during the matching game is an example of physical development contributing to a cognitive learning experience.

Emotional development also contributes to cognitive learning. Mandy's trust in and comfort with her environment enable her to explore and therefore experience with confidence. This greatly facilitates her learning; she can make choices and find activities that have meaning for her. The major accomplishments of toddlerhood include "growing independence . . . self-help skills such as dressing, feeding, washing and toileting. . . . Learning to use the toilet, like all the other self-help skills, is a physical feat, as well as an intellectual and emotional one" (Gonzalez-Mena, 1986).

Temperament/Personality

The health questionnaire identifies Mandy as "sometimes shy, sometimes outgoing, friendly, cautious, and easygoing." The daily log chart indicates that Mandy is cheerful, adapted to routines, and most often in a positive mood. Her activity level is high. She moves easily from one activity to another and is eager to explore new materials in the environment. While Mandy approaches new situations with confidence, it is important to allow her to join the experience at her own pace. She will often watch for a few minutes before joining in.

Transitions pose little problem for Mandy. She listens to instructions and is usually eager to please when asked to do something. Her continuing need for independence should be fostered by caregivers. Mandy responds best when given choices that ultimately encourage the desired behavior, rather than when direct demands are made.

Mandy's cheerful disposition and positive interactions with caregivers and peers can always be depended on. She loves to engage caregivers in her games, especially pretend play, and is able to extend the play experience as it progresses. A dress-up activity turned into a major cleaning out of the dress-up bench--trying on new outfits throughout the activity! Her mother is quite right about Mandy's friendliness. As she matures, pro-social and helping skills are emerging, and her ready smile makes her a positive influence on everyone in the room.

The Whole Child

Mandy's development in all domains meets the norms for her age (2 years) and in some areas exceeds normative expectations. While this analysis looks at each domain separately, it is important to note that development remains integrated in toddlerhood. Balance is needed to facilitate development: "Overemphasis in one area or limited involvement in another may create unnecessary stress or it may delay development for the child" (Wilson, Douville-Watson, & Watson, 1995, p. 35).

The fact that Mandy was born eight weeks prematurely (see health report) does not seem to have delayed her development in any area. Her physical stature is small (she weighs about 21 lb.--the average identified in Allen and Marotz (1994) is 26 to 32 lb.); however, her physical capabilities fall within the norm. Two-year-olds typically weigh about four times their birth weight; this puts Mandy right on the norm (birth weight was 5 lb. 2 oz.). She is emotionally able to take risks. Her natural curiosity encourages lots of exploration in her environment; this is significantly facilitated by her physical competence, which also contributes greatly to her feelings of confidence.

Mandy's excellent language skills are also critical to her overall development. She can express her needs and desires verbally, understand simple directions and questions posed by caregivers, assert her independence positively, understand the meaning of symbols facilitating symbolic representation and pretend play activities, and expand her knowledge of the world around her via verbal expression and receptive language.

Overall, Mandy is a normal toddler, actively exploring her world, eagerly trying new things, all the while asserting her independence. Her egocentricity is beginning to give way as emerging pro-social skills are observed. She is liked by her peers and rarely gets into power struggles with other toddlers. Her sunny disposition makes her a positive influence in the toddler room.

References Used

Allen, K.E., & Marotz, L.R. (1994). *Development profiles: Prebirth through eight* (2nd ed.). Albany, NY: Delmar.

Barrett, K.C., et al. (1995). *Child development.* Westerville, OH: Glencoe.

Biracree, T, & Biracree, N. (1989). *The parents' book of facts: Child development from birth to age five.* New York: Facts on File.

Brazelton, T.B. (1992). *Touchpoints: Your child's emotional and behavioral development.* Reading, MA: Addison-Wesley.

Foundations: Observation and development [Handout, course CY-106]. Toronto: Centennial College.

Gonzalez-Mena, Janet. (1986, November). Toddlers: What to expect. *Young Children.*

Greenspan, S.I., & Greenspan, N.T. (1985). *First feelings: Milestones in the emotional development of your baby and child.* New York: Viking.

How language develops and what you can do [Handout, Toddler Development]. Toronto: Centennial College.

Intellectual development. (1995). *Readings Package,* 8b iv. Toronto: Centennial College.

McCaie, L. [Supervising teacher, Child-Care Center]. Personal conversations.

Outline of expected ages and stages in the development of spoken language. (1995). *Readings Package,* 8b vii. Toronto: Centennial College.

Sheridan M.D. (1975). *The developmental progress of infants and young children* (3rd ed.). London: Her Majesty's Stationery Office.

Skarakis-Doyle, Elizabeth. (1988a). Language development. Tuscon, AZ: Communication Skill Builders.

Skarakis-Doyle, Elizabeth. (1988b). Speech development. Tuscon, AZ: Communication Skill Builders

Weir, M. [Mandy's mother]. Personal interviews.

Wilson, L.C., Douville-Watson, L., & Watson, M.A. (1995). *Infants and toddlers: Curriculum and teaching* (3rd ed.). Albany, NY: Delmar.

Observation Sample

This report, presented to the parents at the time of a portfolio review meeting, briefly outlines the contents of the portfolio, the child's developmental profile, and new program plans. It summarizes the inferences made in the portfolio analysis, stating them clearly and concisely for the benefit of the parents.

PORTFOLIO REVIEW MEETING REPORT

Child's name: Jill   **Date:** November 21, 1997
D.O.B./age: Nov. 22, 1996/1 year old   **Meeting called by:** Art (ECE student)
Those present: Art, Adam and Dulcie (parents), and Tina (teacher)
Intention of meeting: To review portfolio

Review of recent additions to portfolio: Photographs, art work, and summaries
Changed context, social, or family circumstances: None
Development summary given by: Art

Summary details: Observations (time sampling, checklist, and running record), health report, ecological systems, family tree, videotapes, baby book from parents, daily logs

Cognition: Jill understands the use of many everyday objects. She understands simple directions and has an understanding of object permanence.
Personality: Jill is striving for independence right now and is starting to enjoy doing things on her own, such as eating. She has demonstrated curiosity in new experiences.
Language and communication: Jill babbles typically for a child her age. She also has demonstrated the beginning of her vocabulary by saying "hello." Jill is always able to convey her needs, whether it's by reaching up toward what she wants or by falling down when she does not want to move.
Emotional development: Jill shows no fear of strangers or of being hurt by her actions, which is typical for an infant of her age. She also has demonstrated consistently her wants and needs.
Physical development: Jill's physical development is consistent with a child of her age; however, she does need some encouragement in the area of stair climbing. Her gross motor skills are very advanced and her fine motor skills are also extremely good for her age; she grasps and passes items from one hand to the other.
Social skills: Jill is egocentric, which is quite usual at this age. She seems to enjoy the company of other adults and is not afraid to approach them and ask to be held.

Curriculum implications: Activities are being planned to help Jill in her social skills such as playing beside other children in parallel play. Also there are activities to help her stair-climbing motor skills.
Program plan strategies: Activities involving more pro-social, self-help skills and social interaction will benefit Jill at this time and should be offered to her throughout the day.

Measuring Outcomes

9

Whether students learn something well is more important than when they learn it.

Waterloo County Board of Education (1993)

From the perspective of educators, learner outcomes are a discrete expression of a philosophy of education.

Gayle Mindes, Harold Ireton, and
Carol Mardell-Czudnowski (1996)

A primary supposition of outcome-based education is that all children can learn.
Another OBE mantra is that grades have no meaning.
OBE is meant to do away with time-based learning.

Ron Sunseri (1994)

Outcome-based education assesses a child's mastery of specified learning outcomes based on knowledge, skills, and dispositions.

Focus Questions

1. Why are there such wide differences of opinion about the philosophy of outcome-based education (OBE)?

2. What might you observe in a school or other agency that might lead you to think that OBE was being practiced?

3. What makes OBE approaches to assessment the same as or different from any other assessment approach?

4. How are learning outcomes stated so that they can be assessed?

5. What methods of assessment are compatible with OBE?

6. What issues would you need to resolve if you were to implement a new OBE assessment system?

Learning Outcome

Learners will assess the measurability of learning outcomes and devise ways of observing and documenting their achievement.

History Notes

Outcome-based education (OBE) and its partner, **outcome-based learning** (OBL), result in a different approach to assessing learning than is found in completely open-ended portfolio assessment. OBE and OBL consider "exit outcomes" to be the driving force for educational organization, curriculum design, and assessment. They developed from **objectives**-based philosophies through mastery learning and **competency**-based approaches to the purest forms of OBE/OBL practice, transformational education. Not only educational and psychological theories but also changes in social, political, and economic thinking have driven the development of OBE.

For centuries, academic systems focused on the content of curriculum—that is, what should be *studied*, rather than what specific *learning* results or *how* that learning comes about. The systematic study of how learning happens is a relatively new pursuit. In the early twentieth century, the theory of **behaviorism** led teachers to decide which behaviors they wanted to reinforce in children and which they wanted to modify or eliminate.

In the 1920s and 1930s, teachers in North America and Europe considered that education was beneficial in bettering both the individual and society. Further shifts in thinking about who should be able to access education, its function, and its primary goals led sociologists to see the possibility of a more democratic society, in which everyone could find appropriate employment and have the opportunity to be personally successful. Educators, armed with a new psychology, felt able to be part of this equitable way of thinking. Behavioristic theory could support social goals through the determination of stated objectives in teaching.

Bloom (1956) developed a classification system of educational objectives: knowledge, comprehension, application, analysis, synthesis, and evaluation. He emphasized "mastery learning" through the identification of learning objectives. Krathwohl (1964) classified affective (or emotional) objectives: receiving, responding, valuing, organizing, and characterizing by value. Restated as outcomes, these affective components are a strong element of OBE and tend to incite the strongest criticism because of concern relating to what "affect" is considered desirable. A classification system for psychomotor objectives (Harrow, 1972; Simpson, 1972) received greater acceptance because this hierarchy was clearly observable and less open to misinterpretation.

Meanwhile, Tyler (1965) and Mager (1962) developed systems for curriculum design and instruction, based on statements of clear objectives. These texts became the standard for teachers and confirmed the need for educational purpose, content, organization, and evaluation to be in agreement, with the results both observable and measurable.

The work of William Spady drove the OBE movement in the 1970s. He declared the need for "exit outcomes" that could be demonstrated through **knowledge, skill,** and **disposition** (Spady, 1977). His idea was to make programs more focused and possibly more accountable for achieving their intended goals. OBE evaluation processes typically involve alternative assessment techniques including **observation, role performance,** and **work sampling**. They use, as criteria for assessment, the outcomes that are expected at a stage or grade level. Spady believed that certain problems in American society could be addressed by restructuring education.

Another strand of change was taking hold in the United States and Canada at about the same time, influenced by the emerging schools of developmental psychology. The newer theories offered insights into developmental stages of cognition. The ideas of Jean Piaget and others were adopted in various forms to make the process of learning more child-centered and experiential, and less teacher directed. This style of teaching, usually called "open classroom," involved "active" and "discovery" learning. The philosophy was rooted in **constructivism**, a theory of developmental psychology that emphasizes how learners construct an inner web of meaning from their experience.

Constructivism can be a core concept in OBE although, unlike OBE, it focuses on *processes* of learning rather than on *what* is to be achieved. Some critics of developmental and constructivist theories link them to OBE and argue that these notions lead to a lowering of academic standards in schools. Supporters, on the other hand, typically state that their programs offer developmental learning opportunities that are different from, not less than, the standards of the academics.

Canada, Australia, and New Zealand, along with some European countries, have adopted Spady's principles. Lewington and Orpwood (1993) suggest that, in Canada, various interest groups—including parents, teachers, administrators, businesspeople, and politicians—bring conflicting agendas to any discussion of education: "The uncertainty is heightened by a clash of ideologies, values and expectations about schools; for example, is education primarily a tool of economic renewal, a force for social justice or an exercise in character building?" (p. 2). They clearly condemn OBE and think that OBE could not and *should* not re-engineer or transform society.

Reports of OBE activity in the United States are not entirely positive. Several states have dropped OBE, and fewer districts are willing to launch it. Spady has said that he feels OBE has been misunderstood. In his view, the "program alignment" model of OBE is likely to be the most successful, emphasizing congruence of curriculum and assessment with more traditional outcomes. This stance is, as one critic suggests, "a far cry from the 'transformational' OBE model Spady has long fought for" (O'Neil, 1995). Some educators who do not believe in OBE advocate other types of reform; for example, Sunseri (1994) has supported the "back to basics" movement, which is designed, in part, to counter Spady's view of transformational education.

OBE has met with mixed responses and is practiced differently across North America and Europe. Many teachers who find themselves being required to document learning in this way want to do so while still holding fast to their own philosophies that include naturalistic observation and authentic forms of assessment.

Features of Outcome-Based Education

Outcome-based education (OBE) can take a variety of forms. It tends to focus on the following principles:

1. All people can learn.
2. The outcomes of education should be stated.
3. Curriculum should be designed to ensure that the outcomes are achievable.
4. Outcomes are measurable and observable.
5. This approach to education will help society solve its problems.

Some forms of OBE emphasize self-directed learning as an essential component of the philosophy, although OBE specifies neither exactly how learning occurs nor what the content of the curriculum should be. How learning should occur, how it should be stated as outcomes, and how that learning can be measured are issues open to a variety of interpretations. Since, however, the philosophy of OBE usually implies that individuals construct their own meaning from experience, the underlying practice of OBE is typically based on cognitive learning theory and **constructivism**.

Because OBE is part of a evolving philosophy of education, it may not always be clearly identified. Specific elements may appear as part of a stated OBE approach, may be merged with other educational philosophies, or may exist without any relation to OBE.

Watch out!

You may find that OBE is labeled "mastery learning," "competency learning," or some other name!

Observable components of OBE

The following elements will help you recognize OBE environments:

- Mission statements address how all children can learn, and their goals include issues of social justice.
- The curriculum is framed as learning outcomes.
- Learning is identified in areas of knowledge, skill, and disposition (or attitude).

- Programs offer an integrated and/or thematic curriculum.
- Child-directed learning is emphasized.
- Rote learning is eliminated.
- Children are encouraged to learn from each other.
- The assessment criteria are the learning outcomes.
- Assessment is ongoing and without "failure."
- Assessment involves work sampling and student conferences.
- Dispositions such as being cooperative, being open to teamwork, and being empathetic and pro-social are valued.
- Social studies are a high priority in the curriculum.
- Teachers act as motivators and facilitators.
- Teachers work in teams.
- Computers are used for teaching and for portfolio record keeping.
- Collectivism is the norm for teachers and children.
- Age groups are mixed.
- Children are promoted to the next grade whatever their assessment results.
- Children with special needs are integrated into the class or room.
- Parents are considered to be partners.
- Social interventions may be offered to those "in need."
- The school may be called a "community of learners."

OBE assessment

 Definition: Outcome-based education assessment

> Outcome-based education (OBE) assessment measures an individual's demonstrated competence against specified learning outcomes.

The outcome-based education approach to assessment usually uses alternative assessment techniques—naturalistic observations, role performance demonstrations, and work samplings—rather than traditional testing to summarize the acquisition of knowledge, skills, and dispositions (or attitudes) as related to certain criteria called **learning outcomes**.

OBE curriculum is delivered and outcomes are assessed differently according to the individual philosophy of a school or agency and the localized practices of school boards and administrations. The OBE approach is most often found in school settings, although child-care centers may articulate and assess their own outcomes.

Learning outcomes

Definition: Learning outcome

A **learning outcome** is a broad statement that indicates the knowledge, skill, and disposition that will be acquired through experience or from an educational program.

Each learning outcome should be measurable, achievable, and observable. A child's **role performance**, or demonstration of the **competency**, is evaluated for

- **knowledge:** the information that the child must demonstrate he or she knows
- **skill:** the action that the child must perform (often demonstrating the knowledge)
- **disposition:** the manner in which the skill is performed, or the demonstrated value

Learning outcomes are usually written in broad general terms. For example, the outcome "uses patterns and relationships of the fundamental concepts found in mathematics" implies mathematical understanding and focuses on general rather than specific skills.

The three aspects may not always be stated implicitly in the outcome. Some learning outcomes may state only a skill while implying the knowledge needed for their demonstration. For example, the outcome "communicates ideas in complete sentences" states a skill but also implies that the individual has knowledge of the language. Learning outcomes may exclude dispositions because they are not measurable. For example, the outcome "attends to orally presented stories and poems" requires the demonstration only of attention, not of enthusiasm.

Most learning outcomes specify performance criteria. For example, the outcome "uses a variety of construction materials to build three-dimensional models" requires the understanding of the properties of construction materials, the concept of three-dimensional models, and the connection between these two concepts through the demonstration of a specific skill.

Sometimes learning outcomes are articulated at differing levels of performance on a **rating scale**, such as the following (used by the York Region Board of Education):

1. beginning to work toward mastery
2. not yet consistent demonstration of mastery
3. consistent demonstration of mastery at grade level
4. demonstrating performance beyond expectations

Levels could also be described as

a. skill demonstrated
b. skill emerging
c. skill not yet demonstrated

In some cases, levels of performance may be indicated by the way in which the learning outcome is stated. The outcome statement may be made more complex when the type of skill demonstration is also specified. The following examples show the conditions of performance in brackets:

1. identifies characteristics of mammals living on land (by drawing and labeling diagrams)
2. compares and contrasts characteristics of mammals living on land (by discussing the characteristics in essay form)
3. analyzes the characteristics of mammals living on land to hypothesize possible processes of adaptation (by conducting literature and scientific research and documenting the results)

These learning outcomes indicate the levels of critical thought required for their demonstration. The least challenging might be number 1, the most challenging number 3. The conditions for demonstration may be considered to follow the same sequence of difficulty for many people. However, for some children, drawing might in fact be more challenging than writing an essay or conducting research.

Learning outcomes may be derived from **standards**. These standards may be broken down into performance criteria that are listed within the learning outcome.

- **Standard:** The learner will gain self-help skills that enable that individual to be self-sufficient in modern society.
- **Learning outcome:** A range of self-help skills will be demonstrated that enable the individual to function independently in order to earn a living, live independently, access resources, feed and clothe herself or himself, and become mobile within the local community.

Learning outcomes and educational objectives

Learning outcomes may appear to be similar to the **objectives** that are articulated as part of the process toward achieving educational goals, and some people use the terms "outcomes" and "objectives" interchangeably. Although both are statements of learning that are measurable and reflect the intentions of the educator, there are some significant differences between them.

Learning outcomes	Educational objectives
• use broad statements of learning	• use more specific statements of learning
• refer to end products	• refer to a step toward a stated goal
• focus on integrated learning	• focus on separate "pieces" of learning
• are rooted in OBE philosophy	• are rooted in behavioristic philosophy
• do not relate to a time frame for learning	• typically have a specified time frame
• do not indicate the curriculum content	• may emanate from a set curriculum
• do not imply how the learning will occur	• may imply a process of learning
• include skills and dispositions	• focus on knowledge and skills
• may imply knowledge base	
• are written so that they are measurable, achievable, and observable at the end of an experience or educational program	• are written so that the discrete pieces of learning can be assessed during a formal course of learning
• can fit with authentic assessment processes	• usually require more traditional methods of assessment

Expressing curriculum as learning outcomes

The following excerpt from a Grade 2 music curriculum shows how the curriculum can be expressed as learning outcomes. These particular outcomes focus on knowledge rather than specific skills. The references to the children's aesthetic sense show how dispositions can be included in outcomes.

Source: Ontario Ministry of Education and Training, *The Arts: The Ontario Curriculum, Grades 1–8* (1998).

The OBE controversy

It is impossible to include a chapter about measuring learning outcomes without mentioning that OBE is a controversial philosophy of education. Those who disagree with the approach offer such strong philosophical and political criticisms as the following:

* OBE is an exercise in social engineering.
* OBE contradicts some religious beliefs.
* OBE manipulates personal values and attitudes.
* OBE is a move away from content-based education.
* OBE reduces the family's role in the child's nurturance and education.
* OBE diminishes educational standards.
* OBE represents a move from individualism to collectivism.

Many people may have a problem with only one or two components of OBE or may be uncomfortable about some local practices related to OBE. Others may be challenged by an aspect of the "new age" practices without determining their source or appreciating the interconnected nature or real goals of OBE philosophy. Teachers may be concerned that some OBE practices are not labeled as such or that the origins of OBE are unclear.

Proponents of the purer forms of OBE believe that, if implemented thoroughly with teachers who are well aligned with its principles, OBE offers an opportunity for broad-based and far-reaching educational improvement. They see the potential for significant social impact, enabling those who were traditionally disadvantaged to be more successful and to make a more positive contribution to society by being more productive. They believe that a more equitable society is possible if the educational process in general, and the educators in particular, facilitate the acquisition of relevant knowledge, allow for the development of needed skills, and reflect the dispositions that are compatible with social justice. These elements are the basis of the child's learning outcomes according to OBE.

Using outcome-based assessment

The advantages and disadvantages of OBE assessment are perceived differently by those on each side of the debate. The following lists outline some of the most common arguments for and against the system.

Advantages

- Learning outcomes are articulated criteria for assessment.
- Assessment of learning outcomes addresses knowledge and skills.
- Dispositions can be evaluated.
- Values are stated rather than assumed.
- Assessment methods can be flexible.
- Learning outcomes are comprehensive.
- OBE assessment is congruent with OBE curriculum.
- Learning outcomes can be understood by all.
- Learning outcome measurement is fair and applied equitably.
- OBE and OBE assessment are catalysts for social transformation.
- OBE and OBE assessment are congruent with other types of school reform.
- OBE assessment can incorporate other types of assessment.
- OBE assessment is simple and straightforward.
- OBE assessment ensures that learning occurs so that it can be measured.

Disadvantages

- Learning outcomes themselves must be assessed for their appropriateness.
- Knowledge components may be implied rather than stated.
- Many educators are concerned about assessing values and attitudes.
- The stated values may not be acceptable to everyone.

- Assessment methods may be subjective.
- Some learning outcomes are limited to certain subject areas and are not open to interrelated learning.
- If OBE philosophy is found disagreeable, then OBE assessment is also not acceptable.
- Some learning outcomes are open to interpretation.
- The learning outcome criteria are no fairer or more equitable than any other articulated criteria.
- OBE and OBE assessment have the potential to manipulate social systems and beliefs.
- Although educational reform might be necessary, there is disagreement about the nature of OBE.
- OBE assessment may neglect significant developmental assessment.
- OBE assessment assumes that learning only occurs when outcomes are taught or assessed; it does not assess learning that is not included in the stated outcomes.

Measuring Outcomes

Measurement methods

The simplest way to assess learning outcomes is to list them and check off whether or not the child has achieved them. However, the child's performance may not be assessed very accurately, because this method would offer little evidence of *how* the learning outcome had been achieved. The assessment might be improved if the list had a rating scale attached, but this in itself would not increase objectivity or offer details about the performance. If a list or rating scale included observational evidence and used **work sampling** as evidence, the outcomes could be evaluated more meaningfully.

An alternative approach might be to make naturalistic **observations** and, from this recorded data, complete a checklist or rating scale of the expected outcomes. If this method was supplemented by work sampling, the assessment might be more appropriate and reliable. A sample list of learning outcomes with observational evidence can be found on page 302; a sample list with both observational evidence and a rating scale can be found on page 303.

A **rubric** is a scoring system that identifies the criteria for assessing a piece of work or the achievement of a learning outcome. Rubrics might be used as either a template for expectations or as a grading grid. This method might offer more refined assessment, but the results would only be as good as the rubric is valid. Using prepared rubrics that have been tested for reliability and validity may go against the philosophy of OBE, because they are likely to produce results that categorize student performances or even grade them, which might appear to encourage inappropriate competition. Many advocates of OBE, as well as proponents of philosophies of **developmentally appropriate** practice (DAP), think that grades are unhelpful when measuring the competence of young children.

Both **normative** and **criterion-referenced assessments** may be problematic for OBE advocates. Norms could be considered contrary to the philosophy of continual advancement and may be thought to be potentially detrimental for cultural reasons, or minority groups might be seen as disadvantaged or underrepresented in the normative profile. Any criterion other than the learning outcomes themselves may well be considered incompatible with OBE. OBE systems may use developmental profiles such as **checklists** as part of their assessment processes, but this practice does not fit OBE in a pure form.

Self-evaluation may be part of the assessment process even for very young children. Some institutions encourage this practice and ask preschool and kindergarten children to comment on their work and play and to select "best work" items as portfolio samples. Older children can be provided with methods for more careful reflection, which may involve using happy and sad faces, devising a visual rating scale, recording their verbal comments, or, as they become literate, writing their own reflections. Personal **learning logs** and reaction papers may also encourage self-assessment.

On occasion, **peer evaluation** may be used. Children are frequently subjective in their reactions; their evaluation of another child's work may be based more on whether they like that child than on a true evaluation. When asked to comment on a peer's drawing, a child might be influenced by whether or not the drawing is representational of an object. If peer evaluation is used carefully as part of the learning process, it can have some merit—for example, in highlighting the teacher's own biases—but it must be undertaken with great sensitivity.

Here is a summary of some possible measurement methods:

1. Use the learning outcomes as a checklist for each child.
2. Use a list of learning outcomes and add a rating scale for each child.
3. Use the learning outcomes as a checklist with observational evidence for each learning outcome.
4. Use the learning outcomes as a rating scale with observational evidence for each learning outcome.
5. Use the learning outcomes as a checklist with observational evidence and work samples for each learning outcome.

6. Use the learning outcomes as a rating scale with observational evidence and work samples for each learning outcome.

7. Record naturalistic observations (**running records** and **anecdotal records**) and, on the basis of this data, check off learning outcomes on a checklist or rate them on a rating scale.

8. Record naturalistic observations, check off learning outcomes on a checklist, and use a variety of forms of evidence (photographs, videotapes, and so on) to support findings.

9. Use prepared learning outcome documentation portfolios.

10. Design customized portfolio or other assessment processes on paper or in computerized record-keeping systems.

Any of the above methods might be supplemented with the use of screenings, standardized tests, or developmental checklists, although these do not measure the learning outcomes directly. In addition, the process might include the child's self-evaluation, peer evaluations, and parental observations.

Thinking About School

Name: _____

How I feel about school	☺ ☹ ☹
How I feel about my friends	☺ ☹ ☹
How I feel about reading	☺ ☹ ☹
How I feel about math	☺ ☹ ☹
How I feel about art	☺ ☹ ☹

My favorite activity is _____

I don't like _____

I am going to get better at _____

This self-evaluation form for Grade 2 students allows children to reflect on their own performance and interests.

Levels of OBE assessment

There are three levels of OBE assessment, reflecting varying degrees of complexity and frequency of information gathering. The lists below show the common assessment documents used at each level; the asterisked (*) items would only be used for elementary grades, not for preschool or kindergarten.

Basic level OBE assessment

• learning outcome checklist

At the basic level, the checklist is usually completed on a weekly or monthly basis. Assessment reports are sent home twice a semester.

Intermediate level OBE assessment

• as above and . . .
• running record observations
• anecdotal record observations
• learning outcome **inventory**
• checklist and observational evidence
• art samples
• work samples*
• photographs of learning outcome performances
• prepared learning outcome portfolios
• parent conference reports

At the intermediate level, information is gathered on a fairly frequent basis, with assessments occurring when they are needed or at least every month. Curriculum may be shaped as a result of whole-class assessments.

Advanced level OBE assessment

• as above and . . .
• video sequences of performances
• contextual information
• health data
• parental observations
• self-chosen work samples
• self-evaluations*
• student conference reports*

At the advanced level, information is gathered and sorted on an ongoing basis. Assessments are made regularly, every two or three weeks, with parent and child participation. In this model, curriculum is adapted to fit individual learning needs as those needs become apparent.

Evaluating learning outcomes as assessment criteria

Learning outcomes need to be measurable, achievable, and observable. Only when these conditions are met can outcomes be used as the criteria for assessment. Teachers should evaluate the outcomes before they are used for any form of assessment.

Watch out!

The fact that a learning outcome is measurable and achievable does not mean that it is a worthy achievement!

Use the following checklist to evaluate learning outcomes as assessment criteria. The answer to each question should be "Yes."

1. Are the learning outcomes up to date?
2. Were the learning outcomes developed in accordance with community agreement?
3. Are the learning outcomes relevant to the local community?
4. Are the learning outcomes consistent with prevailing and minority religious perspectives?
5. Are the learning outcomes congruent with the range of political thought expressed in the community?
6. Do the learning outcomes allow various forms of demonstration for different learning styles, varying cultural experiences, and individuality?
7. Are the learning outcomes reasonable expectations developmentally?
8. Are there separate learning outcomes developed for children with special needs within the institution?
9. Are the core learning outcomes based on typical maturational levels for the age/stage of the child?
10. Are the learning outcomes progressive from level to level?
11. Are the learning outcomes achievable within the given time constraints?
12. Are all subject areas represented in the learning outcomes?
13. Is there an equal distribution of learning outcomes among subject areas?
14. Is the curriculum geared to providing the opportunity to acquire the knowledge required in the learning outcomes?
15. Is the curriculum geared to providing the opportunity to acquire the skills required in the learning outcomes?

16. Can all children experience some success?
17. Are there learning supports in place to achieve the learning outcomes?
18. Are the learning outcomes stated in understandable language and not open to interpretation?
19. Are the learning outcomes sufficiently broad to allow for contexts of demonstration to change?
20. Is the listing of the learning outcomes comprehensive in all subject areas?
21. Does the set of learning outcomes reflect the philosophy of the institution?
22. Is the set of learning outcomes congruent with the curriculum delivery model?
23. Do all the teachers and parents (and children where appropriate) understand the learning outcomes?
24. Can the school provide extra supports for those experiencing difficulties in achieving the learning outcomes?
25. Is there opportunity for children to progress beyond the learning outcomes?
26. Is there a regular process for refining and updating the learning outcomes?
27. Is there a process to ensure that the learning outcomes are measured appropriately?
28. Is there a confidential process to assess achievement of the learning outcomes?
29. Is there a process to ensure program accountability?
30. Is there regular in-service training for teachers in OBE and assessment?

Responding to measured outcomes

It might seem that the job is done when a child's learning has been assessed. In fact, this is only one part of the learning cycle. Assessment should lead to action. The next step is to evaluate the effectiveness of the program and to determine whether the program is meeting the learning needs of some, or all, of the children. One or more of the following responses may be appropriate:

- **Individualize the program.** If some children are not successful, determine why and address the issues; for example, a child may speak English as a second language, be socially isolated, have joined the group late, or be experiencing stress. Children who have not been learning well do not necessarily lack potential, but they may require appropriate learning conditions. Observe individual performance carefully; children with unusual personalities or different learning styles may be more successful than you first thought.
- **Fill in the gaps.** Teachers may address the outcomes that are not yet fully achieved by providing activities, experiences, or program content to bridge the gap.

- **Continue the program.** Many teachers decide to keep their responsive program running as it is in the belief that development cannot be hurried.
- **Continue with the current plan but lengthen the time frame.** Allowing more time is consistent with OBE, but changing the time frame may be impossible since classes and grades are usually structured on an annual cycle.
- **Continue evaluating.** Some children acquire learning rapidly (and unexpectedly).
- **Have the child repeat the program.** Repeating a level fits with the idea that some people take longer than others to achieve the same outcomes; however, lack of promotion may have counterproductive social and emotional implications.
- **Offer an intensification of the program.** Special help may be offered within the classroom. Some children need more direct "teaching" while others are more self-directed. Children with special needs and disabilities may require resource teachers or assistants to help them.
- **Offer extra help outside the classroom.** Some children need one-on-one help to attain certain skills. People may dislike special treatment and argue against withdrawing a child from the class, but the real problem comes from labeling the child (which can be a self-fulfilling prophecy).

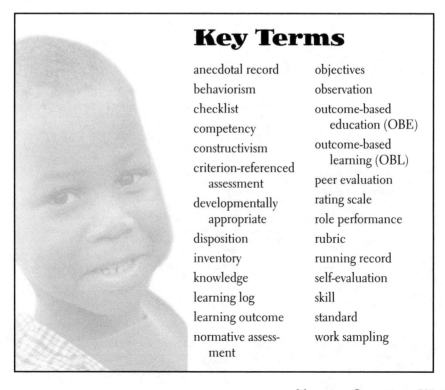

Key Terms

anecdotal record

behaviorism

checklist

competency

constructivism

criterion-referenced assessment

developmentally appropriate

disposition

inventory

knowledge

learning log

learning outcome

normative assessment

objectives

observation

outcome-based education (OBE)

outcome-based learning (OBL)

peer evaluation

rating scale

role performance

rubric

running record

self-evaluation

skill

standard

work sampling

Observation Sample

This excerpt from an assessment shows how observational evidence can be used to measure a child's achievement.

Learning Outcomes in the Arts: Grade 3

Child's name: ___Ben___   Recorder: ___Rhonda___

Age/D.O.B.: ___8 years, 5 months___   Date: ___January 16, 1998___

By the end of Grade 3, students will

Outcome	Observation	Achievement
Understand that many aspects of a work of art contribute to its effect	Ben liked the kinetic art at the gallery and tried to copy it using coat hangers and ping-pong balls. Ben noticed the use of white, blue, and gray in a Monet print.	Ben is alert to these ideas but needs more experience of variety.
Understand that each of the arts requires specific skills	Ben was unsuccessful at his first attempts at making a mobile. Ben acknowledged the difficulty of building a model boat that another student brought in.	Ben is very aware of these skills and has made some efforts to increase his repertoire.
Use the right terms in discussing ideas and techniques in works of art, as well as their own artistic ideas	Ben mentioned several techniques when he discussed painting, collage, and model making.	Ben has the interest as well as the terminology.
Understand that the arts of different cultures have similarities as well as differences	Ben received our work on Native art positively. He suggested that the simple lines in the drawings were bold and quite like cartoons telling a story.	Ben's appreciation of art is impressive, and he has sensitivity to the different art forms and links to culture.
Understand that technology can be used in creating works of art	Ben uses CorelDraw to create images. Ben noticed the large metal modern sculptures outside the bank towers. He said, "They must be pretty well built so they don't fall down on people."	Yes.
Be aware that certain aspects of works of art, such as rhythm and balance, have a wider appreciation in daily life	Ben responds to music and likes strong beats and clear lyrics, which he says are like some of the pictures we have discussed in class.	Ben's attitude is open; he needs time and experience.

Source: Adapted from Ontario Ministry of Education and Training, *The Common Curriculum, Grades 1–9* (1993).

Observation Sample

This excerpt from a child's assessment shows how a rating scale and observational evidence can be used to measure the learning outcomes.

Learning Outcomes: Kindergarten

Child's name: __Anjana__   Recorder: __Carolee__

Age/D.O.B.: __5 years, 2 months__   Date: __February 2-25, 1998__

Time in kindergarten: __4 1/2 months in senior kindergarten__

Context: __informal observations in classroom and outdoors__

Key: 5 = achieved outcome; 4 = emerging skill; 3 = attempts performance;
2 = engaged but not ready; 1 = not yet engaged in performance

What children will know and be able to do at the end of kindergarten:

Culminating performance	Progress	Observation/inference
8. Children will demonstrate basic understanding of the concepts of time, quantity, shape, distance, speed, space, seasons, size, weight, floating and sinking, sorting, matching, seriating, mass, and other core ideas using appropriate descriptive language.	3	- some understanding may be limited by language - uses language associated with all math concepts (except mass and floating--no experience yet) - explores properties of materials and uses them appropriately - counts to 25+ by rote and counts objects correctly to 6 - sorts items according to one characteristic - seriates 3 items correctly - matches items by where they belong
9. Children will identify similarities and differences between objects.	4	- points out similarities between items using color labels - ? limited by language to describe differences
10. Children will represent their understanding of the world through a variety of creative media.	4	- uses painting to express ideas enjoys working with clay but does not make obvious representations
11. Children will estimate what will happen in basic situations.	3+	- guessed "what would happen if . . ." (some correct answers)
12. Children will memorize short poems, songs, and rhymes.	4	- joins in with songs and rhymes - recites sounds (meaning?)
13. Children will retell an event, describe objects, and identify the key features in a story.	2	- language limitations but will point to images representing key ideas in a story
14. Children will count items accurately up to ten and continue counting in sequence up to twenty.	5	- as in #8 above
15. Children will demonstrate their understanding of cause and effect in basic situations.	3	- repeats actions that create a response - demonstrates some logic in guessing some relationships

Screening and Assessment

10

Our society has embraced the formal testing mode to
an excessive degree.

Howard Gardner (1993)

The basis of screening is the comparison of the baby's
level of development with that of an average baby of the
same chronological age; it follows that a thorough
knowledge of the "average" or "normal" is essential.

Ronald S. Illingworth (1990)

The ultimate goal of testing should be to help a child in
some way—physically, developmentally, educationally,
or emotionally—if this is not the case, why do it in the
first place?

Virginia E. McCullough (1992)

The most effective evaluations
of a child's skills are achieved
in natural settings. Absorbed
in a creative experience, this
girl with Down's Syndrome
demonstrates a longer-than-
expected concentration span
and extraordinary attention
to detail.

Focus Questions

1. What efficient method of recording information would let you see if one or more children in a group are in particular need of attention?
2. How can you decide if a ready-made test is of any use to you?
3. What is the difference between an observation and a test?
4. If you were to read a psychologist's test results for a child in your care, how might you react?
5. Can you be as objective as a visiting psychologist or other professional assessor in evaluating a child in your care?
6. Why should parents and teachers be wary of standardized testing results that do not match what they know about a child?

Learning Outcome

Learners will identify the place of screening tools, standardized tests, and formalized assessments in the process of early childhood assessment.

History Notes

Evaluation of a child's development was done by informal observation before more scientific measurement methods were devised. In the eighteenth and nineteenth centuries, those interested in educational philosophy—such as the philosopher Jean-Jacques Rousseau and the educational reformers Johann Heinrich Pestalozzi and Friedrich Froebel—focused on identifying children's characteristics and their consequent needs. Their work encouraged innovation and change but brought about little evolution in practice during their lifetimes. They did not advocate testing for individual children, but they did acknowledge the importance of assessing children's needs. It is unlikely that they would have considered formal measurement of development a desirable way of finding this information, but they, with other educational pioneers, precipitated a more scientific approach.

Standardized tests were first developed as scholastic aptitude tests to help evaluate university applicants. Educators then saw a need to make further evaluations of children within the school system. In some cases, children were streamed into achievement levels; in others, testing led schools to offer individualized learning support, make grade level changes, or replan curriculum.

In the United States, educators have become increasingly aware of the dangers inherent in some testing procedures—such as systemic **bias**—and they have gradually demonstrated concern about state-wide tests, although they have been reluctant to let testing go. In Canada, testing systems vary from province to province, but they commonly rely on a standardized curriculum, which is used as a guide for progression as the student develops. Boards of education are bending to the notion that accountability is dependent on testing. The two are obviously related, but standards do not, of themselves, improve simply because outcomes are measured. The tests used for **assessment** are frequently unsuitable for Canadian children because of their inherent biases; even when more valid and reliable, they are often used inappropriately. In societies like Canada, made up of an ethnically diverse population spread over a wide geographic area, educational standards must be both regionally and personally sensitive.

Educators who advocate **developmentally appropriate** practice are increasingly concerned about the "trickling down" to child care and early education of negative elements of educational practices employed in later childhood. Systems that are heavily dependent on overstructured curriculum and testing in narrow competencies are being translated into developmentally inappropriate curriculum and assessment for infants, toddlers, and preschoolers. Anxiety over achievement levels is influencing teachers and caregivers to use methods that will ultimately reduce quality rather than improve it.

The younger the child tested, the greater the cause for concern. **Readiness tests** have been widely used with preschool and kindergarten children to evaluate their skill level and consequently their apparent readiness for the next step. Many educators express alarm at the trend, but the proponents of higher standards claim that these measures are necessary.

Features of Screening and Assessment Tools

Child Development Focus

Screenings and assessments may
- identify a child with a specific need
- confirm or contradict naturalistic observation
- provide detailed developmental profiling
- suggest developmental supports
- imply readiness for a specific program

Screening

Definition: Screening

Screening is a process of reviewing and evaluating specific behaviors or characteristics of individuals across a population or group in order to identify those who are in need of a more thorough assessment or specific support.

Screening procedures usually involve the use of **standardized tests** in assessing a large population of children in a brief, relatively inexpensive manner. They are usually carried out by medical professionals, psychologists, or diagnosticians. Informal screening techniques are used by child-care workers and teachers as they identify children whose development is in some way atypical.

Early identification of a health concern or developmental challenge can make a significant difference to the child's later progress. **Early intervention** programs may be available either through resource teachers at the school or agency or through external consultants. Often the team of professionals will develop an **individual program plan** for the child, indicating the daily interventions and support that the adults can contribute.

▶▶ **Key Features: Screening tools**

- use standardized procedures to evaluate the health or development of a large number of children
- identify children in a special category of need
- usually nonparticipatory
- usually in a testing location

Taking a Special Look: Screening for disabilities

One reason to observe children is to ensure that they are supported in every way possible. Beyond the daily observation of children's development, screening is required to determine whether they are have any specific condition, syndrome, chronic illness, or other exceptionality. The need for ongoing observation and assessment does not stop once a child has been screened; subsequent open-ended observation may reveal other concerns not identified by a tool aimed at screening for one or two specific conditions.

Assessment

Definition: Assessment

Assessment is a process of information gathering, review, analysis, and determination of the needs of an individual. The process may target particular health, developmental, or contextual information, or may be more holistic by including a wide variety of facts and opinions.

The assessment process may take many forms, including informal observation, standardized tests, teacher appraisal, developmental **checklists**, parental observations, **self-evaluation**, medical diagnosis, or any combination of these or other methods. Assessments may be carried out by a variety of professionals such as health professionals, psychologists, social workers, teachers, caregivers, early childhood specialists, and parents; the most effective process involves a team.

▶▶ Key Features: Standardized assessment tools

- review the behavior of a child in a specified developmental domain
- measure performance with reference to a norm or specified criterion
- are considered valid and reliable
- may require trained skills for administration
- sometimes administered in a testing location

Evaluating standardized tests

Even if your early childhood philosophy emphasizes evaluation through naturalistic observation, you will need to recognize the strengths and weaknesses of standardized tests and be able to evaluate the data they provide. The trend has been to use a wide variety of standardized tests to determine **readiness, skill acquisition,** developmental stages, learning disabilities, and so forth. You should acknowledge why some teachers think tests are desirable and useful; you do not have to agree with the approach or follow the trend if you think you can gain the information more easily, naturally, effectively, and cheaply by other means.

Underlying the belief in standardized testing is a philosophy that values some or all of the following ideas:

- A test can measure what it purports to measure.
- A child's behavior can be evaluated by comparison with an expected norm or stage.
- A test situation can elicit objective information.
- The outcome of a test is a predictor of later development.
- Children evaluated to determine deficits in development can benefit from improved programming.
- Teachers and other professionals are able to determine behavioral goals and learning on the child's behalf.
- Test data can increase an agency's accountability.
- Evaluation of published information regarding the **reliability** and **validity** of tests can filter out possible bias or inaccuracies.
- Testing procedures are advantageous to curriculum development rather than detrimental.
- Test results can be interpreted accurately and successfully by teachers, caregivers, and parents.

Professionals frequently use tests to aid their work, in the belief that tests will offer more **objectivity** than other sources of information. Considering the way in which the data are collected, it is doubtful whether the results can be objective; children may not perform the same way in a "test" situation as they would in their natural surroundings. Some tests are administered by someone other than the regular caregiver; here the child might be affected by the strangeness of the test or the tester. Without an appreciation of a child's regularly displayed behavioral patterns, you can tell little about her or his overall progress. With little understanding of the family background, current issues in the child's life, or what is normal for this child, there is limited scope for effective evaluation.

Watch out!

Standardized tests are only one of the useful tools available to teachers. Dependence on test results can lead to incorrect assessments!

Comparisons with norms determined from a general population may give some reference point; but, even if accurate, the norms will tell you little about what to do if a concern is identified. Particularly worrisome is the undetected cultural **bias** of many well-used standardized tests. For example, in some cultures, children do not learn self-help skills early in life because they are fed, clothed, and toileted. This does not mean that they will not develop "normally." Results that reflect acquired skills may not give you more than a quick "snapshot" of current development—in themselves, they do not determine appropriate curriculum.

Watch out!

Avoid making assumptions about children's skills in terms of a race through developmental stages!

If a test has a well-founded theoretical basis, it may indicate the stage through which a child might next progress. When the child will develop particular skills is as much a matter of maturation as a response to the adult's strategy. All that is needed is the construction of an appropriate learning environment and responsiveness to the child's adaptations to that environment. The test serves little purpose.

A key issue in evaluating a test is to determine what exactly it does measure. The title or naming of the test items does not necessarily indicate the content, so you cannot be assured that it actually tests what it is meant to test. For example, an IQ test may not test intelligence but problem solving, which is only one component of IQ. Another example is the readiness test—it may evaluate a set of skills that the test designer believes are important in determining readiness for, say, kindergarten. In fact, it may reflect skill acquisition in some areas, but not all; social skills are commonly left out.

Before administering a test, teachers and other professionals should consider the appropriateness of that test for children with varying language and cultural heritages, ages, personalities, interests, motivations, powers of concentration, and so on. There are so many possible built-in biases, such as skill assessment in one developmental domain being dependent on expressive language, which may not be the area tested. Test items may rely on familiarity with particular domestic items unknown to a child because of her or his culture. Questions may rely too heavily on logical thought, which may be an unfavorable approach for a creative mind. A child's self-esteem may be evaluated as "poor" because the test did not allow for differing emotional responses.

Administrators and teachers who wish to test children to prove their own effectiveness work on the premise that quality programming is measurable in the short term. Significant data are provided only if the "before" and "after" are measured, and then only if the data are viewed in terms of stages of growth rather than adherence to timeliness. There are many other, more successful ways of determining quality programming. Why not spend the time with the children and the money on the learning environment?

Taking a Special Look: Referrals

Observing children can lead us to realize that further assessment is necessary. Some situations require professional skills beyond our scope or from a different discipline. While the parents should initiate contact with any specialist, the teacher or caregiver may prompt the parents to do so by sharing observations. For example, Kerry's teacher observed that Kerry was not responding to questions, was easily distracted at story time, and would sometimes make comments out of context. She shared her observations with Kerry's mother, who took Kerry to an audiologist. Tests showed that her hearing was slightly impaired, and she was fitted with a hearing aid.

Standardized tests as part of authentic assessment

If teachers and caregivers use standardized tests instead of ongoing naturalistic observation, they will miss much of "who the child is." However, there can be a real place for standardized tests, and their results, in a child's **portfolio**. A test may confirm what the teachers have seen naturalistically, in which case they can feel assured that their perceptions are correct. Or the assessment might highlight something that they were unable to detect using everyday techniques. In this case, they might respond in a variety of ways, perhaps questioning the test's outcome, checking its findings in other ways, or seeking another professional opinion.

The amount of formalized assessment material in an average portfolio is likely to be very small. For some children, though, there might be a greater need to consult professionals who use standardized testing. Children for whom there is an increased likelihood of needing formalized assessments include those who

- exhibit behaviors that are difficult to interpret
- have socially disruptive or adaptive difficulties
- suffer chronic health conditions that influence their developmental patterns
- have long-term, serious, or terminal illnesses
- were born prematurely or with low birth weight and continue to have growth or developmental difficulties
- are diagnosed by professionals as having a particular condition or syndrome
- are born into families with genetically inherited conditions
- appear to be developing at a slower rate than expected
- demonstrate particular gifts or talents
- demonstrate discontinuity in their developmental pattern
- regress in their development without obvious reason
- were brain injured
- communicate with difficulty or fail to make attachments
- show particular difficulty in paying attention
- experience traumatic events or changes in their lives
- are "at risk"
- have been physically, emotionally, or sexually abused
- show unusual ways of processing information
- have a sensory deficit
- experience mobility challenges

Interpreting assessment results

Some medical assessments and psychological evaluations look like they are written in a foreign language! In a way they are, because they use professional jargon. The most obvious way of understanding what they say is to ask the person who wrote the report, or to ask for a summary of the findings. It can be helpful to understand some frequently used terminology, but many reports mention syndromes, conditions, and assessment results that even those working in the field would have to look up.

Most important for the adults working directly with the child are the recommendations, interventions, and program plans that they will have to facilitate. These must be very clear; in some cases, parents, caregivers, and teachers may have to acquire certain skills in order to help the child. Ask lots of questions, and offer continued input to the ongoing assessment process by recording plenty of observations as the child is involved in the program.

Using standardized tests

Advantages

- Standardized tests are usually designed and tested by psychologists.
- Tests provide uniformity of administration.
- Tests give a quantifiable score.
- Assessments may be **norm-referenced**.
- The tool will have been tested for validity.
- Repeated use may increase reliability.
- A wide choice of tests is available.
- Standardized tests offer specific information to parents, teachers, and psychologists.
- Tests may be administered to an individual or a group.
- Tests identifies what the child can do.
- Tests may support other informal assessment.
- Tests may identify potential concerns.
- The results may help indicate appropriate curriculum or activity plans.
- The results may be available quickly.

Disadvantages

- Standardized tests may be carried out by adults unknown to the child.
- The child may not respond well to a testing situation.
- Contextual information may not be available.
- Scores may be open to inappropriate interpretation.
- Norms may not consider cultural or language diversity.
- Users of tests are not always aware of validity concerns.
- Reliability within one group does not determine intercultural reliability.
- Users may not have access to an appropriate range of tests.
- Standardized tests are expensive to buy and administer.
- Training may be needed in administration of tests.
- Test scores should not be used alone to determine evaluation and to construct a program for the child.
- Time taken in testing and test preparation might be better used for play or learning.
- Tests may focus on what the child *cannot* do.
- Skills not identified on a test will not be evaluated.
- The child may be able to demonstrate the skill in a nontesting situation.
- A lack of evidence of skill mastery may be incorrectly interpreted as an inability to perform the task.
- Tests may provide insufficient evidence on which to base program planning.

- Most tools lack flexibility.
- Tests may not be based on current teaching principles.
- Some assessment/screening tools are not designed for diagnosis but are frequently accepted as such.
- The outcome may result in inappropriate labeling.
- Screening and assessment tools may be seen as interchangeable (their purpose is quite different).
- There is seldom opportunity for parental input or observation.
- Tests may be used by teachers as a "quick" method of evaluation in preference to naturalistic observation, which can be time consuming but more effective.

Choosing a Test

If you appreciate the concerns regarding testing, you may not wish to use a standardized test. But if you do use one, the following criteria will help you choose a test that best fits your purpose.

1. **Determine your role in the testing procedure.** Are you to be receiving the test results as a teacher, supervisor, administrator, parent, or child-care worker? You will want information that is useful to your role and presented in a way that you can easily understand and interpret. The role of tester may be appropriate for you if the test you choose fits your qualifications and experience. If you need to find a tester, factor this into your decision making. Consider the possibility of receiving training to administer a test.

2. **Identify your reason for wanting a test to be carried out.** Do you want very specific information about one child, screening for all children in your care, or an assessment system to be used over a period of time? Whatever your reason, evaluate the tests available to you to see if they can give the screening or assessment data you wish. Are you sure a test measures what you want it to measure?

3. **Determine the type of assessment you need.** Are you focusing on health, development, or particular skill development? You will have to find a test that contains the criteria for evaluation that fit your needs.

4. **Ensure that the test covers the age and developmental stage levels that you need.** Are you choosing a test because the title sounds correct, but the span of developmental stages is insufficient? To re-use a test over a period of time, check for the inclusion of a wide developmental range.

5. **Check that the test will offer information in each of the developmental domains or skills you are seeking.** Are you sure that these domains or skill

areas are sufficiently detailed to give information about the quality as well as the presence of the behaviors you want tested?

6. **Review the test material for objectivity, use by others, and published critiques.** Have you read only the information produced by the writers and publishers of the test material, or have you checked it out more thoroughly? Here you will want to look at test validity, reliability, and usefulness.

7. **Find out if the test can be easily obtained, and how much it costs.** Do you have a budget that allows for the testing you want? Many testing procedures require updating or use of duplicate forms that have to be purchased after the initial kit is obtained. Pieces of the testing equipment may also get lost, so check that you can replace these easily. Some tests have copyright prohibitions that prevent you from copying the evaluation forms. A few tests may need computer access for scoring; you will need to ensure that your hardware is compatible. Most of the recognized tests and inventories require a verification of professional qualifications before materials can be bought.

8. **Evaluate the test items for possible bias (cultural, gender, or language).** Will the test be appropriate for the particular children you have? You will need to consider test items to ensure that they are not faulty in their expectation of Eurocentric responses or strong dependence on English language skills. If there are such items as a doll in the assessment kit, could you change the type of doll to reflect the ethnicity of the child to be tested? Look to see if there are any built-in biases that might be relevant in tasks such as sequencing a story line or identifying similarities or differences that might be perceived differently by children from various cultural heritages.

9. **Consider the test's ability to give you results that are easily understood.** Can you interpret the statistical information and understand the terminology of test results? Money is wasted in buying testing procedures that are probably quite valid in themselves but have scores or outcomes that the teacher cannot use. This type of information may lead to impressive record keeping but very little help in program planning.

10. **Think about how you will use the test results.** Do you intend to use them for screening or across the group for evaluation? What will you do when you identify a child in need of further assessment or an individual program plan? You need to work out if you can make the necessary responses. What will you do with the information on the progress of each child?

If you use a test with caution and understand its limitations, it can help you be more sensitive to a child's needs and lead you to modify the learning or social environment. If it enables you to work with your colleagues and the child's parents more effectively, you may have chosen an ideal method of testing. You might, though, have collated better information through informal observation and achieved your intentions more effectively and inexpensively by using a parent-involved naturalistic assessment.

The most effective assessments are **portfolio assessments** that involve a variety of information-gathering techniques. This ideal form of evaluation includes a careful selection of observations of the child's spontaneous play and social learning activities, some interpretive checklists of skill development, any necessary screening or test results, examples of the child's art, evidence of academic skills in the child's products, photographs of the child's activities or constructions, video recordings of play, audio recordings of language and music, and any other samples that reflect the child's processes and products of learning. From these, a more accurate, broad, and contextual picture of the whole child can result. The percep-tive teacher can select the methods most pertinent to his or her skills, time, budget, and team of colleagues, as well as to the context, the degree of parental involvement, and the child's stage of development.

Key Terms

assessment
bias
checklist
developmentally
appropriate
early intervention
individual program
plan (IPP)
norm-referenced
assessment

objectivity
portfolio
portfolio assessment
readiness test
reliability
screening
self-evaluation
skill acquisition
standardized test
validity

Environmental Observation and Evaluation

11

A well-planned environment will be safe and healthful, will meet the needs of both children and adults, will facilitate classroom management, will enhance the process of learning through play, and will support the implementation of program goals and objectives.

Carol E. Catron and Jan Allen (1993)

In observing a program it is important to remember that no program can ever be perfect, and that a given day will never be repeated.

Carol H. Schlank and Barbara Metzger (1989)

Outdoor play spaces need careful design. Their safety depends on satisfactory equipment, careful use of space, good supervision, developmental appropriateness, and suitable use.

Learning Outcome

Learners will select and use techniques to record and evaluate components of the environment that influence children's development.

History Notes

Ecological psychology, or studying behavior in natural settings, was a new approach in the early 1950s. It represented a move away from laboratory methods. The ecological approach considers behavior in the light of the **environment** in which it occurs. The dual importance of behavior and environment was underlined by psychological research showing how a child's development could be fostered by stimulating environments.

In the 1950s and 1960s, sociologists identified links between social class and achievement, determined the cultural elements of child rearing, and highlighted the importance of a child's language environment. These and other research outcomes led both sociologists and ecological psychologists to understand that the environment was the strongest influence on a child's development.

A gradual awareness of the implications of Jean Piaget's work changed educational practice. The learning environment was seen as important, because Piaget explained how children learn through discovery. In a process in which the child builds an inner knowledge of his or her world, the teacher's responsibility was to determine that environment. Structuring the environment to maximize the learning experience became a dominant theme in teacher education in the late 1960s and 1970s.

Not only did practice within educational establishments change; the buildings themselves were reorganized to facilitate greater movement and **child-centered** activity. New buildings reflected this philosophy with the use of more open planning for flexible usage. Architects, social policy makers, and educators influenced a generation of educational establishments, creating very different learning environments from those of the early part of this century.

Conflict between traditional teachers and child-centered educators has been significant and has not lessened to this day. Many of the problems with these changed learning environments arose because their users did not always keep pace with, or believe in, the new theories. Success in using a particular environment was consequently variable.

Much recent research focuses on the social and emotional aspects of a child's development. While somewhat abstract, it has offered insights into the importance of the child's social **context**, bonding, attachment, and emotional environment. Bowlby's (1965) classic work on bonding has been superseded by a wealth of information on attachment, which supports the notion that adequate caregiving can be offered both inside and outside the family home. Explanations of how children develop a sense of self, form social relationships, and gain moral awareness help us appreciate their needs more fully. This understanding allows us not only to appreciate the stages of a child's development, but also to design, utilize, observe, and evaluate environments to ensure that they support development.

Researchers have taken several different approaches to **environmental evaluation**. Some have evaluated the environment in terms of the children's acquisition of skills in various developmental domains; others have considered the role of parents, the health of the children, or caregiver satisfaction. Methods of data collection have varied, but the outcomes have some similarities. The child–adult ratio is seen as the most important indicator of a good quality environment. The particulars of what constitutes an ideal environment vary, but there is a common belief that the children's individual styles, as well as familial and cultural backgrounds, must be appreciated and taken into account.

The Child's Environment

Previous chapters have focused on the child as an individual and on the way in which the child behaves. This chapter moves away from this approach to observation of the child's whole experience. Here we look at a range of aspects of the child's **environment** and attempt to evaluate them on the basis of overall suitability. Appropriate and high-quality features are determined by research.

Any individual understands the world through interaction with the environment. In the early years before abstract thinking, children internalize information about the environment in an accepting, noncomparing way because that is all that is known to them. Through physical explorations of the environment, they make some sense of everything they perceive. It is for the children's sake that you observe and evaluate their environment. Taking responsibility for their experience of the world necessitates an effort to see the world through their eyes while holding in mind what you think appropriate according to your own attitudes and beliefs about how children develop.

Child Development Focus

Environmental observation and evaluation may
- lead to physically or personally safer environments
- allow for better use of space for all activities
- maximize learning opportunities
- increase inclusion of all children
- improve adult–child relationships

The child's context

Wherever a child spends time is an important place. Any adult involved in a child's life would do well to take time to find out about and observe the child in her or his different settings. The obvious scenarios will include home and a child-care center or school. Time may be spent in other places and in travel between them; these are also significant to the child's experience of the world.

The child's **context** includes all factors that pertain to family composition and lifestyle, residence, geographic location, economic status, social relationships, culture, space, resources, exposure to values, attitudes and beliefs, personal belongings, safety, guidance, religious practices, peers, opportunities in education, and caregivers, as well as the more concrete physical environment.

The child's curriculum

Every part of a child's life is his or her "**curriculum**." Experience takes place at any time of the day or night. There should be few boundaries for caregiving and **nurturance**; emotional needs may have to be met at any time. Physical safety is just as relevant indoors and out, at home or in child care. Routines of sleeping, eating, diapering, or independent self-care are just as significant as peak programming time. **Spontaneous play** and discovery may bring about more learning than a designed curriculum activity and therefore need to be planned for and valued. All the adults and the other children in the child's life are important. These people, what they model, and how they respond to the child are also an integral part of the child's environment.

The view that acknowledges all aspects of the child's life to be important gives the adult a great responsibility.

Watch out!

We may not be able to change some elements of the environment—but those that are inappropriate and *are* changeable must be altered!

Features of Environmental Observation

Definition: Environmental observation

Environmental observation involves observation of a child's surroundings, including those elements that are designed and implemented deliberately and those parts that occur without planning.

Why observe the environment?

Observation of a child's environment may seem overwhelming; there are so many locations and aspects to that environment. You need to decide which components of the child's environment you can reasonably focus on. You may have one or more of the following reasons for observing an aspect of the environment:

- to help understand a child's family context (home life), cultural background, ethnicity, and sociological perspectives, so that appropriate sensitivity and accommodations might be demonstrated
- to help understand a child's behavior and its causes and provide appropriate guidance
- to help appreciate a child's conception of the world and support the child's learning
- to help understand a child's level of social competence and provide appropriate experiences and support to improve the social environment
- to help plan new experiences based on the success or failure of previously planned learning environments
- to facilitate a better routine for the day, to use space effectively, to minimize safety risks, and to promote health and healthy practices
- to support a child's emotional development through improvement of the organization of groups, space, and time
- to determine a child's interests by identifying his or her interaction with the environment
- to maximize the adults' interactions so that the language environment and nurturance are enriched
- to identify the influence of climate, temperature, color, space, and atmosphere on individual or group behavior
- to help appreciate the **hidden curriculum** pertaining to attitudes, beliefs, and practices that influence the atmosphere, self-esteem, and success
- to fulfill a regular process of program evaluation and upgrading
- to ascertain that a balanced curriculum is being offered and to ensure that program planning can be shaped by the children's interests and development

Objective observation of the environment

Ensuring **objectivity** when observing the child's setting is a challenge because we all perceive information according to what is familiar. Family lifestyle, affluence or poverty, social relationships, and accommodation type can be difficult to observe objectively because we are influenced by our own world view. Observations can easily be tainted because a bias is so ingrained that we fail to recognize it. What is overcrowded to one person may be spacious to another; one individual's poverty is someone else's affluence.

A poor physical environment does not automatically lead to poor experience. Adults can shape the physical environment with their attitudes.

Separating observation from **inference** is necessary to observe contexts with the most objective eye. Practice this by first making statements that are matters of fact; then return to the statements, and from them make valid and supported inferences. Dealing with observation and inference as different entities will help you avoid subjective comments about children's lives, which can lead to inappropriate interactions with the family, unjustifiable attitudes, and incorrectly based planning. The difference between observation and evaluation of the child's environment is that the first relates to what you see and the second to how you assess it.

▶▶ Key Features: Environmental observation

- involves observing and recording data on how items in the environment are being used
- identifies all components of the child's environment, including hidden curriculum
- includes observing children's behaviors related to any of these components
- usually naturalistic

What to look for in the child's environment

Anytime and anywhere are the times and places to observe a child's environment. If you observed a child's context only in formal times of organized learning in a planned environment, you would miss most of the child's experiences.

Much of the information regarding a child's context might be gathered directly from the parents. Some parents may, quite fairly, resent your request for this information. Some initial interviews for child care are held in the child's home—if this is the case, avoid the clipboard checking-off approach, as this can seem clinical and off-putting to parents. Seek the information through more natural conversation about the child's home situation, but be clear that you are recording some of the bits of information that the parents reveal. Be sure to record the information source.

```
                        Environmental Information

Child's name: _____    Recorder: _____

Age/D.O.B.: _____    Context: _____

┌──────────────────────┬──────────────────────────────┬────────────────┐
│ Characteristic       │ Observation/objective data   │ Source         │
├──────────────────────┼──────────────────────────────┼────────────────┤
│                      │                              │                │
```

Here are some of the things you might look for that constitute the "environment" in a broad sense.

Home and family

- **nuclear family** composition and size
- siblings, birth order
- health and abilities/disabilities of family members
- extended family location
- changes in family composition, moves
- nonfamily adults or children in child's home
- religious or cultural heritage and practices
- mother's role and guidance
- father's role and guidance
- sibling or others' role in caregiving and guidance
- day-care or school enrollment and attendance
- memberships
- play space, play materials
- books and toys available
- TV/VCR/videogames
- employment of parent(s), hours of work
- finances
- accommodation (rented/owned)
- number of rooms (privacy/shared)
- clothing availability
- laundry facilities

- kitchen, food preparation equipment
- temperature, indoor climate
- practical needs met or not met
- safety of environment
- outdoor space
- transportation, access, mobility
- need for social work, therapy, or other support
- family concerns

Sociological and geographic context

- nation and city of residence
- urban or rural location
- accommodations (rented/owned, etc.)
- neighborhood type
- population density
- building types, age, and history
- transportation, mobility
- shopping amenities
- local industry
- community services and buildings
- banks, finances, economy, taxation, benefits
- cultural mix of local population
- play spaces
- schools
- child-care provision
- community concerns
- religious buildings and practices
- health services
- restaurants, cafés, fast-food outlets
- social organizations
- communications
- climate
- prevalence of disease
- demographic changes
- employment
- social services

Child-care agency/school

- type of establishment
- number and organization of staff, full-time or part-time schedules, supply staff
- funding and budget
- age ranges, hours open, size of group or classes, ratios
- catchment area
- staff qualifications, union membership, gender of staff, representation of ethnic groups
- indoor space and organization
- interior design of space
- philosophy reflected in design
- stated philosophy
- variety of activities (name them)
- washrooms—access, independence level for child
- routines—meals, sleep, etc.
- food preparation and snacks
- policies, procedures, meetings, communications
- guidance strategies
- exterior space and equipment
- emergency plans
- safety precautions indoors and out, first aid
- transportation
- parking available
- resources, space, and access
- involvement by parents, parent education available
- involvement with community—trips, in center
- relationships between staff and children
- types of programs offered
- expendable resources—paint, paper, soap, etc.
- temperature and humidity
- hygienic practices
- sick child provision
- staff liaison with child's home
- entry or acclimatizing plan for new children
- accommodation for children with special needs
- cultural or ethnic mix of those enrolled
- referrals to other services if and when required
- personal belongings, storage
- structure, flexibility, expectations

Recording information about the child's environment

Looking at the world with the eyes of a child is one of the most effective ways to see a child's environment. Recording the context involves much more than checking off the presence or absence of an element of that environment on a list. Compare the checklist and the narrative in the following excerpt from a family context.

Family Context

A. Checklist	Yes	No
Child has own room		✓
Child has personal storage space in bedroom	✓	
Child has appropriate toys	✓	
Child owns books	✓	

B. Narrative

Sian lives in a downtown third-floor apartment with her mother and two older sisters, with whom she shares a small bedroom. The apartment offers space for Sian to play between the kitchen and living room where Mom can watch over her. The three girls go to the library with their father alternate Saturday mornings when he has custody. The shared arrangement with the father is amicable, according to Mom, who said she liked to have a little time to herself when the girls are out. When they returned to sleep at home on Saturday night, I observed Mom playing with Sian. Her toys are not all new but seem to challenge Sian without causing her much frustration. . . .

You can see that the **narrative observation** offers much more detail and background than the yes/no approach of a **checklist**. While open to greater interpretation, the narrative description also indicates pertinent information that explains the content of the checklist. Neither is incorrect, but each tells a different version of the situation. Checklists can be handy when you want to record lots of information quickly, and they serve as a reminder to look for particular criteria. The narrative takes much longer but is more open-ended, so it can include what the observer thinks pertinent.

A compromise between these two methods of collecting information is possible. A series of directed statements, prompts, or questions can have a yes/no component but leave room for comment. Open-ended questions can be added to ensure the possibility of including any information that comes to light. The environmental observation on page 348 records comments on a list of criteria.

Visual representations of the environment can be made using photographs, video recordings, and **mappings**. Any of these might be useful additions to checklists, narratives, or **rating scales**, and they offer a record of the context that may be quicker, more detailed, and lasting. Recording the environment in one of these ways enables the observer or evaluator to consider the depiction away from the site or after the context has changed.

Acetates designed for overhead projection can be used for floor plans and overlaid to make comparisons of the use of space. Alternatively, a blank floor plan can be drawn and photocopied so that room arrangements can be planned.

Features of Environmental Evaluation

 Definition: Environmental evaluation

Environmental evaluation involves consideration of all the planned and unplanned aspects of a child's surroundings to ascertain their appropriateness or quality.

- evaluates any or all components of the environment against the stated philosophy of care and education
- determines the effectiveness of any or all components of the environment for safety, inclusion, nurturance, learning potential, or other criteria
- develops plans to improve environmental conditions in line with program goals
- usually naturalistic

Measuring the environment

The narrative or checklist approach to observation can give a relatively unbiased account of a child's environment. This account is desirable for the purpose of understanding what constitutes the child's context, but it does not offer direct evaluative information from which a social worker might determine intervention, a caregiver might decide on compensatory measures, or an educator might appreciate contextual barriers to learning. An assessment of the child's environment requires a much deeper understanding of all the component parts of the child's experience and how they interact. A **qualitative evaluation** of any environment must be based on a clear understanding of the philosophy underlying the construction and use of the environment. For example, it would be difficult to assess a curriculum for its **anti-bias** characteristics if the concept of anti-bias education is not appreciated.

The simplest evaluation format is the checklist. The items must be clear, focused, and as complete as the writer can determine. A more open-ended checklist may have space for inclusion of "add-on" items. A rating scale can be attached to the list of environmental criteria, allowing a more qualitative response rather than a simple indication of presence or absence or a "good" or "bad" response to the item.

Checklist for Quality Inclusive Education

I.1.c Visual displays reflect equity in representation.   F   O   S

I.1.c.16. Do I display photographs and pictures of children involved in a variety of activities? e.g.,

- girls in nontraditional activities   ☐   ☐   ☐
- boys in nontraditional activities   ☐   ☐   ☐
- children with varying abilities engaged in active play   ☐   ☐   ☐

Examples:

	F	0	S
I.1.c.17. Do I balance displays of children in special, traditional clothes in appropriate situations (e.g., celebrations) with displays of children in their everyday clothes?	☐	☐	☐

Examples:

I.1.c.18. Do I use visual displays that represent diversity?

	F	0	S
• varying physical, visual, and sensory abilities	☐	☐	☐
• varying ages	☐	☐	☐
• varying appearances	☐	☐	☐
• different beliefs	☐	☐	☐
• multicultural backgrounds	☐	☐	☐
• different family compositions	☐	☐	☐
• females and males	☐	☐	☐
• multiracial backgrounds	☐	☐	☐

Examples:

F = frequently   0 = occasionally   S = seldom

Source: Rachel Langford et al., *Checklist for Quality Inclusive Education: A Self-Assessment Tool and Manual for Early Childhood Settings* (1997).

Standardized checklists prepared by an authority are checked for **validity** and **reliability**, but reflect a particular philosophy. The best-known, most reliable, and most user-friendly environment rating scales are Harms and Clifford's *Early Childhood Environment Rating Scale* (1998) and Harms, Cryer, and Clifford's *Infant/Toddler Environment Rating Scale* (1989). Another rating scale developed by Harms and Clifford, the *Family Day Care Rating Scale* (1989), is appropriate for evaluating home-based child care.

These scales can be used in a variety of early childhood settings, and can be administered by a wide variety of professionals, including teachers and assistants. They include a rating of each item on a scale of 1 to 7 and space for comment. Each of the major categories is divided into several components, which have clearly identified criteria for grading. The procedure is straightforward, but good results are dependent on general early childhood training and familiarity with some terminology. Checklist and rating scale results can be gathered from both parents and professionals. If the criteria are clear, the perspectives of both parties may offer insight; frequently the outcomes will be similar.

FAMILY DAY CARE RATING SCALE

Name of lead caregiver _Roberta Poole_

No. of caregivers present _1_

Most children attending at one time _5_

Number of children present today _5_

Ages of children enrolled (youngest to oldest in months) _9 mos._ to _40 mos._

Name of rater _Pam Eckard_

Position of rater _Resource and referral trainer_

Date _June 29, 1998_

SPACE AND FURNISHINGS FOR CARE AND LEARNING

1. Furnishings for routine care and learning
   1 2 3 ④ 5 6 7
   Children kneel on chairs—not adapted for their size.

2. Furnishings for relaxation and comfort
   1 2 3 4 ⑤ 6 7

3. Child-related display
   1 2 ③ 4 5 6 7

4. Indoor space arrangement
   1 2 ③ 4 5 6 7
   Space safe and adequate.

5. Active physical play
   1 2 3 4 ⑤ 6 7
   Fenced outdoor area. Uses activity records indoors on rainy days.

6. Space to be alone
   a. infants/toddlers
   1 ② 3 4 5 6 7
   Doesn't interact frequently enough.

   b. 2 years and older
   1 2 3 4 ⑤ 6 7
   Private space used for older children's games.

Total Space and Furnishings (Items 1–6)
_27_

BASIC CARE

7. Arriving/leaving
   1 2 3 4 5 6 ⑦

8. Meals/snacks
   1 2 3 4 ⑤ 6 7

9. Nap/rest
   1 2 3 4 ⑤ 6 7

10. Diapering/toileting
    ① 2 3 4 5 6 7
    Doesn't wash hands after each child.

11. Personal grooming
    1 ② 3 4 5 6 7
    Children's hands not washed before eating.

12. Health
    1 2 3 ④ 5 6 7
    Not careful about preventing spread of germs; no set rules for giving medicines to children.

13. Safety
    1 2 ③ 4 5 6 7

Total Basic Care (Items 7–13)
_27_

FAMILY DAY CARE RATING SCALE

Quality Control: A Manual for Self-Evaluation of a Day Care Agency (Campbell, 1987) offers a format for assessment covering all the functions of a child-care center. Supervisors and day-care operators may find this a useful overview of the center's effectiveness in general. It may not offer sufficient detail to help educators examine the learning environment in a specific area. The steps for program evaluation are, however, clear and applicable even when used with other evaluation systems. Another strength of the evaluation is that it includes parental input. Based on a rating scale attached to "Standards of Performance Statements," parents provide their scoring of components including administration, facilities, staffing, admissions, and the program.

Measurement of the home and family environment has intrigued many researchers, who have thought that there is a link between characteristics of families and IQ or achievement. Caldwell (1979) devised a measure of the environment called the HOME inventory (Home Observation for Measurement of the Environment). A series of yes/no questions are scored by an evaluator who makes observations and interviews the parent about a typical day in the family, interactions with the child, and the material environment. The original intention was to see if the HOME inventory scores and the children's IQs were correlated, which they were. Replication of these studies has highlighted the importance of some of the components of the inventory, but the reasons for the correlations are not all completely understood. The studies do, however, agree that features of children's home environments do have an impact on their performance, competence, or IQ. While the inventory was designed for research purposes, it could be used for evaluation of individual families. What to do with the results is less certain—intervention in the family style and interaction can take place only when there is clear dysfunction that has been identified by the relevant professional.

Evaluation tools are devised as the need becomes evident. A standardized procedure may fulfill your need, but you might find it more useful to make a tool to fit your specific requirements. Modification of or additions to existing measurement tools may also be helpful, but you should be aware of the possible reduction of validity and reliability if you alter the tool.

Appropriate environments

"Appropriate practice" is a commonly used phrase in child-care circles, but its meaning varies. A holistic and child-centered approach is the philosophy of the American organization called the National Association for the Education of Young Children (NAEYC), which has identified the components of **developmentally** appropriate practice. Based on research into the determinants of quality programs, the NAEYC publication *Developmentally Appropriate Practice in Early Childhood Programs Serving Children from Birth Through Age 8* (Bredekamp, 1987) serves as a manual of good practice. It can be used to evaluate an existing program or to help develop provision from scratch. The age–stage integrated components of appropriate and inappropriate practice cover goals, ratios, and teacher qualifications as well as specific developmental practice. If each item is used with a rating scale, putting appropriate practice at one end and inappropriate at the other, the charts become an evaluative tool. The items can be used as a focus for discussion with parents or staff as well as in a more structured environmental evaluation.

Integrated Components of Appropriate and Inappropriate Practice for 4- and 5-Year-Old Children

	Appropriate Practice	Inappropriate Practice
Teaching Strategies	• Teachers prepare the environment for children to learn through active exploration and interaction with adults, other children, and materials.	• Teachers use highly structured, teacher-directed lessons almost exclusively.
	• Children select many of their own activities from among a variety of learning areas the teacher prepares, including dramatic play, blocks, science, math, games and puzzles, books, recordings, art, and music.	• The teacher directs all the activity, deciding what children will do and when. The teacher does most of the activity for the children, such as cutting shapes, performing steps in an experiment.
	• Children are expected to be physically and mentally active. Children choose from among activities the teacher has set up or the children spontaneously initiate.	• Children are expected to sit down, watch, be quiet, and listen, or do paper-and-pencil tasks for inappropriately long periods of time. A major portion of time is spent passively sitting, listening, and waiting.
	• Children work individually or in small, informal groups most of the time.	• Large group, teacher-directed instruction is used most of the time.
	• Children are provided concrete learning activities with materials and people relevant to their own life experiences.	• Workbooks, ditto sheets, flashcards, and other similarly structured abstract materials dominate the curriculum.

	Appropriate Practice	Inappropriate Practice
Teaching Strategies	• Teachers move among groups and individuals to facilitate children's involvement with materials and activities by asking questions, offering suggestions, or adding more complex materials or ideas to a situation.	• Teachers dominate the environment by talking to the whole group most of the time and telling children what to do.
	• Teachers accept that there is often more than one right answer. Teachers recognize that children learn from self-directed problem solving and experimentation.	• Children are expected to respond correctly with one right answer. Rote memorization and drill are emphasized.

Source: Sue Bredekamp, *Developmentally Appropriate Practice in Early Childhood Programs Serving Children from Birth Through Age 8* (1987).

A program can be observed and evaluated by turning performance objectives into questions. Schlank and Metzger (1989) developed an easy-to-use, open-ended tool that uses a minimum of jargon. The questions could be answered in a yes/no way but are likely to provoke some explanation. This type of evaluation allows for parental input and is clear in its philosophy because each component starts with a statement of intention.

Learning (physical)

It is important for young children to gain awareness of their bodies and to develop their physical capabilities. They may need help to feel okay about their differences in size, appearance, strength, and agility.

Is there opportunity for active physical play?

Does the caregiver encourage children to become involved in physical activities?

Is there large equipment such as a climber, large boxes, or a rocking boat for large muscle development? Is there adequate space indoors or outside for physical activity?

Are there activities to help children develop an awareness of their bodies in space? For example, are there activities such as walking on a line, moving to music, and jumping in place?

Are there materials such as blunt scissors, peg boards, and puzzles for the development of small muscle coordination?

Source: Carol H. Schlank and Barbara Metzger, *A Room Full of Children* (1989).

Devising Your Own Environmental Observation or Evaluation Tool

Informal methods

A list of environmental components may be sufficient for your observation purposes. Serving as a reminder of things to look for, it may help refine your perceptions. As you form the list, you will probably become aware of the philosophy behind the criteria; the fact that you include an item means that it is important to your belief system. You might want to explore the philosophy some more to ensure that the listing is complete and organized. As you work, you may see the size of your task and decide to limit it to a more specific focus. You might also want to structure it under separate headings so that the parts become more manageable. As the list evolves, you might phrase the items throughout more consistently as questions with a yes/no reply or as statements to be graded. Trial use of the checklist or rating scale will probably reveal some gaps and items that need to be restated. This kind of tool can be useful as it fits the setting well, but remember that it may not be as inclusive or objective as other tested tools, or may not be valid or reliable if used elsewhere.

Watch out!

We can evaluate a child's environment only if we have articulated what, to us, is the optimal environment!

Structured methods

An effective tool records or measures what it intends to measure. To devise an effective tool for environmental observation or evaluation, you would need to work through the following process:

1. Identify the need for evaluation.
2. Specify the area(s) to be observed/evaluated.
3. State the goals of the project and the philosophy underpinning the tool.
4. Seek team/committee support.
5. Assign the roles and responsibilities of team members.

Philosophy Statement and Indicators

We believe that . . .

Children's development needs to be observed, understood, and supported for it to occur at an optimum level. Objective recording of ongoing observational information guides decision making in all elements of our work with children.

In our lab schools, the indicators that this is being practiced are as follows:

Indicators	Yes	No	Examples of practice
1. Children are observed daily and written notation made.			
2. Observed information reflects the whole child and does not only focus on problem areas or difficulties.			
3. Daily observations are used as a basis for program planning and are obviously reflected in activity plans, room arrangement, schedule, etc.			
4. Developmental assessments are completed biannually and shared with parents in formal meetings.			
5. Ongoing observations of children are shared with parents through daily interactions and written notation.			
6. The opportunity is provided, and parents are encouraged, to share their observations about their child.			
7. Ongoing observations of children are shared with other staff in a professional manner to facilitate problem solving and program adjustments to better respond to children's needs.			
8. Students' assignments requiring the collection of observational information are welcomed and supported.			

Source: Centennial College Early Childhood Education Programs and Child Care Centres, *Philosophy Check-In* (1998).

6. Clarify the process through which the tool is to be devised.
7. Agree on a time line.
8. Arrange for a trial of the tool.

The methods for devising a tool may include any or all of the following activities, separately or simultaneously and in any sequence:

- researching existing tools
- reviewing stated philosophies
- evaluating the environment using different tools
- brainstorming ideas
- surveying parents, professionals, and /or the community to determine opinions and needs
- revising previously used tools
- identifying component parts of "environment"—that is, stating criteria
- editing
- trial runs with items used as checklists, rating scales, or open-ended criteria
- clarifying grading criteria

Some advantages of using a more structured method for devising a tool are that the tool is more likely to fit the need, to reflect a common philosophy, and to be more detailed and inclusive than an informally put-together checklist. It will probably have wider acceptance and be more reliable in its use.

As fashions come and go and research supplies us with new information, you are likely to find your existing observation and evaluation tools less effective than you would want. Updating, changing, and recreating will continue to be necessary. The qualitative methods are most likely to need modification because the purely observational approaches make fewer inferences and are more open.

The aspects of the environment most frequently reviewed by caregivers, parents, and educators include the health and safety, quality, appropriateness, and effectiveness of the environment. You do not have to keep these categories if other concepts are more suitable. Each major category can have many component parts that you will need to identify. Where evaluation is based on an interpretation of observed information, the specifics will need to be clarified. For example, the definition of "high family involvement," "low ratio," or "type of accommodations for special needs" would have to be specific. A qualitative observation or evaluation relies on the recorder's consistent use of terms.

Indicators of appropriate environments for young children

The following lists show broad components that warrant consideration when observing, evaluating, or planning group care environments. Specific criteria may be itemized according to needs and settings. When defined, these components may be used as a checklist, as the criteria for a rating scale, as the basis for a narrative description, as the focus of group discussion, or as a starting point for plans to create or modify an agency. The items are not prioritized.

Environmental Evaluation

Rating scale:

5 = exemplary performance: maintains high standard
4 = good performance: exceeds minimum standard
3 = adequate performance: meets minimum standard
2 = below adequate performance: falls short of minimum standard
1 = poor performance: fails to meet minimum standard

Indicator	Observation	Identification of need	Rating

This chart can be used to evaluate environmental indicators. Depending on the school or agency, the standard against which performance is measured may be determined by the province or state, by a local board, or by the agency or school itself.

General indicators of a quality environment

- clearly stated philosophy based on researched indicators of quality
- small group size
- low ratios
- demonstration of meeting individual needs
- appropriate and stimulating learning environment
- developmental appropriateness of design, activity, and guidance
- high degree of staff training
- high level of parental involvement and partnership
- positive quality of interactions with children
- effective teamwork with parents and professionals

- low staff turnover
- positive communications among staff
- optimal safety, health, and nutrition
- regular program evaluation

Inclusion

- clearly stated anti-bias policy and practice
- welcome and **inclusion** of all children whatever race, appearance, class, ethnicity, ability, gender, origin, religion, or beliefs
- high level of staff training in **diversity**, anti-bias education, and acceptance of diverse life styles
- avoidance of superficiality, **tokenism**, **stereotypes**, and **touristic approaches**
- presentation of cultural and ethnic variety of music, images, scripts, artifacts, food
- sensitivity to range of familial backgrounds
- accommodations made for differing needs and abilities
- resources available for children with **special needs**
- support of first language and cultural heritage

Every area of the curriculum needs to be assessed for its inclusion. The effectiveness of an anti-bias curriculum can be measured by environmental checklists and observation of the children within the setting.

- developmentally and individually appropriate activities and experience
- activities in which children of all abilities can participate and cooperate
- large-group and small-group activities that allow children to participate at their own level
- range of activities and playthings to allow independence but also provide challenges to children of varying abilities
- active encouragement of community involvement in program
- effective communication and partnership with parents
- knowledgeable and sensitive communication with all children, demonstration of respect to all
- avoidance of labeling
- access to support resources to aid inclusion
- ongoing evaluation of all books, images, toys, playthings, and materials for their appropriateness
- policies and practices that address racism, prejudice, judgmental behaviors, and exclusion
- effective communication with parents and involvement of families
- acknowledgment of a wide variety of parenting styles and child-rearing practices

Taking a Special Look: Inclusion and integration

In recent years, the **integration** of children with special needs into mainstream care and education has become an important trend. The benefits of this practice include a more natural environment for all children and an openness to diversity. However, child-care agencies and schools that advocate integration face challenges related to time, equipment, support, and expertise. These issues need to be resolved before inclusion and integration become feasible in many mainstream settings.

Physical well-being

- good **hygienic practices** that control spread of infection
- policies, practices, and protective measures for physical and emotional safety
- minimizing of inappropriate stressors
- clearly stated policies and procedures for health, safety, and nutrition
- first aid provision
- demonstration of meeting physical and emotional needs
- adequate kitchen equipment, food storage, preparation, and serving
- nutritious and healthful snacks and meals

- adequate space and opportunity for physical play
- positive **role models**
- resources and support available to parents on health-related issues
- provision for sick children
- toileting and washroom adequacy
- protection from extreme weather conditions
- health education for children
- regular program evaluations and review
- environment constructed for safe use and healthy development
- routine safety checks
- supervision adequate for well-being
- maintenance of a safe environment
- risk taking encouraged with safety boundaries
- provision for rest, sleep, and quiet
- high level of cleaning, sanitizing, and sterilizing appropriate to building, furniture, and materials
- pollution monitoring
- appropriate waste management
- reporting to parents of changes in behavior, health conditions, and general development
- effective communication with parents
- maintenance of appropriate temperature, humidity, and air quality
- confidential and complete health records
- adequate water supply
- community health resources accessed
- adequate training and professional development in health, safety, nutrition, and first aid for all staff
- compliance with local, provincial or state, and federal legislation and regulations
- sensitive consideration of parental wishes
- accident and serious occurrence records
- documentation and sensitive handling of allergies and medical conditions
- regular and continuous observations concerning health and behavior
- early identification of behavioral changes and indicators of concern
- demonstrated positive attitudes to well-being
- appropriate storage of materials
- accommodations for specific abilities and disabilities
- separation of areas for different purposes
- maintenance of health and management of stress of caregivers

Nurturance

- small group size
- low child–adult ratio
- personal space for belongings
- acceptance of individual styles and behavioral patterns
- opportunities for personal attachments
- demonstration of enjoyment, fun, and enthusiasm
- sensitivity, responsiveness, and attunement to individual children
- positive role models that demonstrate the range of human feelings
- opportunity for play activity with peers
- consistency of caregivers
- **routines** and patterns that are flexible in order to meet individual needs
- stability of family and home circumstances
- positive approaches to changes in accommodation, caregiving, and parenting
- positive communications between parents and caregivers
- maintenance of stable, consistent program
- opportunity for family involvement in the program
- design of agency for contrasts to suit mood and temperament
- acceptance of cooperative and solitary activity
- play encouraged as therapeutic activity
- observation and monitoring of the program's emotional climate, with adaptation as necessary
- demonstration that feelings are acknowledged and allowed
- encouragement of emotional expression
- open exploration of reality and fantasy
- positive communication with children about feelings, changes, crises
- encouragement and modeling of empathy
- encouragement of objects that link home and agency
- support to develop strategies to cope with strong feelings
- acceptance of diversity in action and voice
- practical indication of support for self-identity
- opportunity for self-categorization and self-discovery
- support for positive body image awareness
- fostering of creative thinking and success
- demonstration of support in separations and reunions
- catering to needs for privacy and quiet
- clear indication of the parameters of behavior and the consequences of noncompliance

- opportunity for making choices
- open-ended activities that avoid correct/incorrect responses or winners and losers
- process-focused activity
- authentic praise and encouragement
- support of adults for each other
- common philosophy of nurturing among caregivers

Learning

- design meets children's needs
- child-sized furniture and materials
- opportunity for choices
- self-direction allowed
- spontaneous play valued
- focus on process of activity
- freedom of movement enabled
- developmentally appropriate programming
- observation of children to help determine needs and programs
- opportunity for experimentation/discovery
- sensitivity to the child's stage of understanding
- space organized for movement flow
- child's lead followed
- demonstrated adult enthusiasm for child's efforts
- activity extended (but not directed) by adults
- curriculum evolved from child's interests
- activities that allow for success and minimize failures
- communication of ideas encouraged
- open-ended and evolving program
- stimulation in all developmental areas
- focus on hands-on activity and participatory learning
- avoidance of limiting structure and rigid timetabling
- family contribution and participation encouraged
- natural curiosity encouraged
- provision for imitative, fantasy, and sociodramatic play
- language supplied to help children classify and conceptualize new experiences
- adult interactions that help children focus on learning
- knowledge extended from the base of the child's current understanding

- language, print, symbols, and literature promoted
- sensory exploration promoted
- strategies to overcome challenges offered
- role models and support of moral understanding
- clear direction regarding expectations and behavior
- program changes made at differing pace according to needs
- wide range of traditional and nontraditional curriculum components
- child's range of feelings acknowledged
- interactive learning and construction of knowledge
- understanding of similarities and differences encouraged
- sensitivity to different needs of members of the group
- plans for individual and collective needs
- **therapeutic** or **compensatory care**
- programming responsive to changing needs
- well-trained staff who share a philosophy of how children learn
- cooperation and communication in partnership with parents
- regular program evaluation
- regular observation of children
- learning planned from what is known to what is unknown
- open-ended activities and materials to encourage creativity
- curriculum that makes appropriate and achievable challenges
- higher-order thinking promoted
- success encouraged and errors treated as a learning experience
- skill development monitored
- program justified in measurable ways
- community resources used and dialogue maintained with community representative
- compliance with all regulatory bodies

Responding to an Environmental Evaluation

We can move toward better planning and programming by carrying out an environmental evaluation. But before we attempt to change things, we need general agreement among the team members that change is necessary. Change can be unsettling and can make people feel that they have been failing at their jobs; consequently, certain team members may need some time and encouragement before they are ready to adapt their program or way of doing things. In some circumstances, change is directed by administrators or even driven by legislated requirements, and it may be necessary to move forward without complete agreement. An efficient and effective process of change is most likely to facilitate a successful outcome. If the process is agreed on at the start, and all parties have an opportunity to participate, people are more likely to "buy into" the need to make changes.

What to change

Evaluating the environment may, like any other kind of evaluation, tell us what the problem is, but evaluation does not usually tell us how to fix the problem. Review your evaluation outcome and do some collective problem solving to determine how to address each issue. Some issues may be related, so one solution may address several problems.

Remember that not everything is within your power or scope to change. You may not be able to improve your budget or change the staffing situation overnight! You might want to filter your results according to what you all consider possible. Some flexible people may prefer to take a look at whatever needs changing, however challenging it may appear. As a group, you might decide to be undaunted by some of the obvious limitations. The bigger issues, concerning philosophical issues or values, are harder to address. If it becomes necessary to look at these big issues, you should do so, but accept that they will take effort and heart-searching.

List the things that need to be changed, with or without reference to the relative difficulty of achieving the change. Examine the list to see if the items are superficial and cosmetic or whether they indicate a more profound problem. Your evaluation may indicate several unconnected items, or they may be clustered in a particular area. Scattered items are more likely to be bits and pieces that can be "fixed" quickly. A group of related things is more likely to show a need for philosophical reflection or deeper evaluation of the program achievement or direction. It is also possible that your bits and pieces actually relate to deeper issues; check for any connection.

You may need to prioritize your activities according to available time, money, and professional development opportunities.

Taking action

After reviewing and discussing the data comes action, preferably with a time line and responsibility designations. Time lines need to be realistic; keep in mind that a transition period might be harder to deal with than the change itself will be when fully implemented. The scale of the change also makes a difference to how the change should be accomplished. If you need to move some furniture, few people may resist the change. However, if the change requires a review of policies about inclusion, equity, and anti-bias, you might need a lengthy discussion on the topics.

Depending on the urgency of the issue, the possibility for making changes with speed, and the need for complex negotiation, you will want to create an **action plan**. Using a prepared format can be helpful. A sample action plan can be found on page 349.

The process of evaluation and change needs to be a cycle rather than a "one-off" experience. If environments are evaluated regularly, the process of change will become easier. While individual responsibility for evaluation is commendable, programs for young children are more likely to be of high quality if there is a mandated requirement for regular evaluation. This process requires a budget, encouragement, time, and staff training.

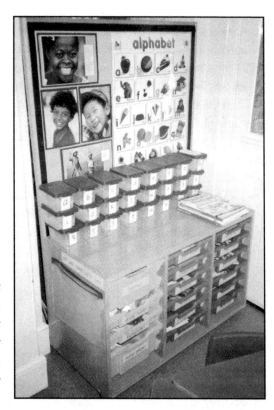

Every element of the environment should be evaluated regularly. An inclusive environment will provide books and other materials suitable for children of varying abilities, and will represent cultural diversity in its materials and displays.

Key Terms

action plan
anti-bias
checklist
child-centered
compensatory care
context
curriculum
developmentally appropriate
diversity
ecological psychology
environment
environmental evaluation
environmental observation
hidden curriculum
hygienic practices
inclusion
inference

integration
mapping
narrative observation
nuclear family
nurturance
objectivity
qualitative evaluation
rating scale
reliability
role model
routine
special needs
spontaneous play
stereotype
therapeutic care
tokenism
touristic approach
validity

Observation Sample

This environmental observation provides comments on various health issues. These observations could be used to evaluate the environment and to suggest changes and improvements.

Environmental Observation: Health

Observer's name: _James_   Date: _December 9-12, 1998_

Setting: _Unionville Child Care Center (a center for 60 children, birth to school age)_

Number of children: _14_   Number of adults: _2_

Ages: _3 years, 3 months, to 5 years, 7 months_

Space available: _L-shaped room. One end used for gross motor activities, sleep, and meals._

Purpose of observation: _To evaluate the environment for its part in supporting the children's healthy development_

Criteria	Observations
1. Good hygienic practices	regular hand washing, disinfecting using a bleach solution
2. Positive role model	teachers follow proper practice
3. Nutritious snacks/meals	bananas, oranges, apples for snack; meal plans appear appropriate
4. Protection for extreme weather	2 sets of clothes are stored (spring/winter)
5. Effective communication with parents	parent board, reports, and communication logs
6. Health education	posters, art supplies, talking
7. Toileting/washroom adequate	2 washrooms (1 large, 1 small)
8. Parent reports	separate reports for everyone
9. First aid provision	box/kit in each room, large in office
10. Parental wishes adhered to	notes taken in communication log and passed on if necessary
11. Separation of areas for different purposes	reading area, blocks, floor toys, table toys
12. Appropriate storage	large cupboard in each room labeled and cleaned regularly
13. Accommodations for abilities and disabilities	minimal stairs, lots of space for gross motor, etc.
14. Accident and serious occurrence records kept	each child has a file, book of "serious occurrences" shown to parents
15. Maintenance and stress for caregivers	separate/comfortable room for breaks and quiet time
16. Demonstrated positive attitudes to well-being	talk about vitamins in oranges, milk, etc., hand washing
17. Documentation and sensitive handling of allergies and medical conditions	lists in every room for every child and separate larger one in individual rooms

Observation Sample

This action plan begins with concerns raised by an environmental evaluation. It outlines how the issues will be addressed and provides a time line and a list of specific responsibilities for each team member.

Action Plan to Improve the Environment

Agency: Yellowknife Center _____ Date: June 1, 1998 _____

Recorder: Julie _____ Date of environmental evaluation: May 22-27, 1998

Context: The ministry suggested that we do a program review because we have had our new supervisor for a year. We used criteria from Martin, *Take a Look.*

Concern	Action to be taken	Time line	Responsibility
Supervision because of safety concern around swings in preschool play space	- Children not allowed to play on swings until a new barrier is erected	Urgent (today)	**JD** will announce to staff that the swings are not to be used until a barrier is put up. **JD** will contact plant operations and request building of barrier. **JD** will inform staff when swings can be used again.
A wider depiction of culture in books, pictures, and playthings	- New pictures to be collected and made into puzzles - New toys to be purchased	Soon (this week) Also long term	**KC** will order new posters from NAEYC. **JD** will ask all staff to collect pictures for use in materials. **JD** will set aside money in next year's budget for dolls and new books.
Staff training in guidance strategies for toddlers	- Investigate budget - Investigate external facilitators/workshops - Investigate internal workshop/resources	Medium term	**JD** will seek funding. **KC** will review literature to find professional development opportunities. **DD** will make contact with possible facilitator. **RC** will bring in guidance video to be viewed on lunch breaks.
Improve observation and record keeping	- Create new portfolio system	Medium term (by end of October)	**JD** will seek funding and review fundraising possibilities. **DD** will develop a plan for communicating portfolio philosophy to parents. **LR** will see if she can find a box system (from pizza boxes). **JD** will organize a series of evening meetings for **group** to plan process.

Glossary of Key Terms

action plan: a plan for change developed as a result of an environmental assessment

analysis: a process of gaining understanding of recorded observational data involving study of the component parts, making inferences, and validating them

anecdotal record: a short narrative account of a child's activity

antecedent event: the event that occurred just before the example of the sampled behavior

anti-bias: active opposition to negative or inappropriate attitudes towards or pre-judgment of groups of people, practices, or things

assessment: measurement of an individual's performance or development, which may be based on observations, tests, or the person's products

assumption: a reaction to a behavior that accepts as true an approach that has not been considered objectively or analytically

attachment: the process of making an affectional bond or emotional connection with another individual

authentic assessment: assessment of learning that focuses on performance of skill or knowledge in a manner that is within an appropriate context

baby book: a book or album used for recording information about a child, frequently used by parents

bar chart: a graph that represents observational material as bars of varying heights along an axis

behavior: the actions and reactions of an individual, that is, anything a person does, whether deliberate or not

behaviorism: a school of psychology that involves the objective study of responses of animals or human beings. Behaviorism views learning as being formed from the outside, by the external environment.

behavior modification: a technique that attempts to change, stop, or modify a demonstrated behavior

bias: a known or unknown perspective or point of view that has personal or philosophical values, attitudes, or beliefs that influence objectivity

biological clock: the force of the individual's program of maturing that is determined by the nature of the organism and by genetic inheritance; one of three forces that drive human development through the life cycle

causality: a supposed connection between events that indicates what brought about one or more of the events

cephalo-caudal principle: a principle of development that states that bodily control typically starts with the head and proceeds downward

chart: a prepared format or map on which observed information is recorded according to specified criteria

checklist: a listing of skills or other behaviors used as a guide for recording the presence or absence of each behavior

child-centered: a philosophy of child care and education that emphasizes the importance of the child's need to direct activity, to make play choices spontaneously, and to learn at a self-determined level

child development: the dynamic process of change and progression that enables each individual to become increasingly independent, knowledgeable, skilled, and self-sufficient

child study: a collection of information about a child, gathered by a student, researcher, or teacher over a period of time, that may be used for record keeping, research, evaluation, or program planning

cognition: the process of knowing, thinking, and understanding

compensatory care: nurturance or education to address negative experiences or deprivations

competency: what an individual is able to do or perform; a component part of a learning outcome that is measurable and observable

confidentiality: the principle of privacy and the practice of storing information securely so that its disclosure is only made to those considered appropriate

consequent event: the event that occurred immediately after the example of the sampled behavior

construction of knowledge: the creation of meaning through personal experience. The child constructs knowledge by experimenting and building "schemes" of understanding.

constructivism: a school of thought that considers learning to be a process of adaptation and that believes that individuals create their own meaning of the world through experience

context: the circumstances, situations, or background in which an observation is recorded

contextual information: family, social, cultural, medical, geographic, economic, or other information about the background of the child that enables a teacher or another stakeholder in the child's life to have some insight into the factors affecting the child's health, growth, or development

criterion-referenced assessment: assessment based on specific and clearly articulated criteria, designed to measure the specified skills and knowledge of an individual

cue: an indication or communication given by a child that is "read" by an adult. A cue may consciously or unconsciously communicate a need or desire and may involve facial expressions, gestures, or changes in posture.

cultural diversity: individuals from varying linguistic, ethnic, or religious backgrounds within the same group

curriculum: the child's whole experience; usually used to mean the teacher's or caregiver's provision for the child's developmental needs

data: the observational facts from which inferences can be drawn, or the information that the analysis produces

developmental diversity: individuals with varying ability levels within the same group

developmentally appropriate: the way in which a program or procedure is suitable for an individual's stage of progress and personal needs

developmental psychology: the school of study that focuses on the individual's progressive change, explaining how that adaptation occurs in terms of a cognitive framework

diary record: a recording made on a regular, usually daily, basis

disposition: the attitude or value demonstrated in a role performance

diversity: a wide range of various abilities, appearance, ethnicity, gender, culture, belief, religion, or place of origin

duration: the length of time a behavior is observed

early intervention: a plan to try to avoid potential challenges in a child's development or relationships, or, if difficulty is already diagnosed, a plan to support the child's development

ecological psychology: a social science concerned with connections between the individual and his or her environment

ecological systems model: a model that explains the components of the environment that influence an individual's life and development (for example, Bronfenbrenner's model)

ecomap: a diagrammatic representation of an individual's environment and his or her relationship to the elements of that environment, including people, activities, and organizations

emerging skill: a learned behavior at a starting or incipient stage

emotion: a feeling or, in observable terms, a change in arousal patterns

emotional intelligence: a term coined by Goleman to describe an ability to understand and use an individual pattern of responses to personal advancement

empirical evidence: information gathered through careful observation or experimentation

environment: an individual's surroundings, including places, objects, and people

environmental evaluation: a consideration of all the planned and unplanned aspects of a child's surroundings to ascertain their appropriateness or quality

environmental observation: observation of the use of a child's surroundings, including those elements that are designed and implemented deliberately and those parts that occur without planning

event: an example of a selected category of behavior

event sampling: an observation method in which occurrences of a preselected category of behavior are recorded

exceptional child: a child whose development is not typical (atypical) of those of a similar age. The child's development may be less advanced, uneven, or gifted.

family tree: a diagrammatic representation of an individual's ancestry

fine motor skills: learned behaviors involving the small muscles of the body

forced choice scale: a rating scale that requires the observer to judge the degree to which a characteristic or quality is evident

formative assessment: in-process, ongoing assessment designed to indicate an educational progression from the identified skill level or to enable the educator to set learning goals for the child

frequency: the pattern or number of occurrences of a specified behavior

genogram: a diagrammatic representation of a family structure, which may include historical and observational information about its style and functioning

graphic scale: a rating scale that is designed to record judgments of characteristics or qualities on a continuum that has predetermined word categories

gross motor skills: learned behaviors involving the large muscles of the body

hidden curriculum: elements of the child's experience that are affected by the unstated attitudes and beliefs of the responsible adult

hygienic practices: all behaviors that promote cleanliness, sanitization, or sterilization of bodies, materials, furniture, buildings, or other aspects of the environment

inclusion: the practice of ensuring that all children are treated equally and given equitable support in their development, regardless of their ability, ethnicity, gender, or beliefs

individual education plan (IEP): an individualized plan of goals and objectives, tailored to the child's needs

individual program plan (IPP): a curriculum, activity, task, or educational plan designed for an individual child

inference: a deduction made from observational data

input/outcome planning model: curriculum planning based on observational information as well as predesigned requirements such as competencies

integration: the practice of including children with special needs within mainstream care and education

interpretive graphic representation: visual presentation of information analyzed from data previously collected

inventory: a complete and comprehensive listing of skills, competencies, or specific requirements

knowledge: what is to be known; may be articulated at varying levels from identification to comprehension to analysis and synthesis

language: a complex means of communication that requires the acquisition of both a vocabulary and the rules governing the structure

learning log: a record-keeping device used to document the objective description of experiences and the child's response to the experiences

learning outcome: a complex role performance requiring knowledge and skill. An outcome may also specify the disposition of the performance.

life book: a book used to record significant people and experiences in a child's life over a period of time, often used by social workers and adoption agency workers

life experience flow chart: a diagrammatic representation of the series of key experiences in an individual's life

mapping: a diagram or map of an area where children are observed, used to record their movements or evaluate the program

media technique: any method of recording or storing observational data that is achieved by mechanical, electronic, or technical means

morality: an intellectual understanding of right and wrong and a social understanding of the consequent social responsibilities. Morality may be rooted in religious or cultural beliefs.

multiple intelligences: the theory, developed by Gardner, that each individual has a specific learning style (or way of being "smart"), made up of one or more different forms of intelligence, including spatial, logical/mathematical, linguistic, bodily/kinesthetic, musical, interpersonal, and intrapersonal

narrative observation: a sequentially written, detailed description of a child's actions

negative behavior: a behavior judged to be undesirable, inappropriate, or socially unacceptable

nonparticipant observation: the observation of an individual or a group by a person who is not interacting with that individual or group

norm: an average level of demonstrated behaviors, skills, results, or measurements determined from statistically significant populations

normal patterns: the expected sequence of development of the individual; what is expected may come from personal experience of children or, more reliably, from a statistically significant sample of a population

normative assessment: assessment based on researched norms of behavior or performance. The norms are stated as average levels of performance and may be expressed as percentiles.

norm-referenced assessment: the process of interpreting data according to an accepted range of performance (usually age related)

nuclear family: immediately related individuals who reside together

numerical scale: a rating scale that requires the observer to quantify the degree to which a characteristic or quality is evident

nurturance: the whole care and experience of the child that fosters development

objectives: the behaviors that are considered necessary to achieve a set goal or aim

objectivity: the pursuit of an approach that is undistorted, impartial, unbiased, analytical, and reliable

observation: the informal or formal perception of behavior of an individual or group of people, or the perceptions gained from looking at an environment or object

observation chart: a prepared chart with sections used for categorizing and recording behavior at the time or soon after it is observed

operational definition: a working, usable description of the behavior to be sampled

outcome-based education (OBE): a philosophy of education that structures curriculum and assessment on learning outcomes

outcome-based learning (OBL): a philosophy of learning that structures curriculum and assessment on learning outcomes

participant observation: the observation of an individual or a group by a person who is interacting with that individual or group at the same time

pattern of development: the sequence of skill acquisition in each developmental area or domain

peer evaluation: the assessment of a performance made by members of the same group

personality: an individual's personal characteristics including temperament, patterns of behavior, awareness of self, and ability to meet challenges

phenomenology: a philosophy that studies personal experiences from the point of view of the subject rather than that of the "objective" world

physical development: an individual's growth and acquisition of gross and fine motor skills and sensory acuity

pictorial representation: any form of recording or interpretation that uses visual presentation to demonstrate collected data

pie chart: a circular diagram that represents "slices" to depict proportions or percentages

play pattern: the recurring sequences of activity that are directed by the child

portfolio: a collection of information about a child's development gathered over time, used by teachers for assessment and record keeping

portfolio assessment: the process of observing, recording, and gathering contextual information about a child in order to evaluate performance, support development, and create appropriate curriculum

positive behavior: a behavior judged to be desirable, appropriate, or socially acceptable

professionalism: the way of behaving that is appropriate for trained, skilled, and practicing workers in performing their roles

pro-social skills: performance of behaviors that are considered positive and supportive of a desired morality

proximo-distal principle: a principle of development that states that bodily control typically starts at the center of the body and proceeds to the extremities

psychological clock: the force of an individual's quest to meet his or her own needs; one of the three forces that drive human development through the life cycle

qualitative evaluation: the process of measurement that involves the kind and degree of developmental change

rating scale: a predetermined list of behavioral characteristics that is accompanied by a numerical, semantic, or other grading system

readiness test: a test designed to evaluate the individual's cognitive functioning in order to determine potential success in a "higher" level program

record of achievement: a record kept by the teacher or student that logs anecdotal notes regarding the student's skill development and achievements

reinforcement: the process of supporting a behavior by offering an inducement or encouragement

reliability: the degree to which a method can be consistent; the degree to which scores for a test or measurement tool remain constant, consistent, or reliable

role model: a demonstration of the behaviors associated with a particular task, employment, or responsibility

role performance: the demonstration of the skill of a learning outcome; may imply knowledge of certain information and demonstration of a specific disposition

routine: a planned or responsive sequence of activity

rubric: a template for grading or assessing levels of performance of specific skills and knowledge

running record: a sequential written account of a child's behavior involving rich description and detail

sampling: an observation in which examples of behavior are recorded as they occur or behaviors are recorded as they are demonstrated at previously decided intervals

scaffolding: a term coined by Bruner that describes the adult's role in assisting the child in learning

scale: a way of measuring information that uses lists of behaviors or other items and rates them according to predetermined values

screening: a process of reviewing and evaluating specific behaviors or characteristics of individuals across a population or group in order to identify those who are in need of a more thorough assessment or specific support

self-evaluation: the process of evaluating one's own performance or creation of a product, involving comparison with a norm, measurement against specified criteria, or a general reflection on one's own process of learning

semantic differential scale: a rating scale that is designed to record judgments of characteristics or qualities on a continuum, listing pairs of opposites

sensitive period: a time in the developmental process when an individual is susceptible to particular kinds of influence

sensory acuity: the degree to which the senses perceive information accurately or in detail

sequential model: a diagrammatic representation of a curriculum plan to design learning on the basis of the breakdown of a competency into a series of stages

severity: the degree to which a behavior has been observed, that is, "irritability" might be described as mild, moderate, or severe (involves making a judgment)

skill: a learned behavior that is observable and measurable

skill acquisition: the process of gaining new behaviors or modifying or refining existing skills

social clock: the force of society's and the family's expectations; one of three forces that drive human development through the life cycle

social emotions: emotions that express feelings shaped by social experiences

social interaction: the process of communicating, sharing, playing, or otherwise interacting with another individual

social play: play activity involving others (seen or unseen)

sociogram: the diagrammatic representation of social relationships of those within a peer group

sociometry: the study of social interactions, which uses pictorial representations to record data

special needs: the necessities required to support the health and development of a child whose development is atypical in one or more domain

specimen record: an extremely detailed, sequential narrative recording of an observation of one child made as the behaviors are observed; frequently uses coding devices to ensure that the particulars are accurate and complete

spirituality: an approach to experience that may involve personal reflections, a connection with a power outside the self, or an appreciation of the significance of people and things; may be directly related to religious or philosophical beliefs about our existence

spontaneous play: naturally occurring, unstructured activity of the child, which is directed by the child

standard: a broad statement of achievement that is accepted as a requirement at a specified level

standardized test: a valid and reliable tool for evaluation that specifies the method of administration, content, and scoring

stereotype: a description or image of individuals or groups that depicts them according to clichés, or exaggerated or erroneous criteria, without regard for actual characteristics or individual differences

subjective: distorted, partial, biased, lacking in analysis, or unreliable

summary: a categorization of the essential parts of an observation, listing and organizing the behaviors observed

summative assessment: the total outcome of a range of assessment procedures or the total result of a particular evaluation tool

tally: a system of marks used to count the observed behavior

temperament: an individual's typical style of response to experiences and situations

therapeutic care: nurturance, education, or special measures that attempt to address negative or missing experiences or trauma

time sampling: an observation method in which random or previously chosen behaviors are recorded at preset time periods

tokenism: the practice of exceptional favor, based on negative prejudice, to "prove" one's fairness

topic planning: planning for children based on predesignated areas of learning

touristic approach: the practice of presenting cultural differences and places of origin in a superficial holiday, festival, or vacation style

tracking: a diagram or map of an area where a child is to be observed, onto which the child's movement is recorded; may be used to identify interests, mobility, concentration span, or interactions

validate: to ensure that the inferences made from observational data are supported or confirmed by one or more reliable authorities

validity: the degree to which a test or observation tool measures what it purports to measure

webbing model: a planning model that relates all curriculum areas through a single topic or focus

whole child: a concept of the child that sees all domains of development as interacting, the child being more than the sum of the domains

work sampling: a teacher's, parent's, or child's choice of work intended to demonstrate a particular competency

zone of proximal development: a phrase coined by Vygotsky that refers to the supposed gap between what the child can do presently in an independent manner and what the child can do in a supported way

Bibliography

Adamson, L.B. (1996). *Communication development during infancy.* Boulder, CO: Westview.

Ainsworth, M.D. (1972). Individual differences in the development of attachment behaviors. *Merrill Palmer Quarterly* 18.

Allen, K.E., & Marotz, L.R. (1994). *Developmental profiles: Pre-birth through eight* (2nd ed.). Albany, NY: Delmar.

Allen, K.E., et al. (1998). *Exceptional children: Inclusion in early childhood programs.* Scarborough, ON: ITP Nelson.

Arena, J. (1989). *How to write an I.E.P.* Novato, CA: Academic Therapy Publications.

Bandura, A. (1977). *Social learning theory.* Engelwood Cliffs, NJ: Prentice-Hall.

Beaty, J.J. (1996). *Preschool appropriate practices* (2nd ed.). Fort Worth, TX: Harcourt Brace Jovanovich.

Beaty, J.J. (1998). *Observing development of the young child* (4th ed.). Upper Saddle River, NJ: Prentice-Hall.

Bentzen, W. (1993). *Seeing young children: A guide to observing and recording behavior* (2nd ed.). Albany, NY: Delmar.

Bergen, D. (1994). Authentic performance assessments. *Educational Leadership,* 70(2).

Berk, L.E. (1994). *Infants, children, and adolescents.* Needham Heights, MA: Allyn & Bacon.

Bloom, B. (1956). *Taxonomy of educational objectives: The classification of educational goals. Handbook 1: The cognitive domain.* New York: Longmans Green.

Bowen, M. (1978). *Family therapy in clinical practice.* New York: Aronson.

Bowlby, J. (1965). *Child care and the growth of love.* Harmondsworth, England: Penguin.

Bredekamp, S. (Ed.). (1997). *Developmentally appropriate practice in early childhood programs serving children from birth through age 8* (revised edition). Washington, DC: National Association for the Education of Young Children.

Bredekamp, S., & Rosegrant, T. (Eds.). (1992). *Reaching potentials: Appropriate curriculum and assessment for young children.* (Vol. 1). Washington, DC: National Association for the Education of Young Children.

Bredekamp, S., & Rosegrant, T. (Eds.). (1995). *Reaching potentials: Transforming early childhood curriculum and assessment.* (Vol. 2). Washington, DC: National Association for the Education of Young Children.

Brian, J., & Martin, M. (1986). *Child care and health for nursery nurses.* Chester Springs, PA: Dufour.

Bronfenbrenner, U. (1979). *The ecology of human development: Experiments by nature and design*. Cambridge, MA: Harvard University Press.

Brown, J.L. (1995). *Observing dimensions of learning in classrooms and schools*. Alexandria, VA: Association for Supervision and Curriculum Development.

Bruner, J.S. (1966). *Toward a theory of instruction*. Cambridge, MA: Harvard University Press.

Bushweller, K. (1995). The high-tech portfolio. *The Executive Educator*, 17(1), 19–22.

Caldwell, B.M., & Bradley, R.H. (1979). *Home observation for measurement of the environment*. Little Rock, AR: University of Arkansas Press.

Campbell, S.D. (1987). *Quality control: A manual for self-evaluation of a day care agency*. Ottawa: Health and Welfare Canada.

Canadian Child Care Federation. (1995). *Towards excellence in ECCE training programs: A self-assessment guide*. Ottawa: Canadian Child Care Federation

Canadian Day Care Advocacy Association. (1992). *Caregiver behaviours and program characteristics associated with quality care*. Ottawa: Canadian Day Care Advocacy Association.

Canadian Paediatric Society. (1992). *Well beings: A guide to promote the physical health, safety and emotional well-being of children in child care centres and family day care homes*. Ottawa: Canadian Paediatric Society.

Catron, C.E., & Allen, J. (Eds.). (1993). *Early childhood curriculum*. New York: Merrill.

Centennial College Early Child Programs and Child Care Centres. (1998). *Philosophy check-in*. Toronto, ON: Centennial College.

Chess, S., & Thomas, A. (1996). *Temperament: Theory and practice*. New York: Brunner/Mazel.

Choate, J.S., et al. (1995). *Curriculum-based assessment and programming* (3rd ed.). Needham Heights, MA: Allyn & Bacon.

Chud, G., & Fahlman, R. (1985). *Early childhood education for a multicultural society*. Vancouver, BC: Western Education Development Group.

Clemmons, J., Cooper, D., & Lasse, L. (1996). *Portfolios in the classroom*. Jefferson City, MO: Scholastic.

Cohen, D., & Stern, V. (1978). *Observing and recording the behavior of young children*. New York: Teachers College Press.

Department of Health, Great Britain. (1988). *Protecting children: A guide for social workers undertaking a comprehensive assessment*. London: Her Majesty's Stationery Office.

Dewey, J. (1963; original ed. 1938). *Education and experience*. New York: Collier.

Doherty-Derkowski, G. (1994). *Quality matters: Excellence in early childhood programs*. Don Mills, ON: Addison-Wesley.

Elkind, D. (1988). *The hurried child: growing up too fast too soon* (revised). Reading, MA: Addison-Wesley.

Elliott, B. (1995). *Measure of success.* Toronto, ON: Association for Early Childhood Educators, Ontario.

Engel, B.S. (1990). *An approach to assessment in early literacy.* In C. Kamii (Ed.), *Achievement testing in the early grades: The games grown-ups play.* Washington, DC: National Association for the Education of Young Children.

Erikson, E.H. (1963). *Childhood and society* (2nd ed.). New York: Norton.

Erikson, E.H. (1994). *Identity and the life cycle.* New York: Norton.

Farr, R., & Tone, B. (1994). *Portfolio and performance assessment: Helping students evaluate their progress as readers and writers.* Fort Worth, TX: Harcourt Brace.

Friendly, M. (1994). *Child care policy in Canada: Putting the pieces together.* Don Mills, ON: Addison-Wesley.

Froebel, F. (1974; original ed. 1826). *The education of man.* Clifton, NJ: A.M. Kelley.

Gardner, H. (1993). *Multiple intelligences: The theory in practice.* New York: Basic Books.

Garmezy, N., Rutter, M. (Eds.). (1983). *Stress, coping and development in children.* New York: McGraw-Hill.

Glaser, R. (1963). Instructional technology and the measurement of learning outcomes: Some questions. *American Psychologist 18,* 519–521.

Goleman, D. (1997). *Emotional intelligence.* New York: Bantam.

Goodrich, H. (1996/97). Understanding rubrics. *Educational Leadership, 54*(4), 14–17.

Goodwin, W.L., & Driscoll, L.A. (1980). *Handbook for measurement and evaluation in early childhood education.* San Francisco: Jossey-Bass.

Greenspan, S.I., & Greenspan, N.T. (1985). *First feelings: Milestones in the emotional development of your baby and child.* New York: Viking.

Hall, G.S. (n.d.). The content of children's minds on entering school. *Pedagogical Seminary.*

Harms, T., & Clifford, R.M. (1990). *Family day care rating scale.* New York: Teachers College Press.

Harms, T., & Clifford, R.M. (1998). *Early childhood environment rating scale.* New York: Teachers College Press.

Harms, T., Cryer, D., & Clifford, R.M. (1990). *Infant/toddler environment rating scale.* New York: Teachers College Press.

Harrington, H.L., et al. (1997). *Observing, documenting, and assessing learning: The Work Sampling System for teacher educators.* Ann Arbor, MI: Rebus.

Harrow, A.J. (1972). *A taxonomy of the psychomotor domain: A guide for developing behavioral objectives.* New York: D. McKay.

Havard, L.A. (1995). *Outcome based education through the school system.* New York: Norton.

Health and Welfare Canada. (1980). *Children with special needs in daycare.* Ottawa: Health and Welfare Canada.

Hedgecoe, J. (1992). *Complete guide to video: The ultimate manual of video techniques and equipment.* Toronto: Stoddart.

Herman, J.L., et al. (1992). *A practical guide to alternative assessment.* Alexandria, VA: Association for Supervision and Curriculum Development.

Hills, T.W. (1992). Reaching potentials through appropriate assessment. In S. Bredekamp and T. Rosegrant (Eds.) (pp. 43–63).

Hornby, G. (1977). *Photographing baby and child.* New York: Crown Publishers.

Illingworth, R.S. (1990). *Basic developmental screening 0–5 years* (5th ed.). Oxford: Blackwell Scientific Publications.

Ireton, H. (1995). *Teacher's observation guide.* Minneapolis, MN: Behavioral Science Systems.

Ireton, H. (1997). Assessment: Appreciating children's development using parents' and teachers' observations. *EarlyChildhood.com* [On-line]. Discount School Supply. Available: http:// www.earlychildhood.com/articles/asmntobs.html.

Irwin, D.M., & Bushnell, M.M. (1980). *Observational strategies for child study.* New York: Holt, Rinehart, and Winston.

Jablon, J., et al. (1994a). *Work Sampling System omnibus guidelines: Kindergarten through fifth grade* (Vol. 2, 3rd ed.). Ann Arbor, MI: Rebus.

Jablon, J., et al. (1994b). *Work Sampling System omnibus guidelines: Preschool through third grade* (Vol. 1, 3rd ed.). Ann Arbor, MI: Rebus.

Katz, L.G., & Chard, S.C. (1989). *Engaging children's minds.* Norwood, NJ: Ablex Publishing.

King, J.A., & Evans, K.M. (1991, October). Can we achieve outcome-based education? *Educational Leadership.*

Klaus, M.H., Kennell, J.H., & Klaus, P.H. (1995). *Bonding: Building the foundations of secure attachment and independence.* Reading, MA: Addison-Wesley.

Krathwohl, M.B. (1964). *Taxonomy of educational objectives: The classification of educational goals. Handbook 2: The affective domain.* New York: McKay.

Langford, R., et al. (1997). *Checklist for quality inclusive education: A self-assessment tool and manual for early childhood settings.* Barrie, ON: Early Childhood Resource Teacher Network of Ontario.

Leavitt, R.L., & Eheart, B.K. (1991, July). Assessment in early childhood programs. *Young Children.*

Lewington, J., & Orpwood, G. (1993). *Overdue assignment: Taking responsibility for Canada's schools.* Toronto: John Wiley.

Lewis, R. (1993). *Learn to make videos in a weekend.* New York: Alfred A. Knopf.

Linder, T.W. (1990). *Transdisciplinary play-based assessment: A functional approach to working with young children.* Baltimore, MD: P.H. Brookes.

Locke, J. (1989; original ed. 1693). *Some thoughts concerning education.* New York: Oxford University Press.

Lorenz, K. (1937). Imprinting. *The Auk, 54,* 245–273.

Mager, R.F. (1962). *Preparing instructional objectives.* Belmont, CA: Lake Publishing.

Martin, S. (1988, September). Your child study: A new approach. *Nursery World.*

McCullough, V.E. (1992). *Testing and your child: What you should know about 150 of the most common educational and psychological tests.* New York: Plume.

McGoldrick, M., & Gerson, R. (1985). *Genograms in family assessment.* New York: Norton.

Meisels, S.J. (1992). *Early screening inventory revised.* Ann Arbor, MI: Rebus.

Meisels, S.J. (1993, July). Remaking classroom assessment with the Work Sampling System. *Young Children.*

Meisels, S.J. (1996/97). Using work sampling in authentic assessments. *Educational Leadership, 54*(4).

Meisels, S.J., & Steele, D. (1991). *The early childhood portfolio collection process.* Ann Arbor, MI: Center for Human Growth and Development, University of Michigan.

Mindes, G., Ireton, H., & Mardell-Czudnowski, C. (1996). *Assessing young children.* Albany, NY: Delmar.

Montessori, M. (1963; original ed. 1913). *Montessori training course.* Ann Arbor, MI: Ann Arbor Press.

Morris, D. (1995). *Illustrated babywatching.* London: Ebury Press.

National Association for the Education of Young Children. (1988). *Healthy young children: A manual for programs.* Washington, DC: National Association for the Education of Young Children.

Nicolson, S., & Shipstead, S.G. (1998). *Through the looking glass: Observations in the early childhood classroom* (2nd ed.). Upper Saddle River, NJ: Prentice-Hall.

Niguidula, D. (1997). Picturing performance with digital portfolios. *Educational Leadership, 55*(3).

North York Board of Education. (1992). *Beginnings—The early years.* North York, ON: North York Board of Education.

O'Neil, J. (1995). Future of OBE is up in the air. *Education Update, 37.*

Ontario Ministry of Education and Training. (1998). *The arts: The Ontario curriculum, grades 1–8.* Toronto: Publications Ontario.

Parten, M.B. (1932–33). Social participation among pre-school children. *Journal of Abnormal and Social Psychology.*

Pastor, E., & Kerns, E. (1997). A digital snapshot of an early childhood classroom. *Educational Leadership, 55*(3).

Pestalozzi, J.H. (1906). *A father's diary.* New York: Appleton.

Phillips, D.A. (Ed.). (1991). *Quality in child care: What does research tell us?* Washington, DC: National Association for the Education of Young Children.

Piaget, J. (1929). *The child's conception of the world.* (J. & A. Tomlinson, Trans.). New York: Harcourt Brace.

Piaget, J. (1954). *The child's construction of reality*. (M. Cook, Trans.). London: Routledge & Kegan Paul.

Picciotto, L.P. (1996). *Student-led parent conferences*. New York: Scholastic Professional.

Pimento, B., & Kernested, D. (1996). *Healthy foundations in child care*. Toronto, ON: Nelson.

Pinder, R. (1987, September). Not so modern methods. *Nursery World*.

Popham, W.J. (1998). *Classroom assessment: What teachers need to know* (2nd ed.). Boston, MA: Allyn & Bacon.

Preyer, W. (1973; original ed. 1888). *Mind of the child*. New York: Arno.

Puckett, M.B. (1994). *Authentic assessment of the young child: Celebrating development and learning*. New York: Macmillan.

Quilliam, S. (1994). *Child watching: A parent's guide to children's body language*. London: Ward Lock.

Robertson, J., & Robertson, J. (1967–71). *Young children in brief separation* (Videocassette series). London: Tavistock Institute of Human Relations.

Rose, V. (1985, November). Detecting problems with growth development charts. *Nursery World*.

Rousseau, J.-J. (1974; original French ed. 1762). *Emile*. (B. Foxley, Trans.). London: Dent.

Sax, G. (1997). *Principles of educational and psychological measurement and evaluation* (4th ed.). Belmont, CA: Wadsworth.

Schermann, Ada. (1990). Learning. In I. Doxey (Ed.), *Child care and education: Canadian dimensions*. Scarborough, ON: Nelson.

Schlank, C.H., & Metzger, B. (1989). *A room full of children: How to observe and evaluate a preschool program*. New York: Rochester Association for Young Children.

Shepard, L.A. (1994). The challenges of assessing young children appropriately. *Phi Delta Kappan, 76*(3), 206–212.

Shinn, M.W. (1975; original ed. 1900). *The biography of a baby*. New York: Arno Press.

Shipley, D. (1994). Learning outcomes: Another bandwagon or a strategic instrument of reform? *Educational Strategies, 1*(4), 3

Simpson, E. (1972). *The classification of educational objectives in the psychomotor domain*. Washington, DC: Prentice-Hall.

Southern Early Childhood Association. *Early childhood assessment* (Special series of reprints from *Dimensions of Early Childhood*). Little Rock, AR: SECA.

Spady, W. (1977). Competency-based education: A bandwagon in search of a definition. *Educational Researcher, 6* (1), 9–14.

Spitz, R.A. (1965). *The first year of life: A psychoanalytic study of normal and deviant development of object relations*. New York: International Universities Press.

Steiner, R. (1982; original ed. 1924). *The roots of education.* London: Rudolf Steiner Press.

Sunseri, R. (1994). *Outcome based education: Understanding the truth about education reform.* Sisters, OR: Multnomah Books.

Tindal, G.A., & Marston, D.B. (1990). *Classroom-based assessment: evaluating instructional outcomes.* Columbus, OH: Merrill Publishing.

Toronto Observation Project. (1980). *Observing children through their formative years.* Toronto: Board of Education for the City of Toronto.

Tyler, L.E. (1965). *The psychology of human differences* (3rd ed.). New York: Appleton-Century-Crofts.

Van Manen, M. (1990). *Researching lived experience: Human science for an action sensitive pedagogy.* London, ON: The Althouse Press.

Vygotsky, L.S. (1978). *Mind in society: The development of psychological processes.* Cambridge, MA: Harvard University Press.

Waterloo County Board of Education. (1993). *Invitations to literacy learning.*

Watson, J.B. (1930). *Behaviorism.* Chicago: University of Chicago Press.

Weitzman, E. (1992). *Learning language and loving it: A guide to promoting children's social and language development in early childhood settings.* Toronto, ON: Hanen Centre.

Whitbread, N. (1972). *The evolution of the nursery-infant school: A history of infant and nursery education in Britain, 1800–1970.* London: Routledge & Kegan Paul.

Wiggins, G. (1996/97). Practice what we preach in designing authentic assessments. *Educational Leadership, 54*(4).

Wilson, L.C., Douville-Watson, L., & Watson, M.A. (1995). *Infants and toddlers: Curriculum and teaching* (3rd ed.). Albany, NY: Delmar.

Wortham, S.C. (1992). *Childhood, 1892–1992.* Wheaton, MD: Association for Childhood Education International.

Wortham, S.C. (1996). *The integrated classroom: The assessment–curriculum link in early childhood education.* Englewood Cliffs, NJ: Merrill.

Zitterkopf, R. (1994). A fundamentalist's defense of OBE. *Educational Leadership, 51*(6).

Index

ABC format, for event sampling, 121–22, 125, 136–40, 141–42
abuse, observing indicators of, 96
action plan, 346–47, 349
activity response chart, 184
activity/routine chart, 185
acuity, sensory, 51
adult's assistance in a child's learning, chart, 70, 81
adult's role as learning facilitator, 72
agency records, 259–60
Ainsworth, Mary, 74
analysis, 19–24, 237
  charts, 35–37
  of checklists, 160
  of child studies, 237
  of running records, 90
  of samplings, 133
anecdotal records, 88, 95–99, 115–17, 240, 297
  charts, 98–99
antecedent event, 121
anti-bias, 329. *See also* bias
appropriate, developmentally, 151, 296, 306, 332–34
appropriate environments, 332–34, 338–44
appropriateness, 156
assessment, 6, 18–24, 90–91, 304–16
  authentic, 4, 311–12
  criterion-referenced, 150, 296
  formative, 242
  normative, 296
  norm-referenced, 150
  outcome-based education (OBE), 289, 294–95, 297–98, 302, 303
  portfolio, 248, 264–66, 275–82, 316
  results, interpreting, 312
  and standardized tests, 311–12
  summative, 242
assistants, 260
assumptions, 86
attachments, 56, 74
  chart, 60
attention deficit disorder (ADD), 20
audio recording, 213, 228–34
  basics of, 229–31
  general principles of, 229
  log, 234
  for observational purposes, 231–34
authentic assessment, 4, 7–8, 311–12

baby book, 95, 239, 244–45
background information. *See* contextual information
bar chart, 202, 203
bar line graph, 210
behavior(s), 4, 86, 88–89, 119, 121, 150, 151, 156–57
  categories of, 122–23
  describing, 86–88
  negative, 189
  positive, 189
behavioral challenges, 123
behaviorism, 3, 46, 85, 286
behavior modification, 128, 134–35
bias, 14–15, 87–88, 124, 157, 190, 306, 310, 315
biological clock, 48, 49
birth weight, low, 187, 249
Bowlby, John, 74, 75
Bronfenbrenner, Urie, 75, 194–95
Bruner, Jerome, 47, 73

caregiver–parent information chart for infants, 183, 205
causality, 121
cephalo-caudal principle, 51
charts
  analysis, 35–37
  anecdotal record, 98–99
  bar, 202, 203
  checklist, 152
  child development, 53, 57, 58, 60, 65, 69, 70, 71
  diary record, 101
  event sampling, 125–128
  life experience flow, 198, 240
  observation, 177, 178–88, 240
  pie, 202, 203
  running record, 92–94
  time sampling, 130–31
checklists, 149–74, 240, 296, 308
  analysis of, 160
  chart, 152
  environmental, 327–28, 329–30
  homemade, 152, 172–74
  open-ended, 327–28
  prepared, 153–55, 161–62, 164–67, 168–71
  recording observations, 157–58
Chess, Stella, 61, 192

resource teachers, 260
Robertson, James and Joyce, 213
role model, 341, 342, 344
role performance, 286, 290
Rousseau, Jean-Jacques, 45, 84, 305
routine, 185, 342
rubric, 295–96
running records, 88, 89–94, 107–11, 112–14,
 240, 297
 analysis of, 90
 charts, 92–94

sampling(s). 118–48. *See also* event sampling;
 time sampling
 how to use, 131–35
 work, 286, 295
scaffolding, 73, 81
scale, 178. *See also* environmental rating
 scales; observation scales; rating scales
school individual records, 247
screening, 307–308
self-evaluation, 296, 297, 308
semantic differential scale, 190, 206–207
sensitive period, 54, 56, 75–76
sensory acuity, 51
separations chart, 60
sequential model, 30
severity, 121, 128
Shinn, Milicent Washburn, 238
sign language, 227
skill(s), 152, 286, 290
 acquisition of, 152, 309
 emerging, 18–19, 95
 fine motor, 51, 87, 152
 gross motor, 51, 87, 152
 pro-social, 62
social clock, 48, 49
social emotions, 59
social interactions, 56
 charts, 57, 58, 79
social maps, 179, 193–99. *See also* ecomaps;
 family trees; genograms; life experience flow chart; sociograms
social play, 56
sociograms, 197
sociometry, 177, 197
Spady, William, 286–87
special needs, 25, 26, 48, 55, 64, 74, 88, 91,
 105, 260, 339
specimen records, 89, 102–103, 240
spirituality, 66–67
Spitz, René, 213
spontaneous play, 89, 226, 321
standard, 291
standardized tests, 240, 306, 307–16
 choosing, 314–16
 evaluating, 308–11

as part of authentic assessment, 311–12
 using, 313–14
stereotype, 74, 339
subjective, 11, 223
summary, 19, 264, 273–74
summative assessment, 242
symptom chart for chronic or special medical
 conditions, 188

tally, 125, 126
teamwork, 15–16
temperament, 61, 192
tests. *See* readiness test; standardized tests
therapeutic care, 344
Thomas, Alexander, 61, 192
time sampling, 119, 129–31, 132, 143–44,
 145–48, 240
 analysis of, 133
 charts, 130–31
 time intervals for, 129
tokenism, 339
topic planning, 31
touristic approach, 339
tracking, 177, 200–201, 208–209
transdisciplinary play-based assessment
 (TPBA), 16

validate, 20
validity, 133, 156, 188–89, 309, 330
video recording, 213, 222–28
 basics of, 223–25
 general principles of, 223
 log, 228
 for observational purposes, 225–28
Vygotsky, Lev, 31, 47, 73

Watson, John B., 46, 85
webbing model, 31, 41
whole child, 23, 68
work sampling, 286, 295

zone of proximal development, 31, 73